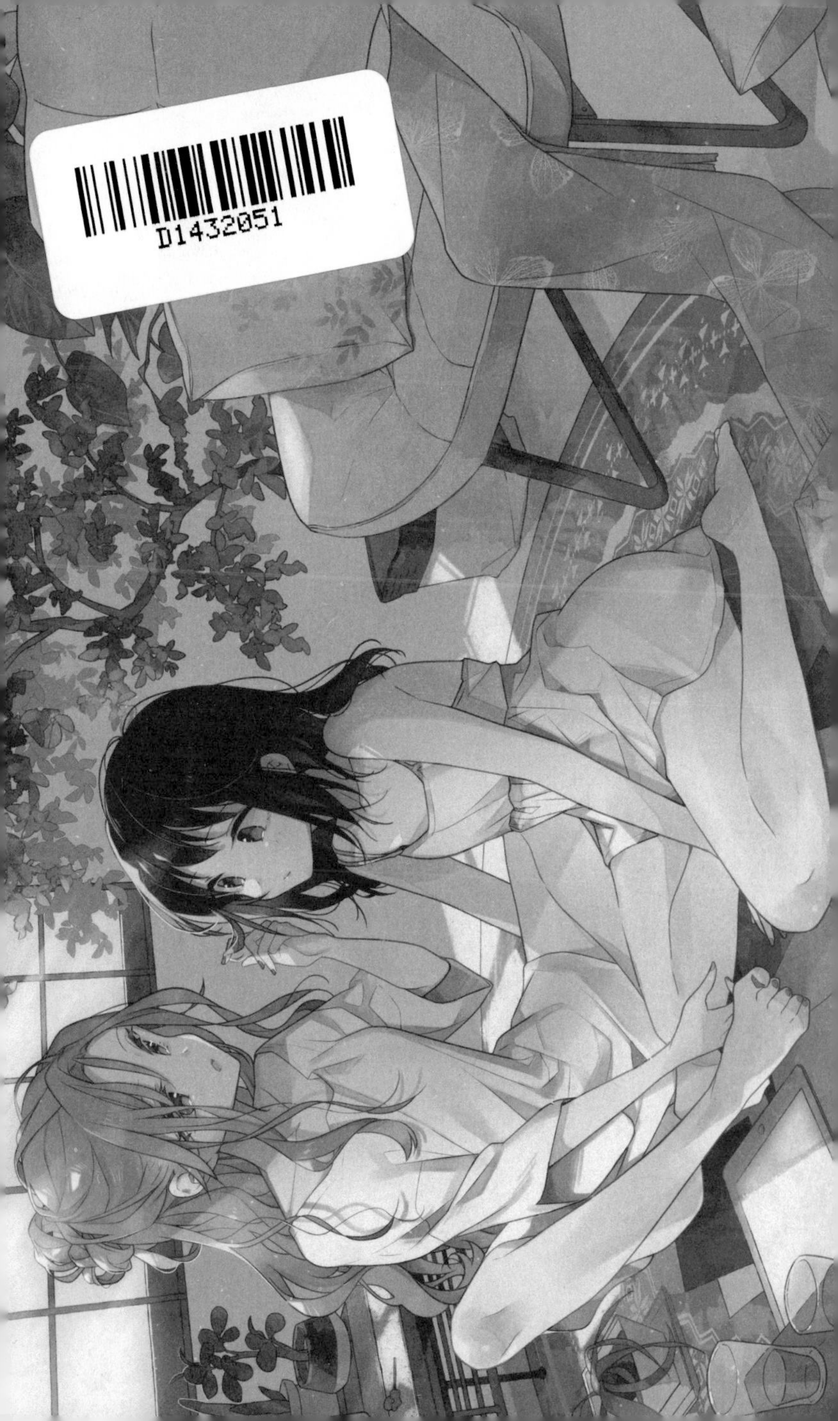

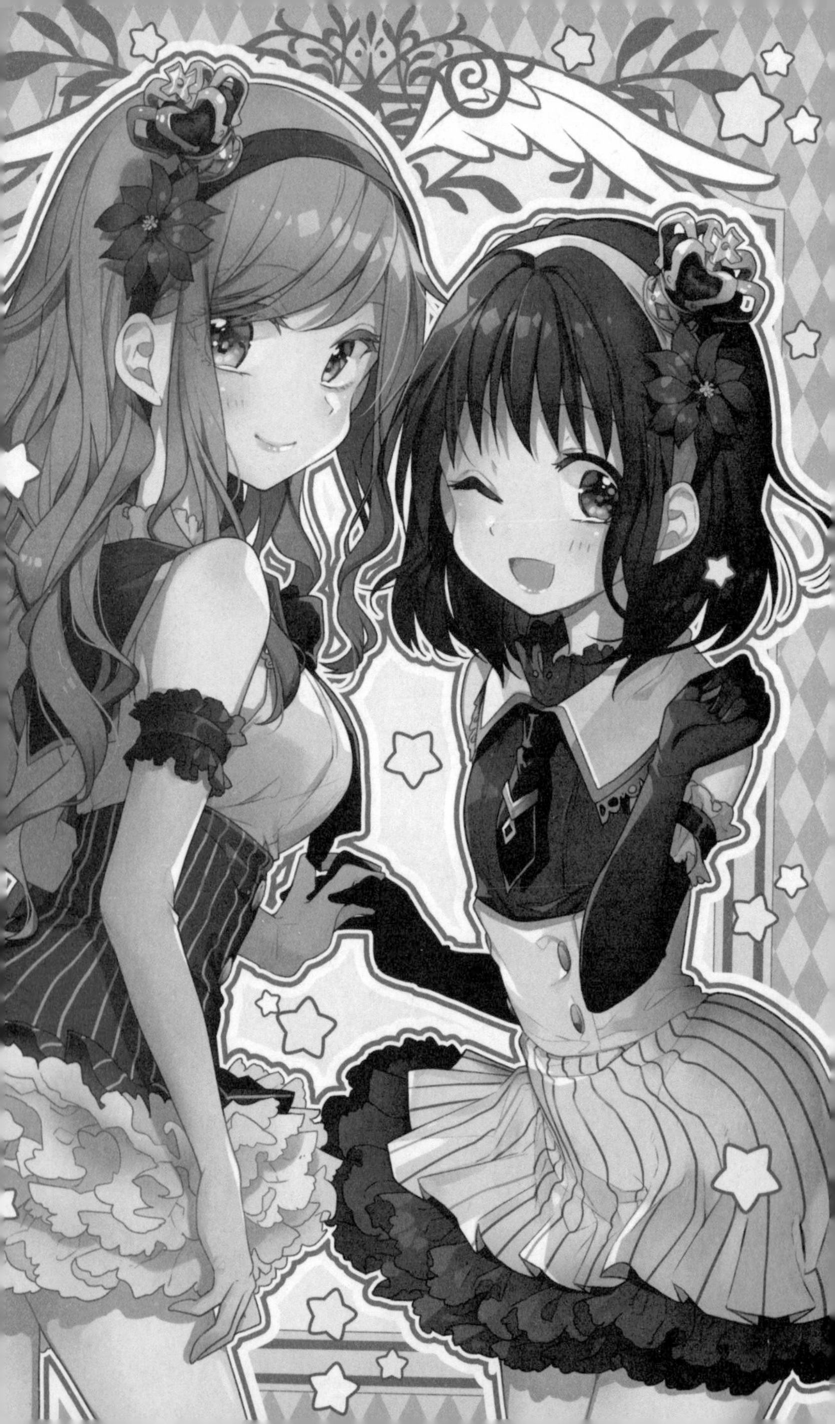

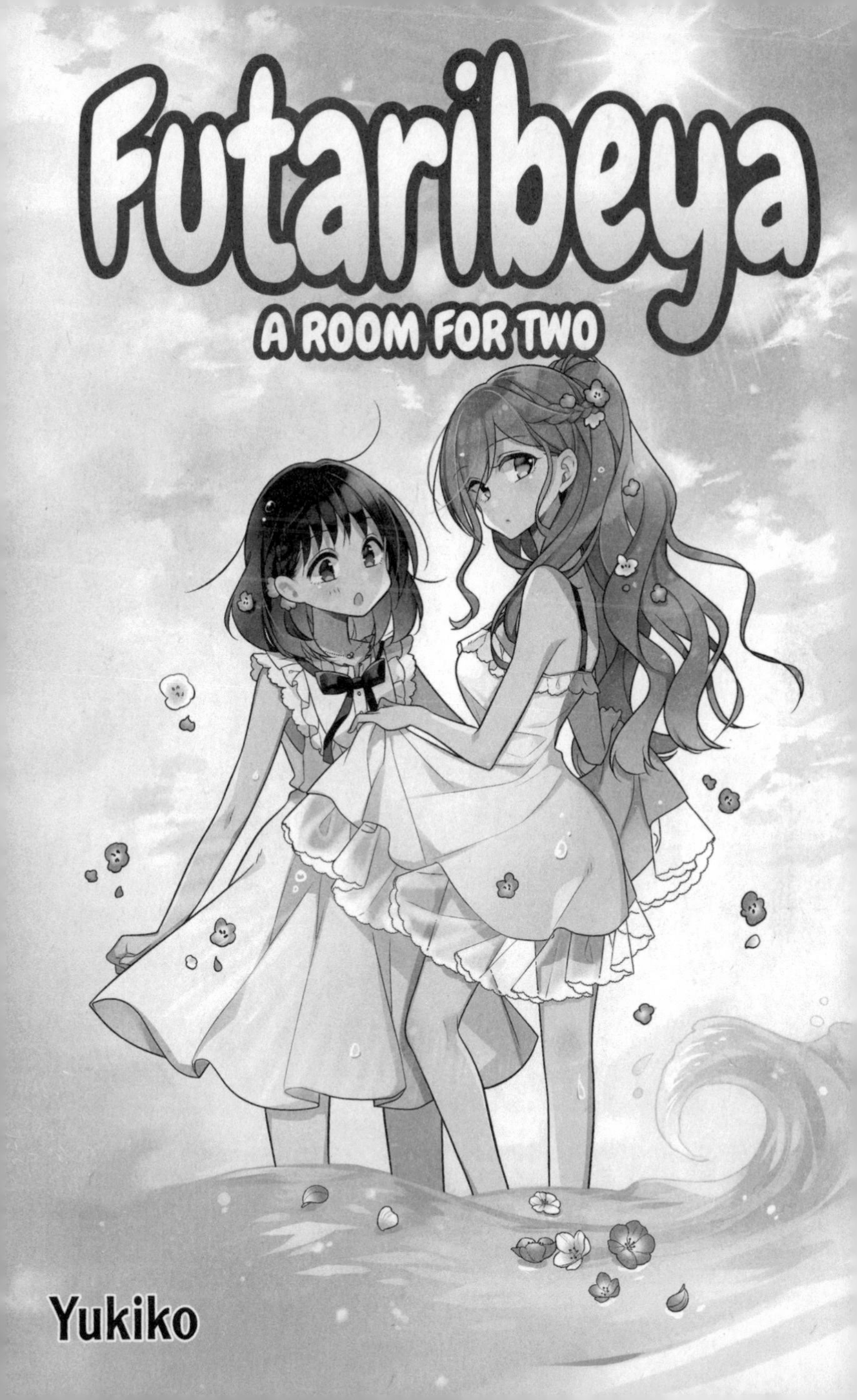
Futaribeya
A ROOM FOR TWO
Yukiko

CHARACTER

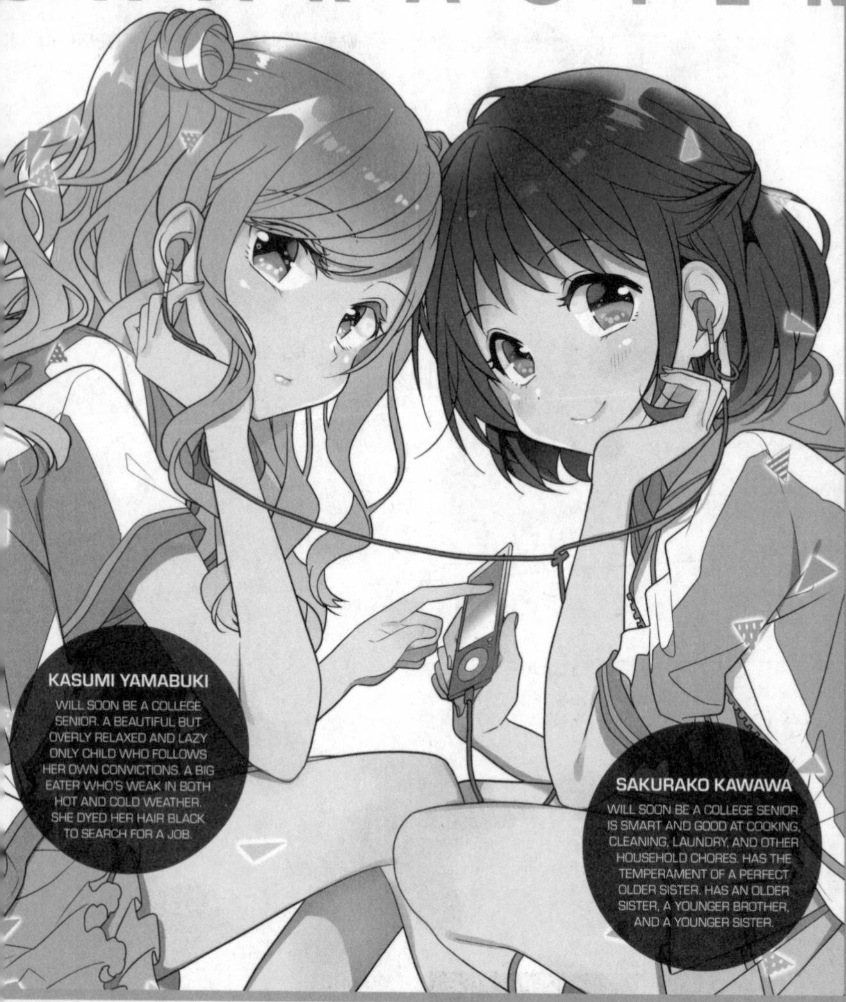
KASUMI YAMABUKI
WILL SOON BE A COLLEGE SENIOR. A BEAUTIFUL BUT OVERLY RELAXED AND LAZY ONLY CHILD WHO FOLLOWS HER OWN CONVICTIONS. A BIG EATER WHO'S WEAK IN BOTH HOT AND COLD WEATHER. SHE DYED HER HAIR BLACK TO SEARCH FOR A JOB.
SAKURAKO KAWAWA
WILL SOON BE A COLLEGE SENIOR. IS SMART AND GOOD AT COOKING, CLEANING, LAUNDRY, AND OTHER HOUSEHOLD CHORES. HAS THE TEMPERAMENT OF A PERFECT OLDER SISTER. HAS AN OLDER SISTER, A YOUNGER BROTHER, AND A YOUNGER SISTER.

SAKURAKO AND KASUMI BECAME ROOMMATES WHEN THEY ENTERED THEIR HIGH SCHOOL'S BOARDING HOUSE, AND THEY ARE GREAT FRIENDS. THEY CONTINUE TO LIVE TOGETHER IN A ONE-ROOM APARTMENT, SHARING A BED. NOTHING HAS CHANGED DESPITE THEIR MOVE AND ENTERING COLLEGE. EVEN THOUGH THEY HAVE DIFFERENT MAJORS, THEY ENJOY LIFE ALONG WITH THEIR COLLEGE FRIENDS KORURI, MOKA, YUKARI, AND THEIR UNDERCLASSMAN, SERI. NOW THAT THEY'RE CLOSE TO BECOMING SENIORS, THEY'VE FINALLY STARTED TO SERIOUSLY LOOK FOR JOBS AND THEIR SCHEDULES ARE JAM-PACKED FULL OF EVENTS!

STORY and

MOKA NENASHI

A PSYCHOLOGY MAJOR LIKE SAKURAKO. SHE HAS A FREE VIEW ON LOVE AND OFTEN STAYS OVER AT KORURI'S HOUSE.

KORURI MASUI

STUDIES IN THE LIFE ENVIRONMENT STUDIES DEPARTMENT WITH KASUMI. SHE HAS A BAD SENSE OF DIRECTION AND IS UNABLE TO THROW THINGS AWAY.

SHOUKO AKASHI

SERI'S FORMER ROOMMATE WHO IS CURRENTLY WORKING. SHE HAS A FRANK PERSONALITY. EVERYONE CALLS HER SHOUKO.

SERI FURUYASHIKI

SAKURAKO AND KASUMI'S UNDERCLASSMAN FROM HIGH SCHOOL WHO GOES TO THEIR COLLEGE. SHE'S A SHELTERED RICH GIRL WHO USES POLITE SPEECH WITH EVERYONE SHE MEETS.

YUKARI

SAKURAKO AND KASUMI'S HIGH SCHOOL CLASSMATE WHO ATTENDS THE SAME COLLEGE AS THEM. SHE EVEN JOINED THE SAME CLUB AND WANTS TO BE A LIBRARIAN.

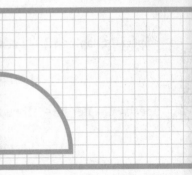

HINAKO

SHE'S SPOILED AND ABSOLUTELY LOVES SAKURAKO AND KASUMI. SHE HAS A TWIN BROTHER NAMED KAKERU.

FUJIHO

HINAKO'S HIGH SCHOOL ROOMMATE. SHE'S ATTENDING A BEAUTY SCHOOL.

Contents

Chapter 59.5

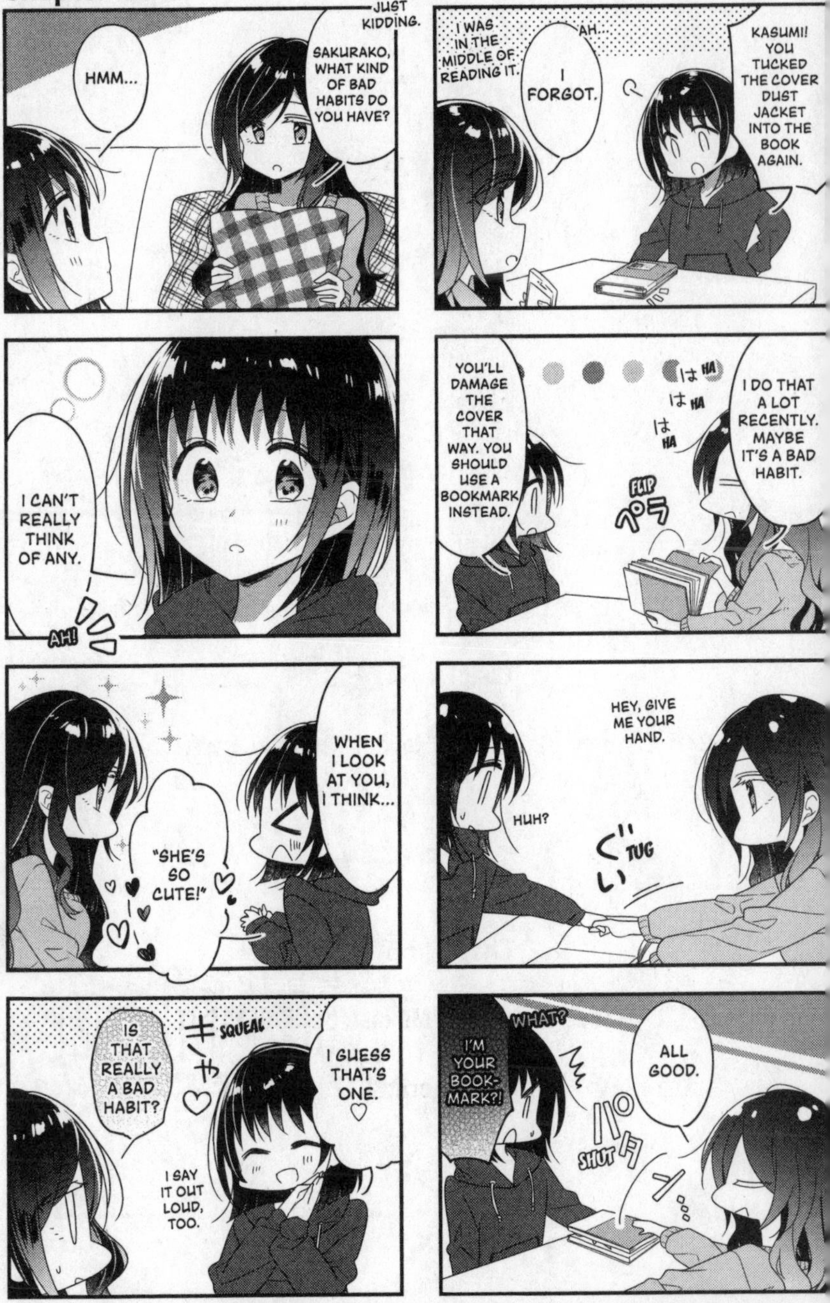
KASUMI! YOU TUCKED THE COVER DUST JACKET INTO THE BOOK AGAIN.
AH...
I FORGOT.
I WAS IN THE MIDDLE OF READING IT.
I DO THAT A LOT RECENTLY. MAYBE IT'S A BAD HABIT.
は HA
は HA
は HA
YOU'LL DAMAGE THE COVER THAT WAY. YOU SHOULD USE A BOOKMARK INSTEAD.
ペラ FLIP
HEY, GIVE ME YOUR HAND.
ぐい TUG
HUH?
ALL GOOD.
パタ SHUT
WHAT?
I'M YOUR BOOK-MARK?!
JUST KIDDING.
SAKURAKO, WHAT KIND OF BAD HABITS DO YOU HAVE?
HMM...
I CAN'T REALLY THINK OF ANY.
AH!
WHEN I LOOK AT YOU, I THINK...
"SHE'S SO CUTE!"
I GUESS THAT'S ONE.
I SAY IT OUT LOUD, TOO.
キャ SQUEAL
IS THAT REALLY A BAD HABIT?

Futaribeya
A ROOM FOR TWO

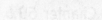

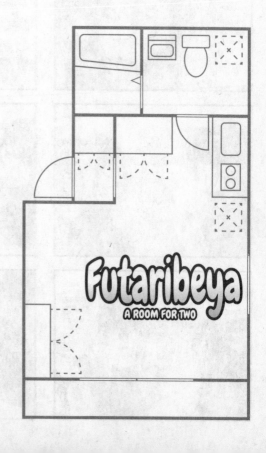

Chapter 60

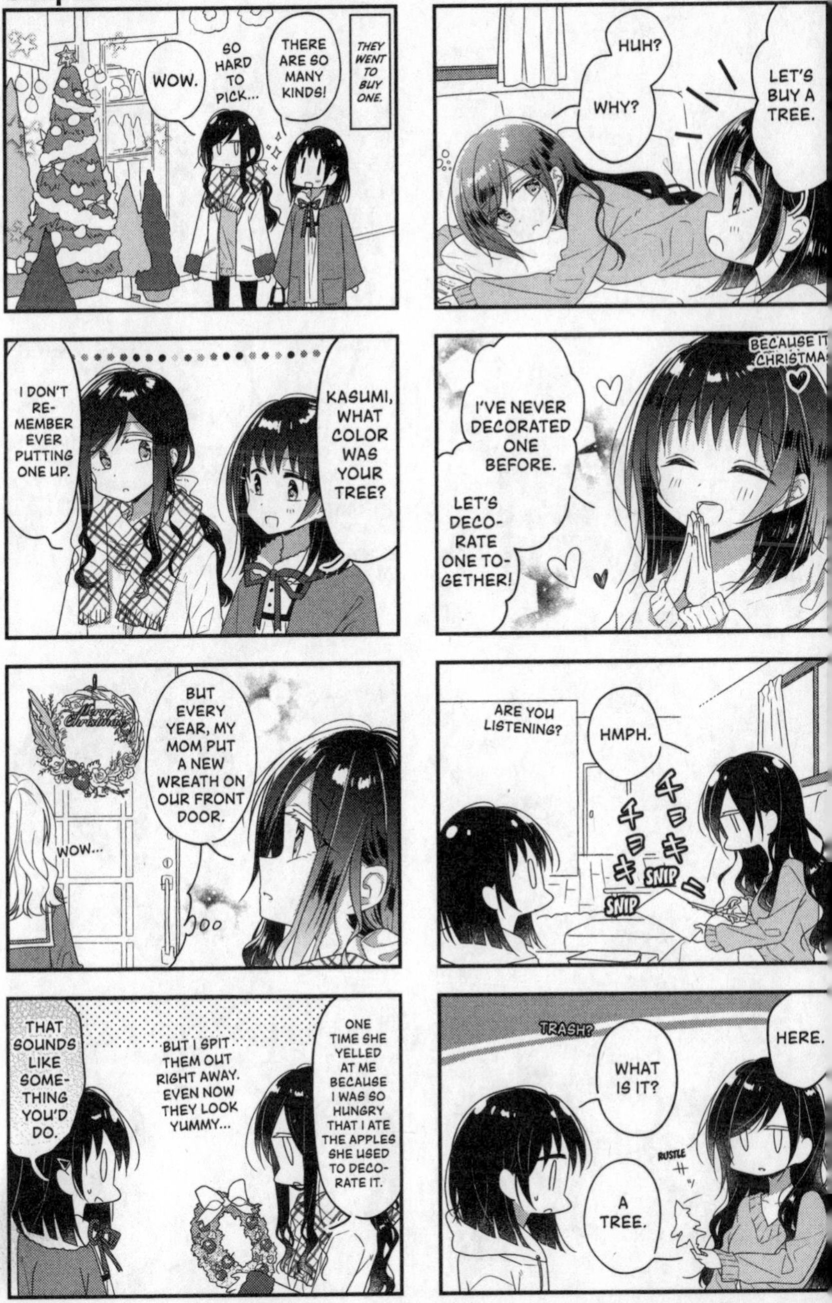
LET'S BUY A TREE.
HUH?
WHY?
BECAUSE IT
CHRISTMA
I'VE NEVER DECORATED ONE BEFORE.
LET'S DECO-RATE ONE TO-GETHER!
HMPH.
ARE YOU LISTENING?
チョキチョキ
SNIP
SNIP
HERE.
WHAT IS IT?
TRASH?
RUSTLE
A TREE.
THEY WENT TO BUY ONE.
THERE ARE SO MANY KINDS!
SO HARD TO PICK...
WOW.
KASUMI, WHAT COLOR WAS YOUR TREE?
I DON'T RE-MEMBER EVER PUTTING ONE UP.
Merry Christmas
BUT EVERY YEAR, MY MOM PUT A NEW WREATH ON OUR FRONT DOOR.
WOW...
ONE TIME SHE YELLED AT ME BECAUSE I WAS SO HUNGRY THAT I ATE THE APPLES SHE USED TO DECO-RATE IT.
BUT I SPIT THEM OUT RIGHT AWAY. EVEN NOW THEY LOOK YUMMY...
THAT SOUNDS LIKE SOME-THING YOU'D DO.

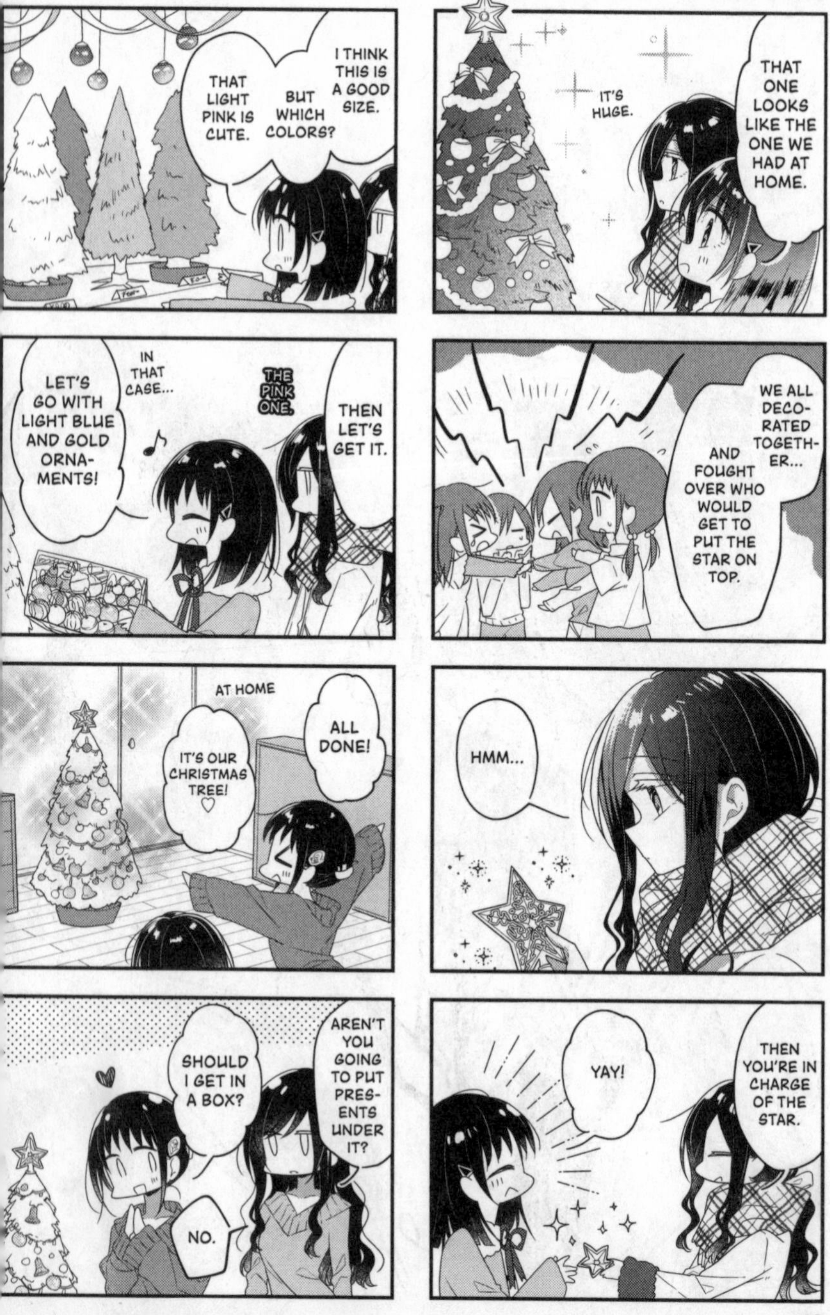
THAT ONE LOOKS LIKE THE ONE WE HAD AT HOME.
IT'S HUGE.
WE ALL DECO-RATED TOGETH-ER...
AND FOUGHT OVER WHO WOULD GET TO PUT THE STAR ON TOP.
HMM...
THEN YOU'RE IN CHARGE OF THE STAR.
YAY!
I THINK THIS IS A GOOD SIZE.
BUT WHICH COLORS?
THAT LIGHT PINK IS CUTE.
THEN LET'S GET IT.
THE PINK ONE.
IN THAT CASE...
LET'S GO WITH LIGHT BLUE AND GOLD ORNA-MENTS!
AT HOME
ALL DONE!
IT'S OUR CHRISTMAS TREE! ♡
AREN'T YOU GOING TO PUT PRES-ENTS UNDER IT?
SHOULD I GET IN A BOX?
NO.

Illustration gallery of Yukike

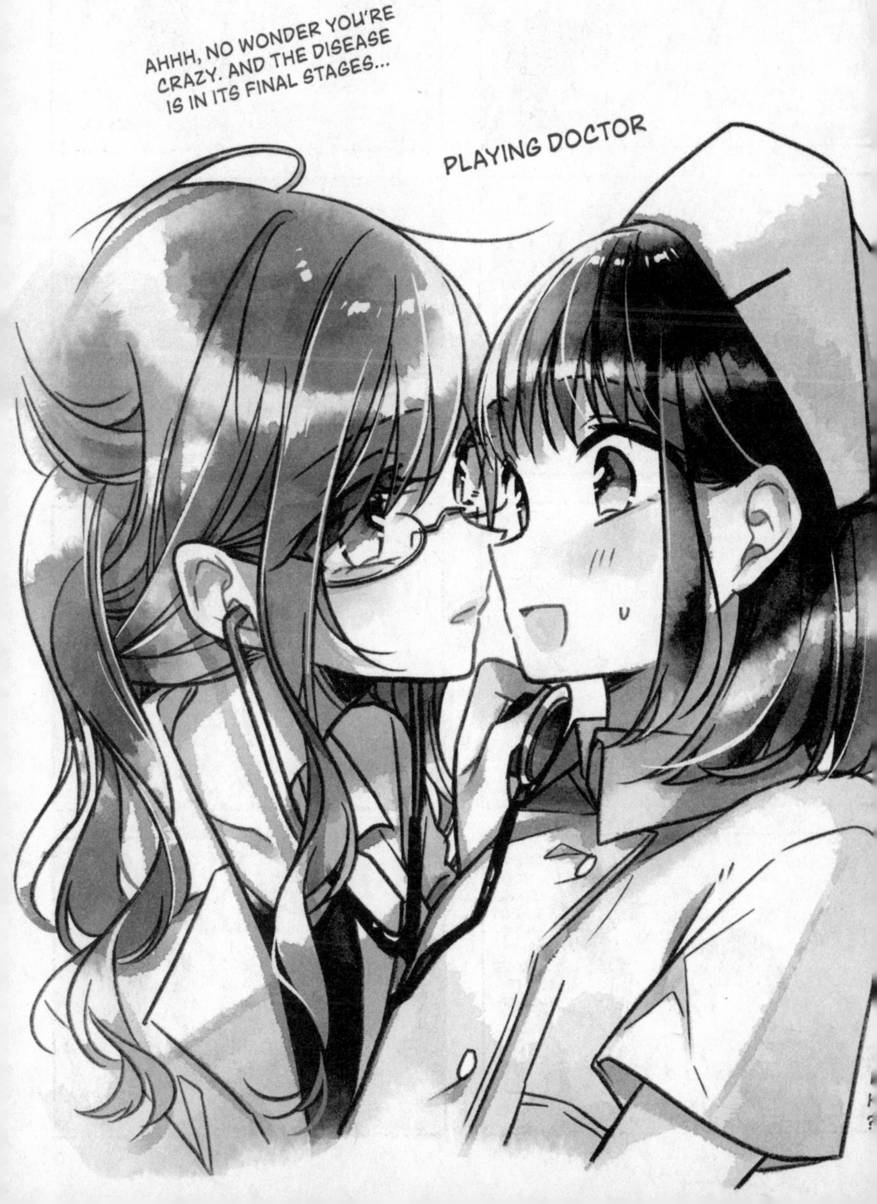
AHHH, NO WONDER YOU'RE CRAZY. AND THE DISEASE IS IN ITS FINAL STAGES...
PLAYING DOCTOR

Futaribeya
A ROOM FOR TWO

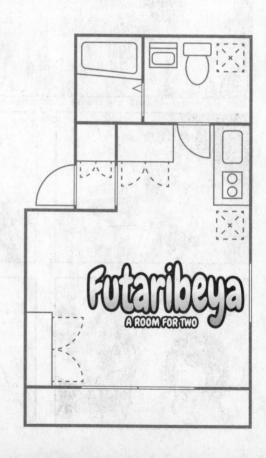

Chapter 61

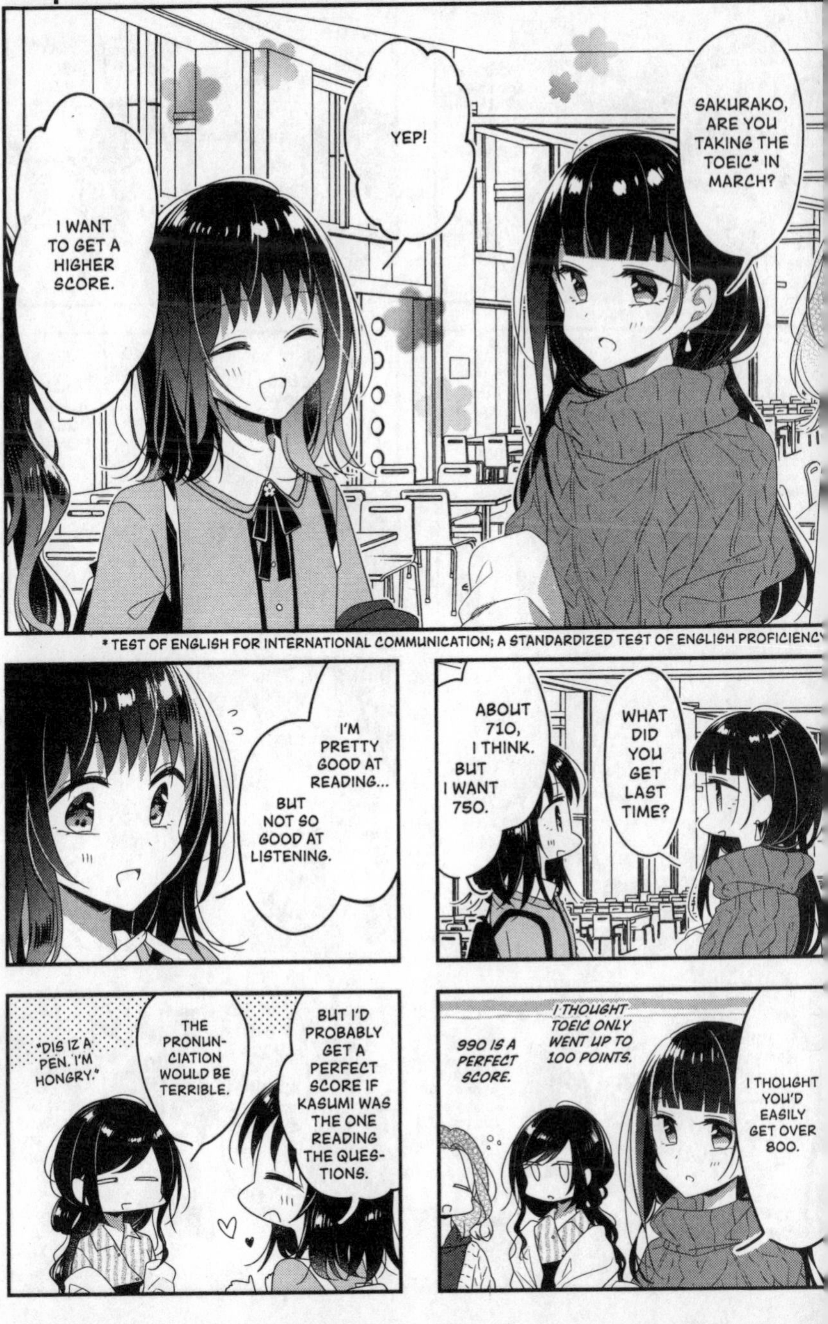
SAKURAKO, ARE YOU TAKING THE TOEIC* IN MARCH?
YEP!
I WANT TO GET A HIGHER SCORE.
WHAT DID YOU GET LAST TIME?
ABOUT 710, I THINK. BUT I WANT 750.
I'M PRETTY GOOD AT READING... BUT NOT SO GOOD AT LISTENING.
I THOUGHT YOU'D EASILY GET OVER 800.
I THOUGHT TOEIC ONLY WENT UP TO 100 POINTS.
990 IS A PERFECT SCORE.
BUT I'D PROBABLY GET A PERFECT SCORE IF KASUMI WAS THE ONE READING THE QUESTIONS.
THE PRONUNCIATION WOULD BE TERRIBLE.
"DIS IZ A PEN. I'M HONGRY."

* TEST OF ENGLISH FOR INTERNATIONAL COMMUNICATION; A STANDARDIZED TEST OF ENGLISH PROFICIENCY

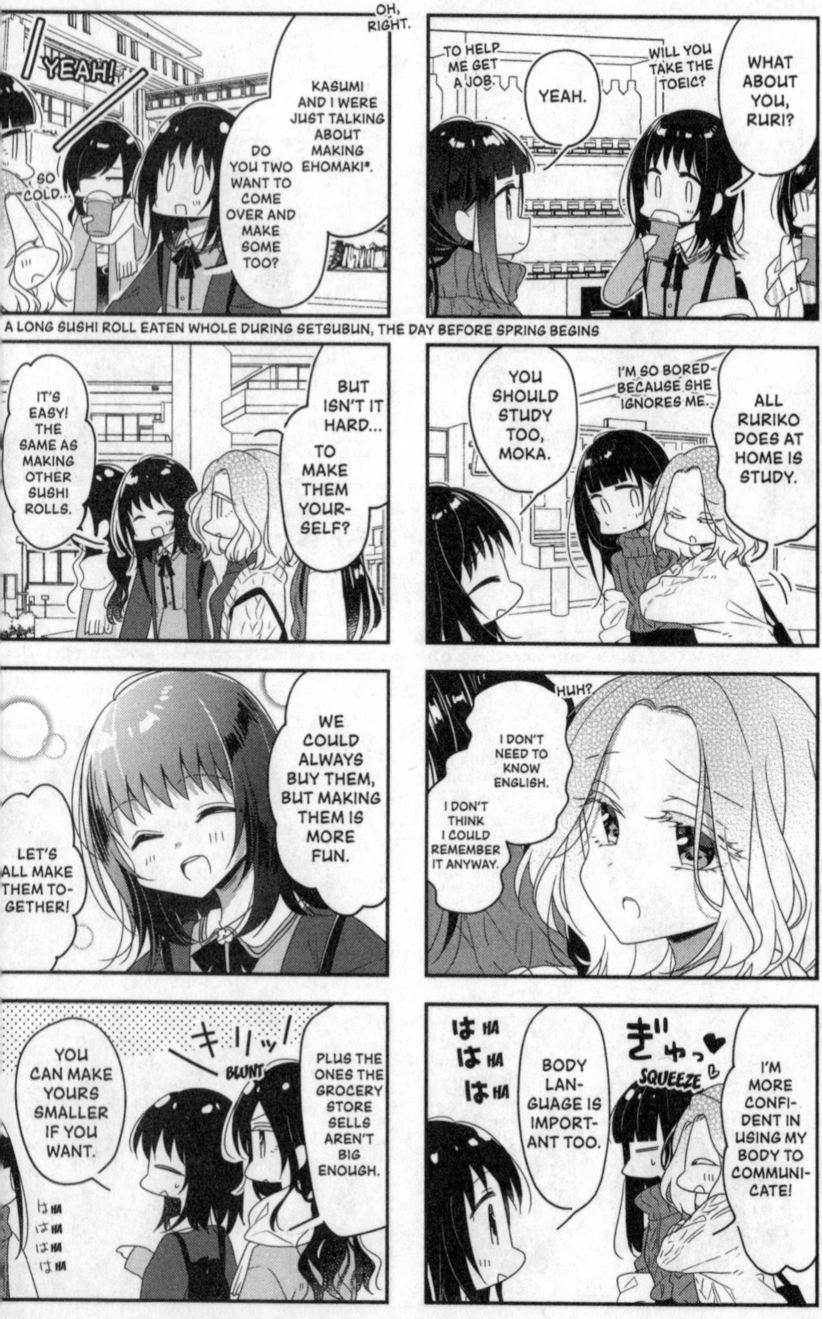
WHAT ABOUT YOU, RURI?
WILL YOU TAKE THE TOEIC?
YEAH.
TO HELP ME GET A JOB.
ALL RURIKO DOES AT HOME IS STUDY.
I'M SO BORED BECAUSE SHE IGNORES ME.
YOU SHOULD STUDY TOO, MOKA.
HUH?
I DON'T NEED TO KNOW ENGLISH.
I DON'T THINK I COULD REMEMBER IT ANYWAY.
I'M MORE CONFIDENT IN USING MY BODY TO COMMUNICATE!
ぎゅっ SQUEEZE
BODY LANGUAGE IS IMPORTANT TOO.
は HA は HA は HA
OH, RIGHT.
KASUMI AND I WERE JUST TALKING ABOUT MAKING EHOMAKI*.
DO YOU TWO WANT TO COME OVER AND MAKE SOME TOO?
YEAH!
SO COLD...
BUT ISN'T IT HARD...
TO MAKE THEM YOURSELF?
IT'S EASY! THE SAME AS MAKING OTHER SUSHI ROLLS.
WE COULD ALWAYS BUY THEM, BUT MAKING THEM IS MORE FUN.
LET'S ALL MAKE THEM TOGETHER!
PLUS THE ONES THE GROCERY STORE SELLS AREN'T BIG ENOUGH.
キリッ BLUNT
YOU CAN MAKE YOURS SMALLER IF YOU WANT.
は HA は HA は HA は HA

A LONG SUSHI ROLL EATEN WHOLE DURING SETSUBUN, THE DAY BEFORE SPRING BEGINS

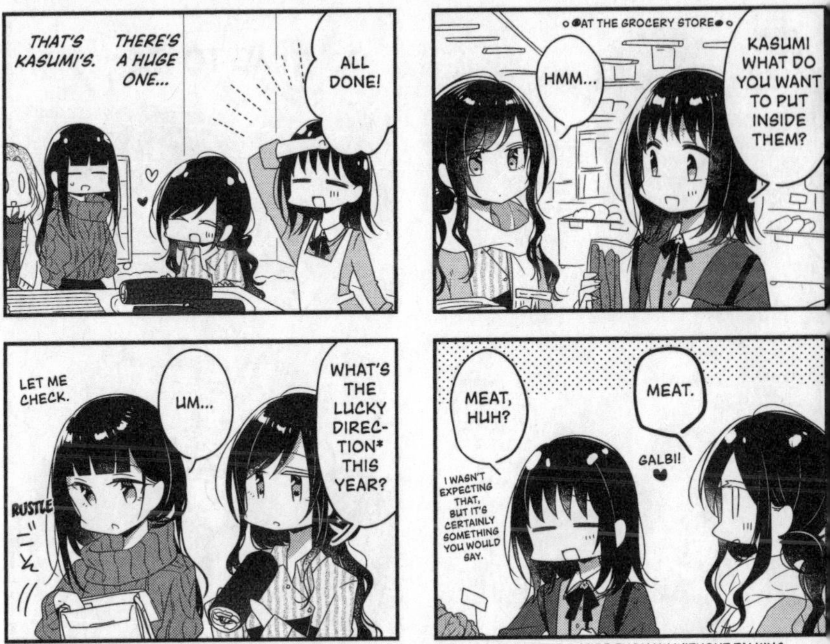
AT THE GROCERY STORE
KASUMI WHAT DO YOU WANT TO PUT INSIDE THEM?
HMM...
ALL DONE!
THERE'S A HUGE ONE...
THAT'S KASUMI'S.
MEAT.
GALBI!
MEAT, HUH?
I WASN'T EXPECTING THAT, BUT IT'S CERTAINLY SOMETHING YOU WOULD SAY.
WHAT'S THE LUCKY DIRECTION* THIS YEAR?
UM...
LET ME CHECK.
RUSTLE

* WHEN EATING EHOMAKI, YOU'RE SUPPOSED TO FACE THE "LUCKY DIRECTION" AND EAT THE ENTIRE EHOMAKI WITHOUT TALKING.

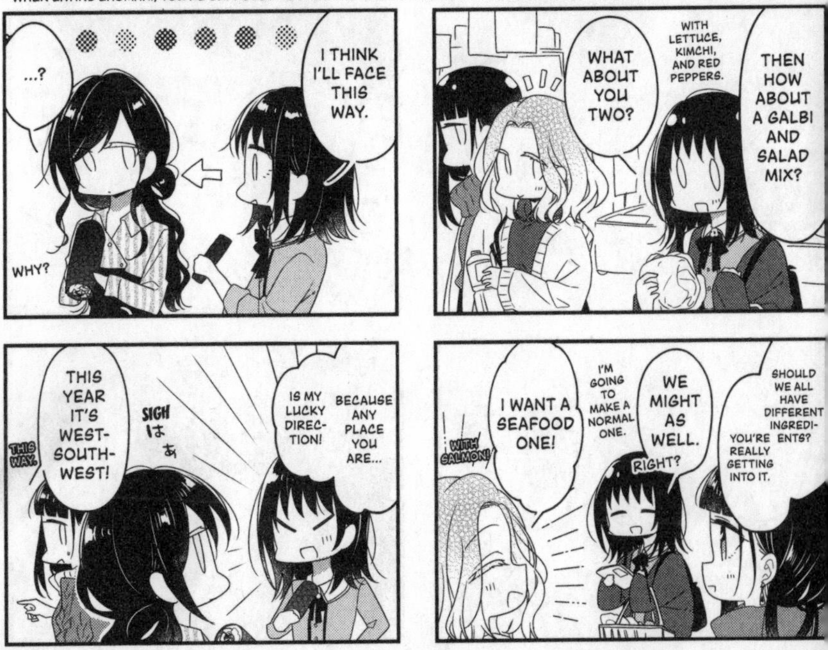
THEN HOW ABOUT A GALBI AND SALAD MIX?
WITH LETTUCE, KIMCHI, AND RED PEPPERS.
WHAT ABOUT YOU TWO?
I THINK I'LL FACE THIS WAY.
...?
WHY?
SHOULD WE ALL HAVE DIFFERENT INGREDIENTS?
YOU'RE REALLY GETTING INTO IT.
WE MIGHT AS WELL.
RIGHT?
I'M GOING TO MAKE A NORMAL ONE.
I WANT A SEAFOOD ONE!
WITH SALMON!
BECAUSE ANY PLACE YOU ARE...
IS MY LUCKY DIRECTION!
SIGH はぁ
THIS YEAR IT'S WEST-SOUTHWEST!
THIS WAY.

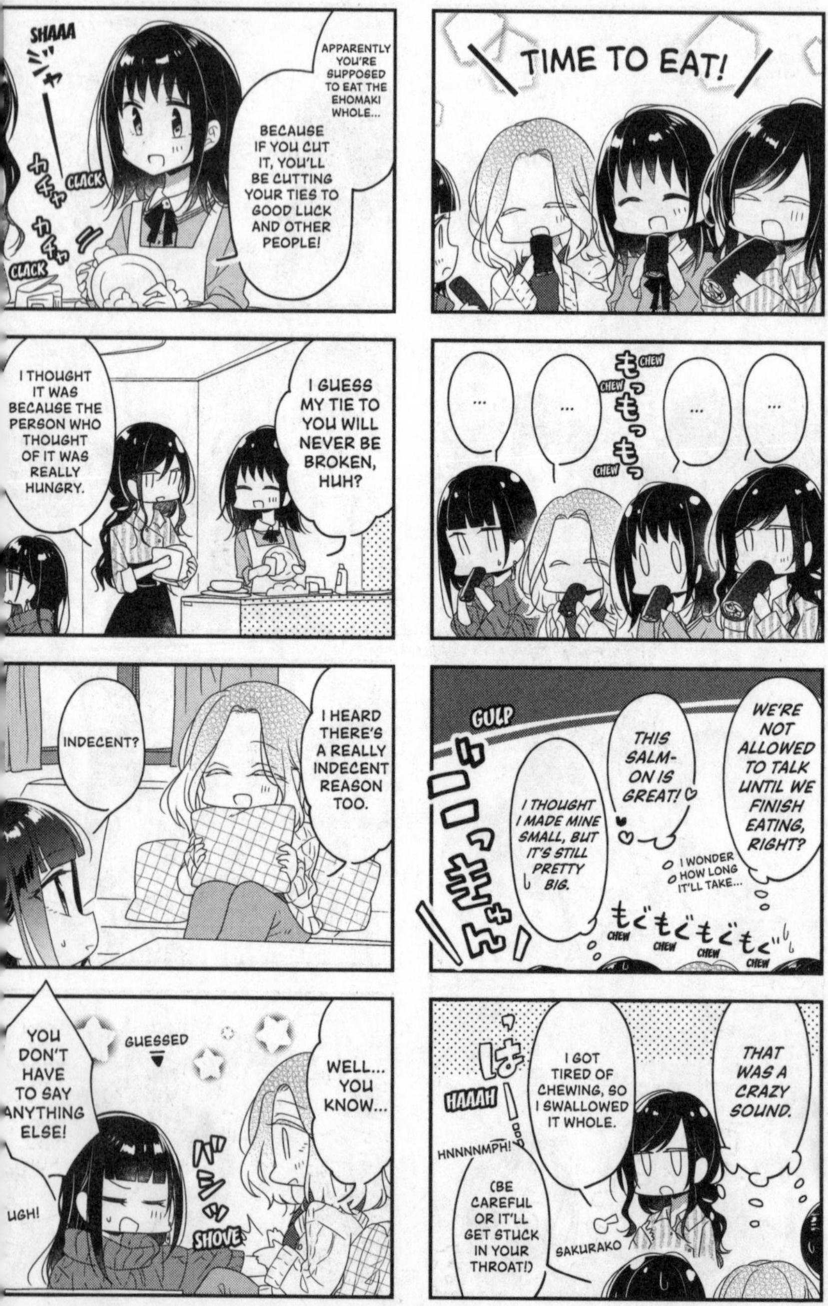
TIME TO EAT!
CHEW
CHEW
CHEW
...
...
...
...
WE'RE NOT ALLOWED TO TALK UNTIL WE FINISH EATING, RIGHT?
THIS SALMON IS GREAT!
I WONDER HOW LONG IT'LL TAKE...
I THOUGHT I MADE MINE SMALL, BUT IT'S STILL PRETTY BIG.
GULP
CHEW
CHEW
CHEW
CHEW
THAT WAS A CRAZY SOUND.
I GOT TIRED OF CHEWING, SO I SWALLOWED IT WHOLE.
HAAAH
HNNNNMPH!
(BE CAREFUL OR IT'LL GET STUCK IN YOUR THROAT!)
SAKURAKO
APPARENTLY YOU'RE SUPPOSED TO EAT THE EHOMAKI WHOLE...
BECAUSE IF YOU CUT IT, YOU'LL BE CUTTING YOUR TIES TO GOOD LUCK AND OTHER PEOPLE!
SHAAA
CLACK
CLACK
I GUESS MY TIE TO YOU WILL NEVER BE BROKEN, HUH?
I THOUGHT IT WAS BECAUSE THE PERSON WHO THOUGHT OF IT WAS REALLY HUNGRY.
I HEARD THERE'S A REALLY INDECENT REASON TOO.
INDECENT?
WELL... YOU KNOW...
GUESSED
YOU DON'T HAVE TO SAY ANYTHING ELSE!
SHOVE
UGH!

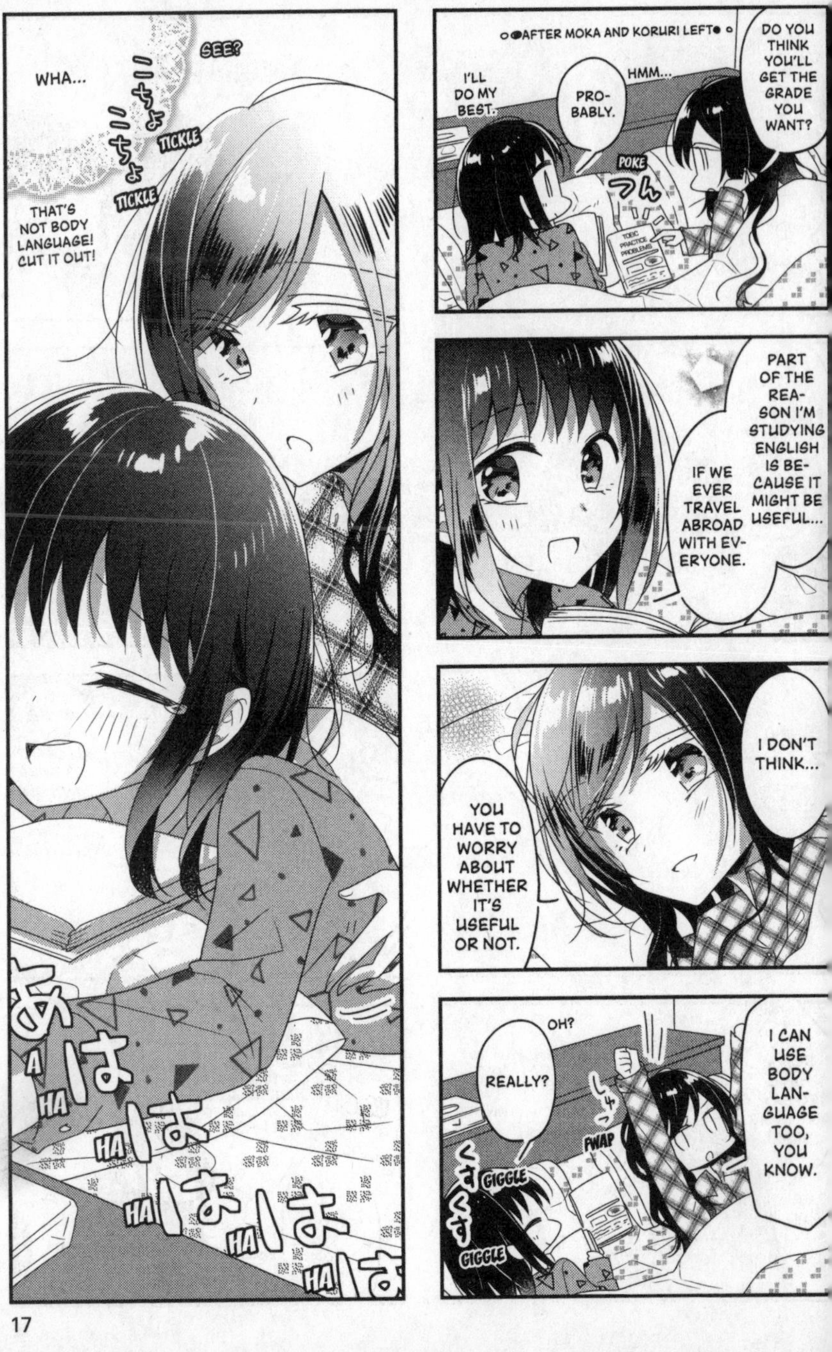
AFTER MOKA AND KORURI LEFT
DO YOU THINK YOU'LL GET THE GRADE YOU WANT?
HMM... PRO-BABLY.
I'LL DO MY BEST.
POKE
つん
TOEIC PRACTICE PROBLEMS
PART OF THE REA-SON I'M STUDYING ENGLISH IS BE-CAUSE IT MIGHT BE USEFUL...
IF WE EVER TRAVEL ABROAD WITH EV-ERYONE.
I DON'T THINK...
YOU HAVE TO WORRY ABOUT WHETHER IT'S USEFUL OR NOT.
I CAN USE BODY LAN-GUAGE TOO, YOU KNOW.
OH?
REALLY?
しゅっ
FWAP
くすくす
GIGGLE
GIGGLE
SEE?
こちょこちょ
TICKLE
TICKLE
WHA...
THAT'S NOT BODY LANGUAGE! CUT IT OUT!
あははははは
A HA HA HA HA HA

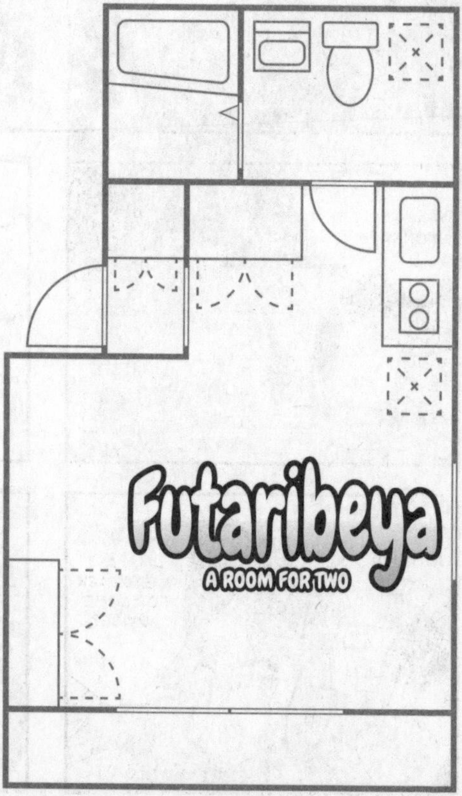
Futaribeya
A ROOM FOR TWO

Chapter 62

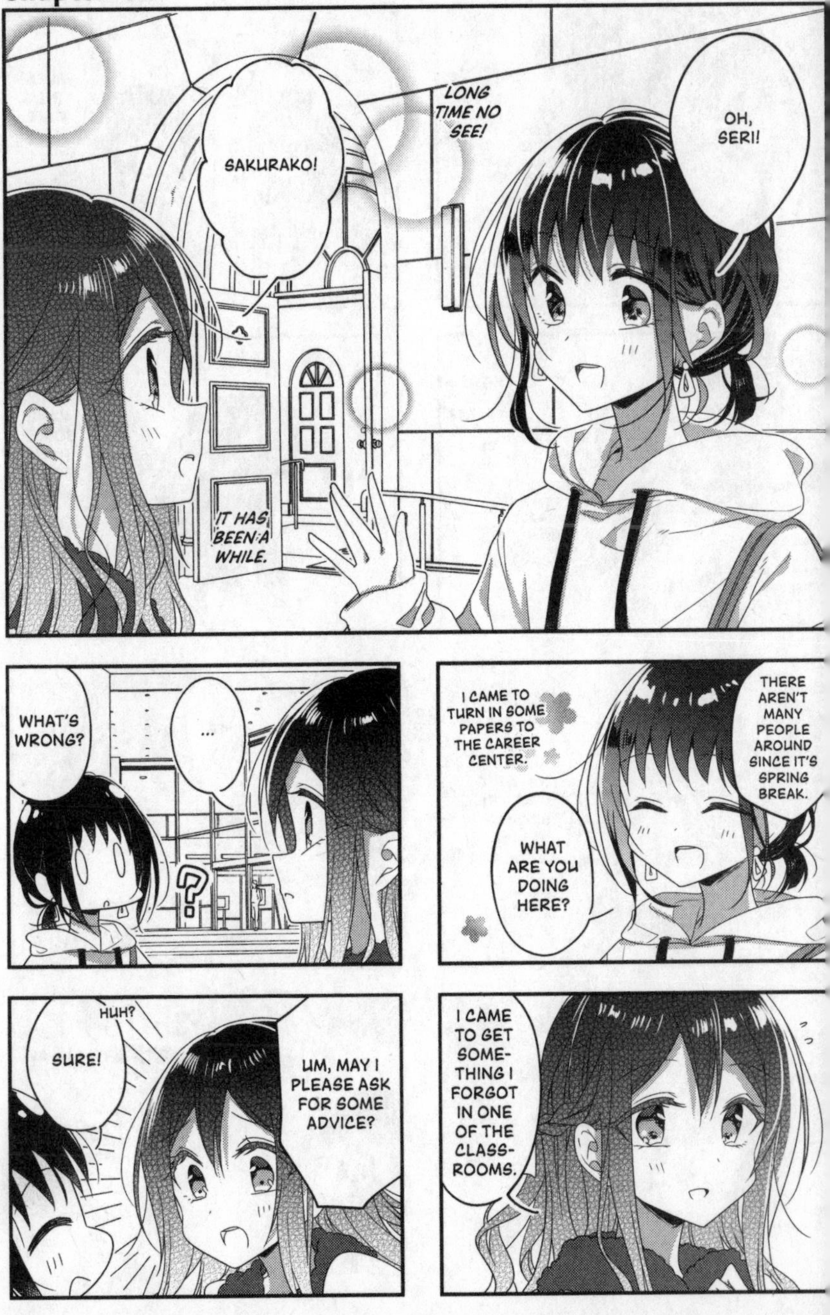
OH, SERI!
LONG TIME NO SEE!
SAKURAKO!
IT HAS BEEN A WHILE.
THERE AREN'T MANY PEOPLE AROUND SINCE IT'S SPRING BREAK.
I CAME TO TURN IN SOME PAPERS TO THE CAREER CENTER.
WHAT ARE YOU DOING HERE?
...
WHAT'S WRONG?
I CAME TO GET SOME-THING I FORGOT IN ONE OF THE CLASS-ROOMS.
UM, MAY I PLEASE ASK FOR SOME ADVICE?
HUH?
SURE!

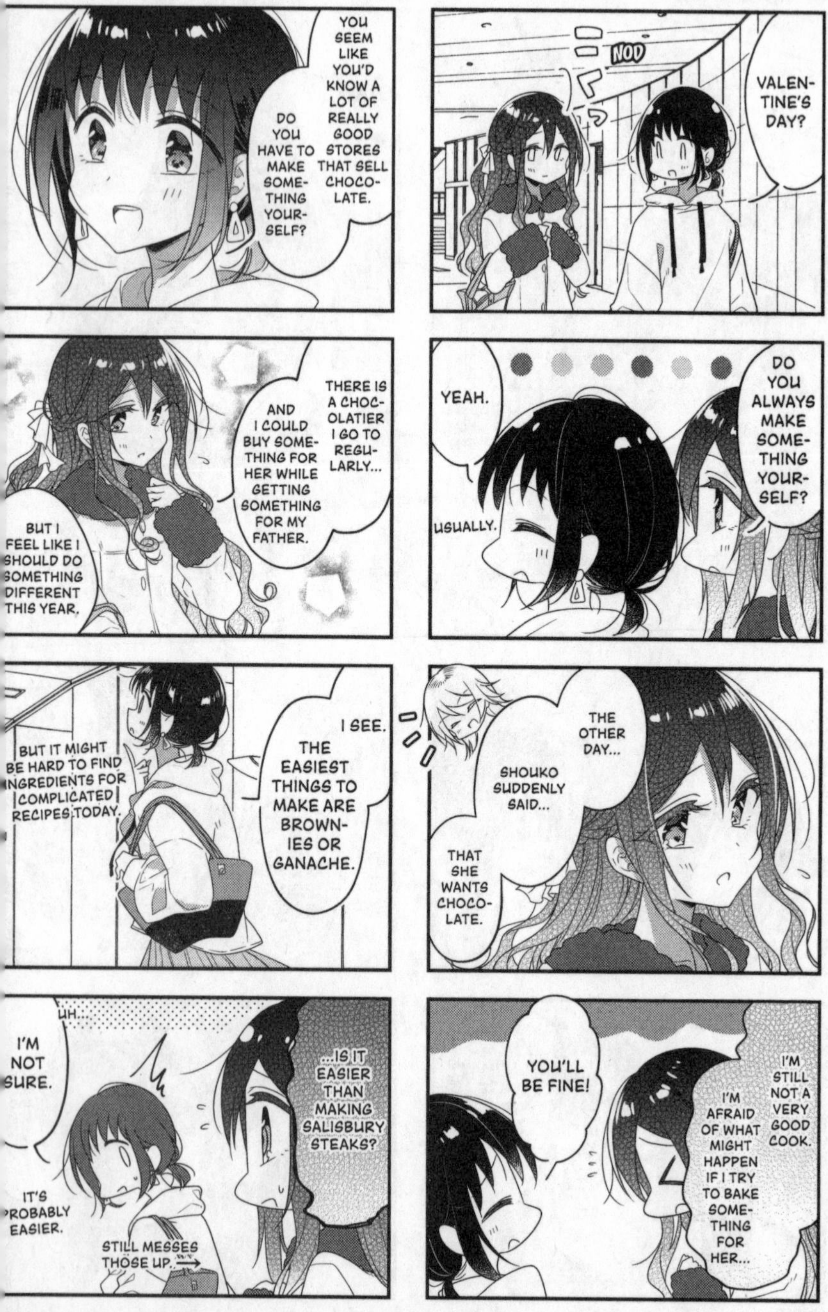
NOD
VALENTINE'S DAY?
YOU SEEM LIKE YOU'D KNOW A LOT OF REALLY GOOD STORES THAT SELL CHOCOLATE.
DO YOU HAVE TO MAKE SOMETHING YOURSELF?
DO YOU ALWAYS MAKE SOMETHING YOURSELF?
YEAH.
USUALLY.
THERE IS A CHOCOLATIER I GO TO REGULARLY...
AND I COULD BUY SOMETHING FOR HER WHILE GETTING SOMETHING FOR MY FATHER.
BUT I FEEL LIKE I SHOULD DO SOMETHING DIFFERENT THIS YEAR.
THE OTHER DAY...
SHOUKO SUDDENLY SAID...
THAT SHE WANTS CHOCOLATE.
I SEE.
THE EASIEST THINGS TO MAKE ARE BROWNIES OR GANACHE.
BUT IT MIGHT BE HARD TO FIND INGREDIENTS FOR COMPLICATED RECIPES TODAY.
I'M STILL NOT A VERY GOOD COOK.
I'M AFRAID OF WHAT MIGHT HAPPEN IF I TRY TO BAKE SOMETHING FOR HER...
YOU'LL BE FINE!
...IS IT EASIER THAN MAKING SALISBURY STEAKS?
UH...
I'M NOT SURE.
IT'S PROBABLY EASIER.
STILL MESSES THOSE UP.

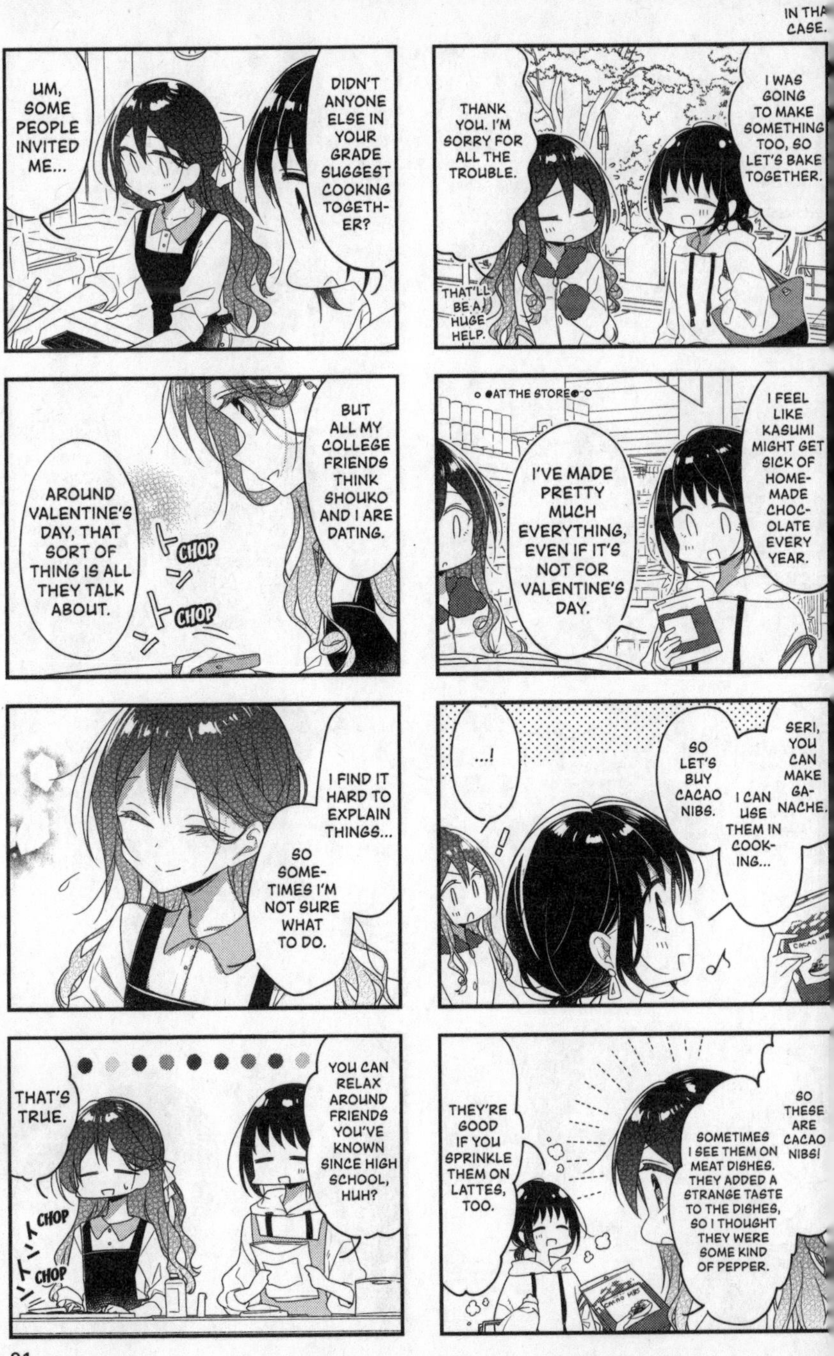
IN THA CASE.
I WAS GOING TO MAKE SOMETHING TOO, SO LET'S BAKE TOGETHER.
THANK YOU. I'M SORRY FOR ALL THE TROUBLE.
THAT'LL BE A HUGE HELP.
●AT THE STORE●
I FEEL LIKE KASUMI MIGHT GET SICK OF HOME-MADE CHOC-OLATE EVERY YEAR.
I'VE MADE PRETTY MUCH EVERYTHING, EVEN IF IT'S NOT FOR VALENTINE'S DAY.
SERI, YOU CAN MAKE GA-NACHE.
I CAN USE THEM IN COOK-ING...
SO LET'S BUY CACAO NIBS.
...!
CACAO NIBS
SO THESE ARE CACAO NIBS!
SOMETIMES I SEE THEM ON MEAT DISHES. THEY ADDED A STRANGE TASTE TO THE DISHES, SO I THOUGHT THEY WERE SOME KIND OF PEPPER.
THEY'RE GOOD IF YOU SPRINKLE THEM ON LATTES, TOO.
CACAO NIBS
DIDN'T ANYONE ELSE IN YOUR GRADE SUGGEST COOKING TOGETH-ER?
UM, SOME PEOPLE INVITED ME...
BUT ALL MY COLLEGE FRIENDS THINK SHOUKO AND I ARE DATING.
AROUND VALENTINE'S DAY, THAT SORT OF THING IS ALL THEY TALK ABOUT.
CHOP
CHOP
I FIND IT HARD TO EXPLAIN THINGS...
SO SOME-TIMES I'M NOT SURE WHAT TO DO.
YOU CAN RELAX AROUND FRIENDS YOU'VE KNOWN SINCE HIGH SCHOOL, HUH?
●●●●●●●●●
THAT'S TRUE.
CHOP
CHOP

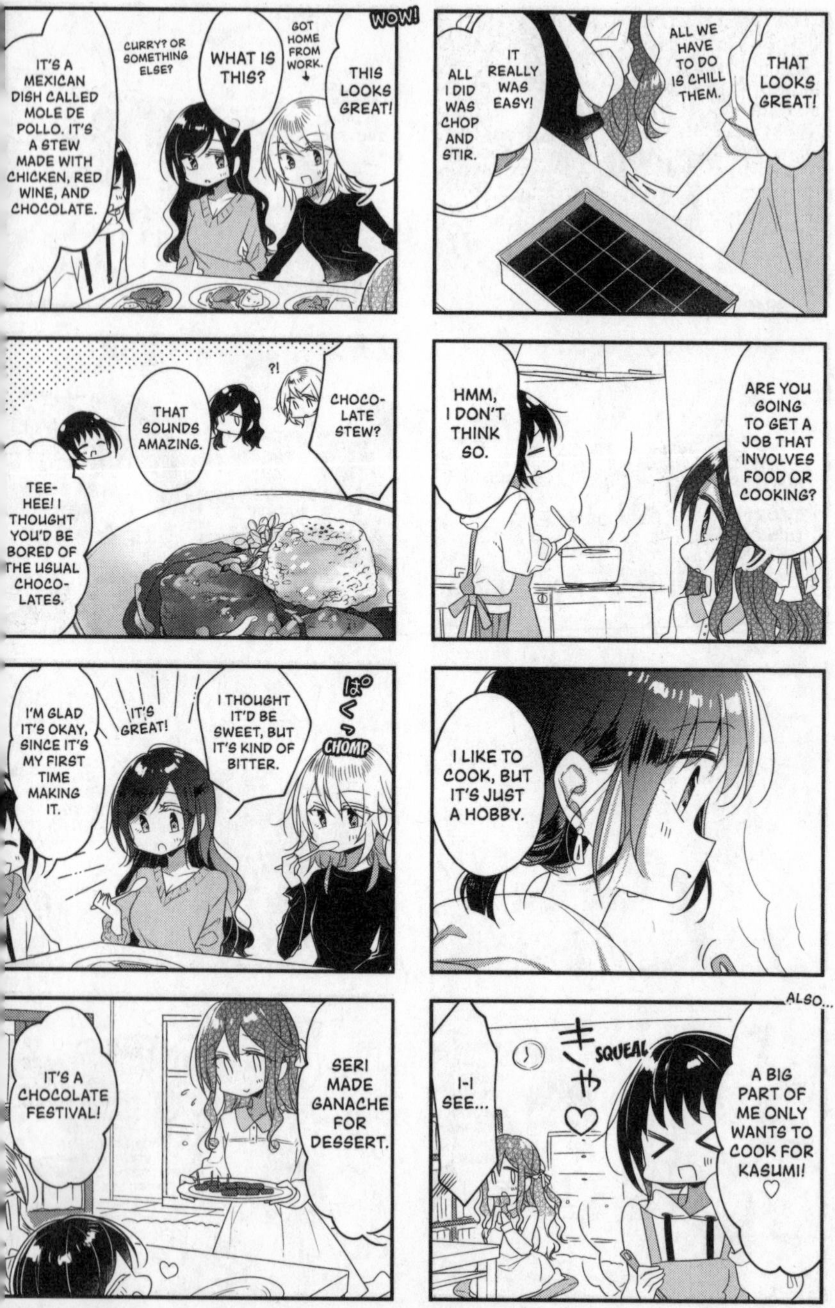
THAT LOOKS GREAT!
ALL WE HAVE TO DO IS CHILL THEM.
IT REALLY WAS EASY!
ALL I DID WAS CHOP AND STIR.
ARE YOU GOING TO GET A JOB THAT INVOLVES FOOD OR COOKING?
HMM, I DON'T THINK SO.
I LIKE TO COOK, BUT IT'S JUST A HOBBY.
ALSO...
A BIG PART OF ME ONLY WANTS TO COOK FOR KASUMI! ♡
きゃ
SQUEAL
I-I SEE...
WOW!
THIS LOOKS GREAT!
GOT HOME FROM WORK.
WHAT IS THIS?
CURRY? OR SOMETHING ELSE?
IT'S A MEXICAN DISH CALLED MOLE DE POLLO. IT'S A STEW MADE WITH CHICKEN, RED WINE, AND CHOCOLATE.
CHOCO-LATE STEW?
?!
THAT SOUNDS AMAZING.
TEE-HEE! I THOUGHT YOU'D BE BORED OF THE USUAL CHOCO-LATES.
ぱくっ
CHOMP
I THOUGHT IT'D BE SWEET, BUT IT'S KIND OF BITTER.
IT'S GREAT!
I'M GLAD IT'S OKAY, SINCE IT'S MY FIRST TIME MAKING IT.
SERI MADE GANACHE FOR DESSERT.
IT'S A CHOCOLATE FESTIVAL!

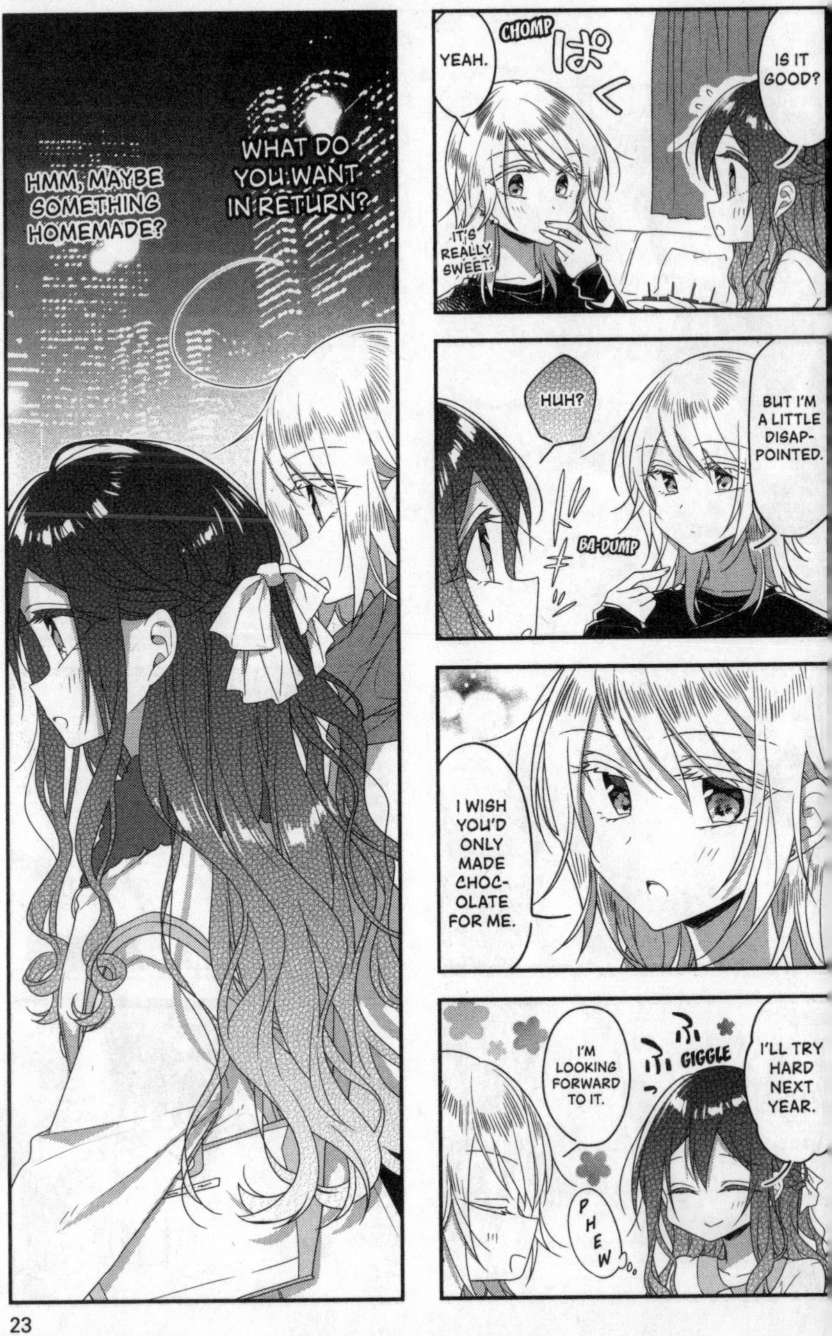
IS IT GOOD?
CHOMP
ぱく
YEAH.
IT'S REALLY SWEET.
BUT I'M A LITTLE DISAP-POINTED.
HUH?
BA-DUMP
I WISH YOU'D ONLY MADE CHOC-OLATE FOR ME.
I'LL TRY HARD NEXT YEAR.
ふふ
GIGGLE
I'M LOOKING FORWARD TO IT.
PHEW
WHAT DO YOU WANT IN RETURN?
HMM, MAYBE SOMETHING HOMEMADE?

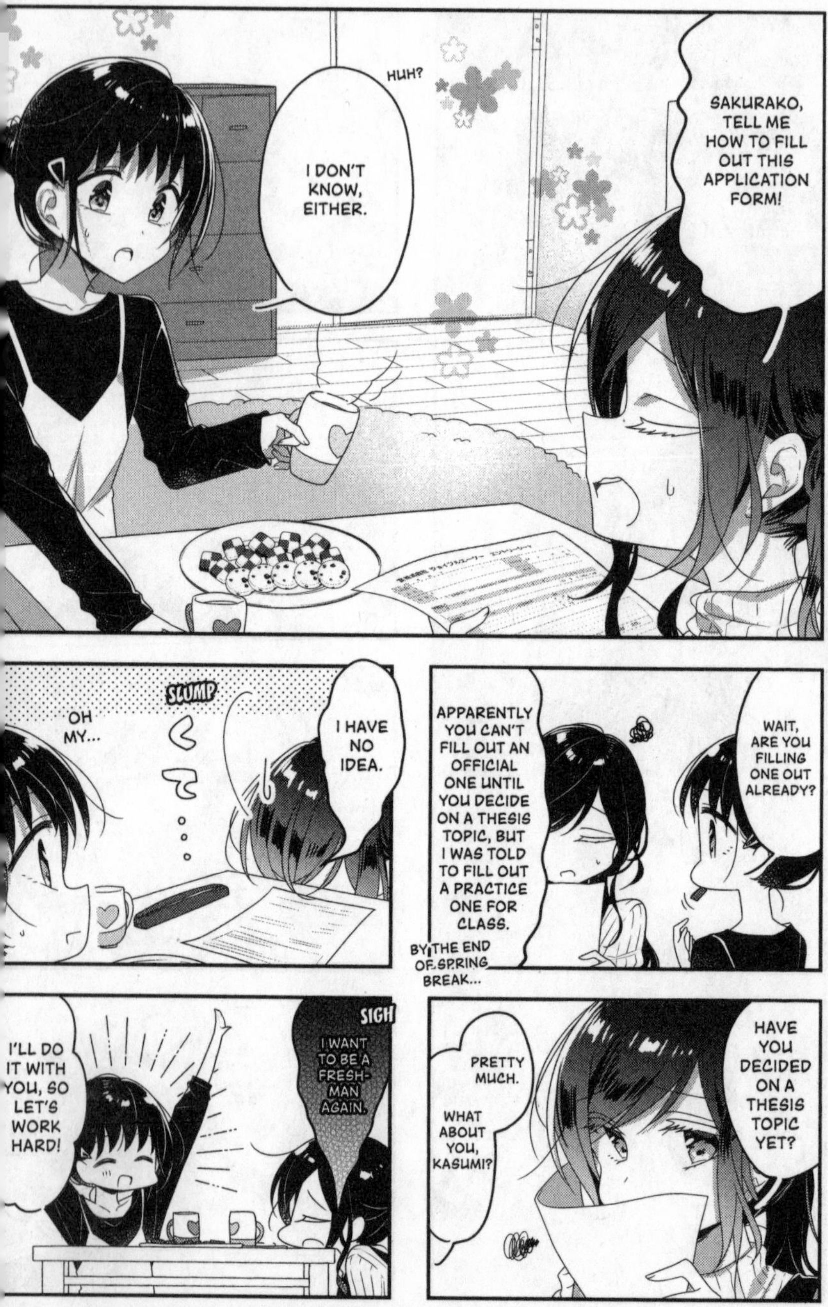
SAKURAKO, TELL ME HOW TO FILL OUT THIS APPLICATION FORM!
HUH?
I DON'T KNOW, EITHER.
WAIT, ARE YOU FILLING ONE OUT ALREADY?
APPARENTLY YOU CAN'T FILL OUT AN OFFICIAL ONE UNTIL YOU DECIDE ON A THESIS TOPIC, BUT I WAS TOLD TO FILL OUT A PRACTICE ONE FOR CLASS.
BY THE END OF SPRING BREAK...
I HAVE NO IDEA.
SLUMP
OH MY...
HAVE YOU DECIDED ON A THESIS TOPIC YET?
PRETTY MUCH.
WHAT ABOUT YOU, KASUMI?
SIGH
I WANT TO BE A FRESHMAN AGAIN.
I'LL DO IT WITH YOU, SO LET'S WORK HARD!

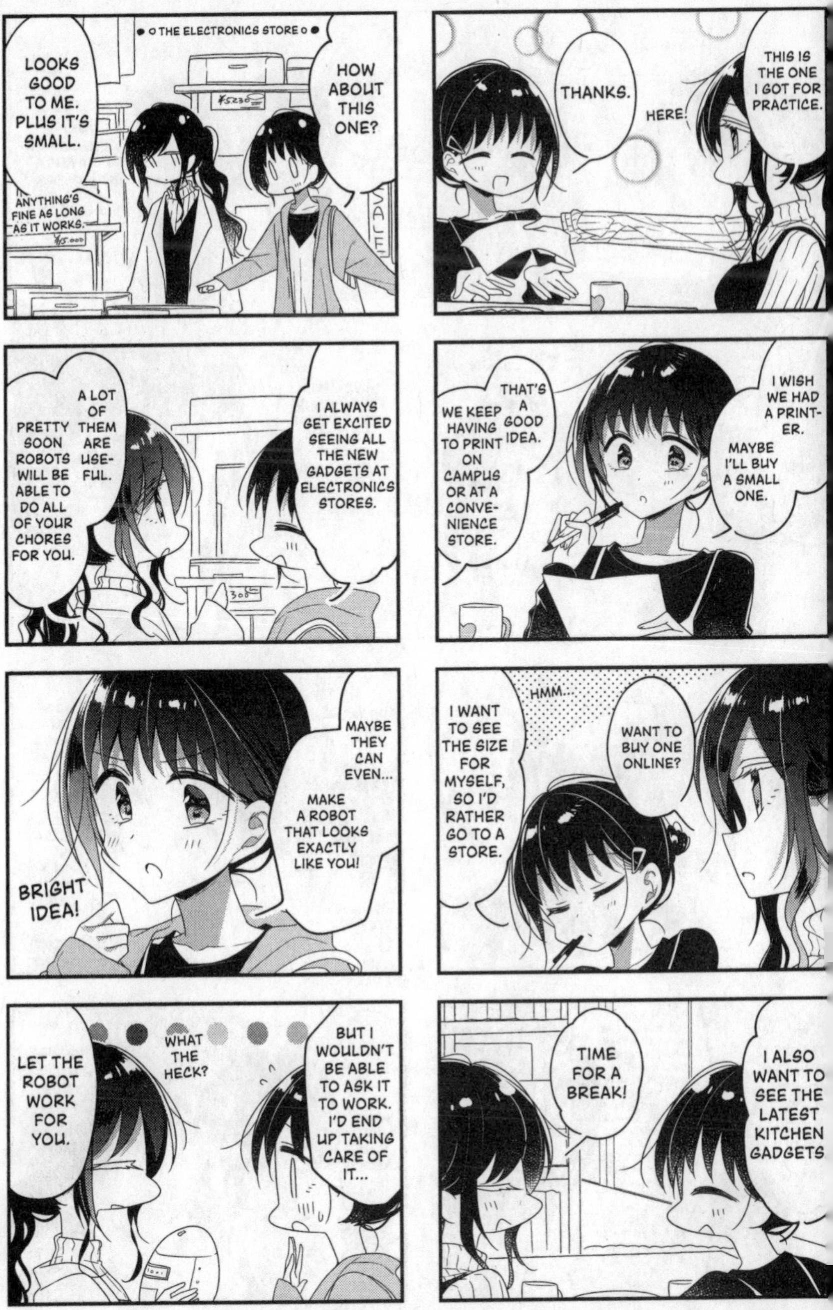
THIS IS THE ONE I GOT FOR PRACTICE.
HERE.
THANKS.
I WISH WE HAD A PRINTER.
MAYBE I'LL BUY A SMALL ONE.
THAT'S A GOOD IDEA.
WE KEEP HAVING TO PRINT ON CAMPUS OR AT A CONVENIENCE STORE.
WANT TO BUY ONE ONLINE?
HMM...
I WANT TO SEE THE SIZE FOR MYSELF, SO I'D RATHER GO TO A STORE.
I ALSO WANT TO SEE THE LATEST KITCHEN GADGETS
TIME FOR A BREAK!
THE ELECTRONICS STORE
HOW ABOUT THIS ONE?
LOOKS GOOD TO ME. PLUS IT'S SMALL.
ANYTHING'S FINE AS LONG AS IT WORKS.
SALE
I ALWAYS GET EXCITED SEEING ALL THE NEW GADGETS AT ELECTRONICS STORES.
A LOT OF THEM ARE USEFUL.
PRETTY SOON ROBOTS WILL BE ABLE TO DO ALL OF YOUR CHORES FOR YOU.
MAYBE THEY CAN EVEN...
MAKE A ROBOT THAT LOOKS EXACTLY LIKE YOU!
BRIGHT IDEA!
BUT I WOULDN'T BE ABLE TO ASK IT TO WORK. I'D END UP TAKING CARE OF IT...
WHAT THE HECK?
LET THE ROBOT WORK FOR YOU.

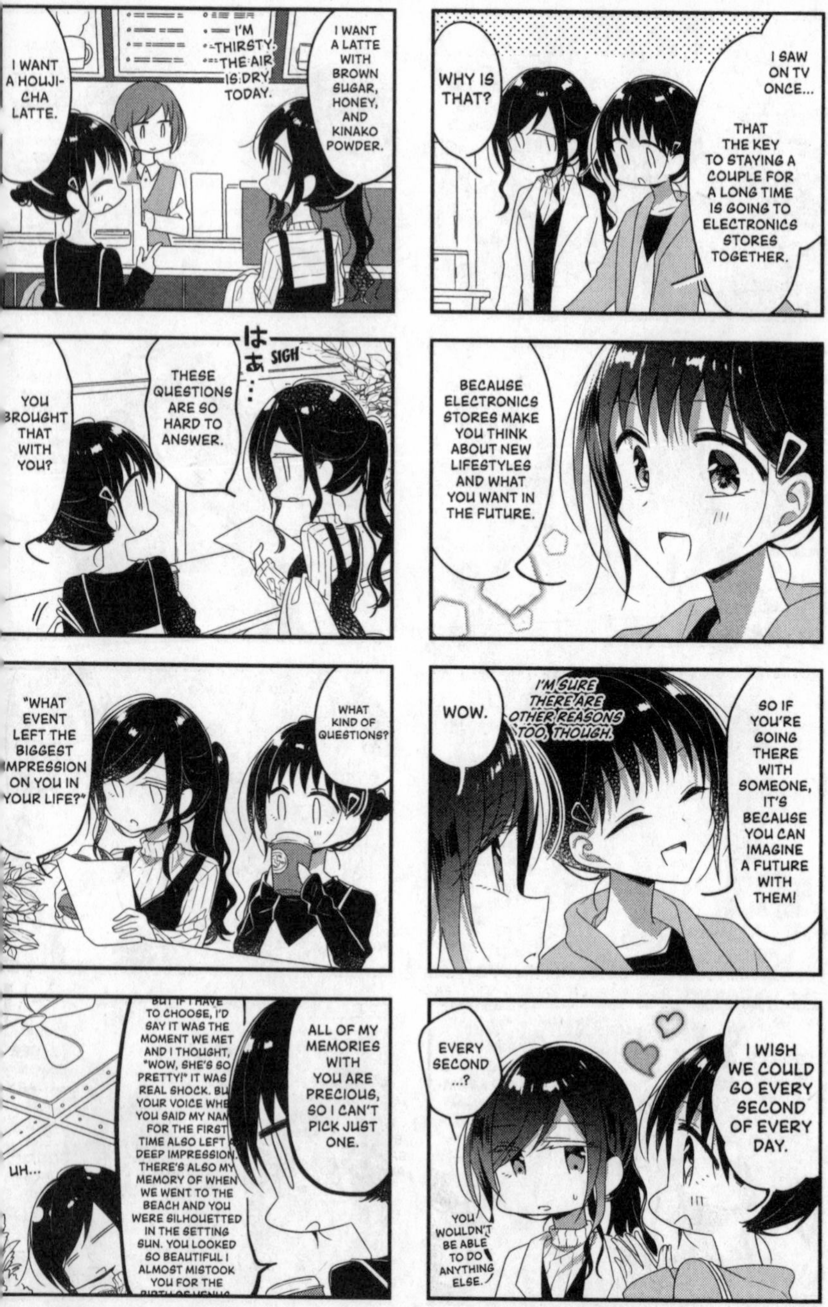
I SAW ON TV ONCE...
THAT THE KEY TO STAYING A COUPLE FOR A LONG TIME IS GOING TO ELECTRONICS STORES TOGETHER.
WHY IS THAT?
BECAUSE ELECTRONICS STORES MAKE YOU THINK ABOUT NEW LIFESTYLES AND WHAT YOU WANT IN THE FUTURE.
SO IF YOU'RE GOING THERE WITH SOMEONE, IT'S BECAUSE YOU CAN IMAGINE A FUTURE WITH THEM!
I'M SURE THERE ARE OTHER REASONS TOO, THOUGH.
WOW.
I WISH WE COULD GO EVERY SECOND OF EVERY DAY.
EVERY SECOND ...?
YOU WOULDN'T BE ABLE TO DO ANYTHING ELSE.
I WANT A LATTE WITH BROWN SUGAR, HONEY, AND KINAKO POWDER.
I'M THIRSTY. THE AIR IS DRY TODAY.
I WANT A HOUJI-CHA LATTE.
はあ… SIGH
THESE QUESTIONS ARE SO HARD TO ANSWER.
YOU BROUGHT THAT WITH YOU?
WHAT KIND OF QUESTIONS?
"WHAT EVENT LEFT THE BIGGEST IMPRESSION ON YOU IN YOUR LIFE?"
ALL OF MY MEMORIES WITH YOU ARE PRECIOUS, SO I CAN'T PICK JUST ONE.
BUT IF I HAVE TO CHOOSE, I'D SAY IT WAS THE MOMENT WE MET AND I THOUGHT, "WOW, SHE'S SO PRETTY!" IT WAS REAL SHOCK. BU YOUR VOICE WHE YOU SAID MY NAM FOR THE FIRST TIME ALSO LEFT DEEP IMPRESSION. THERE'S ALSO MY MEMORY OF WHEN WE WENT TO THE BEACH AND YOU WERE SILHOUETTED IN THE SETTING SUN. YOU LOOKED SO BEAUTIFUL I ALMOST MISTOOK YOU FOR THE
UH...

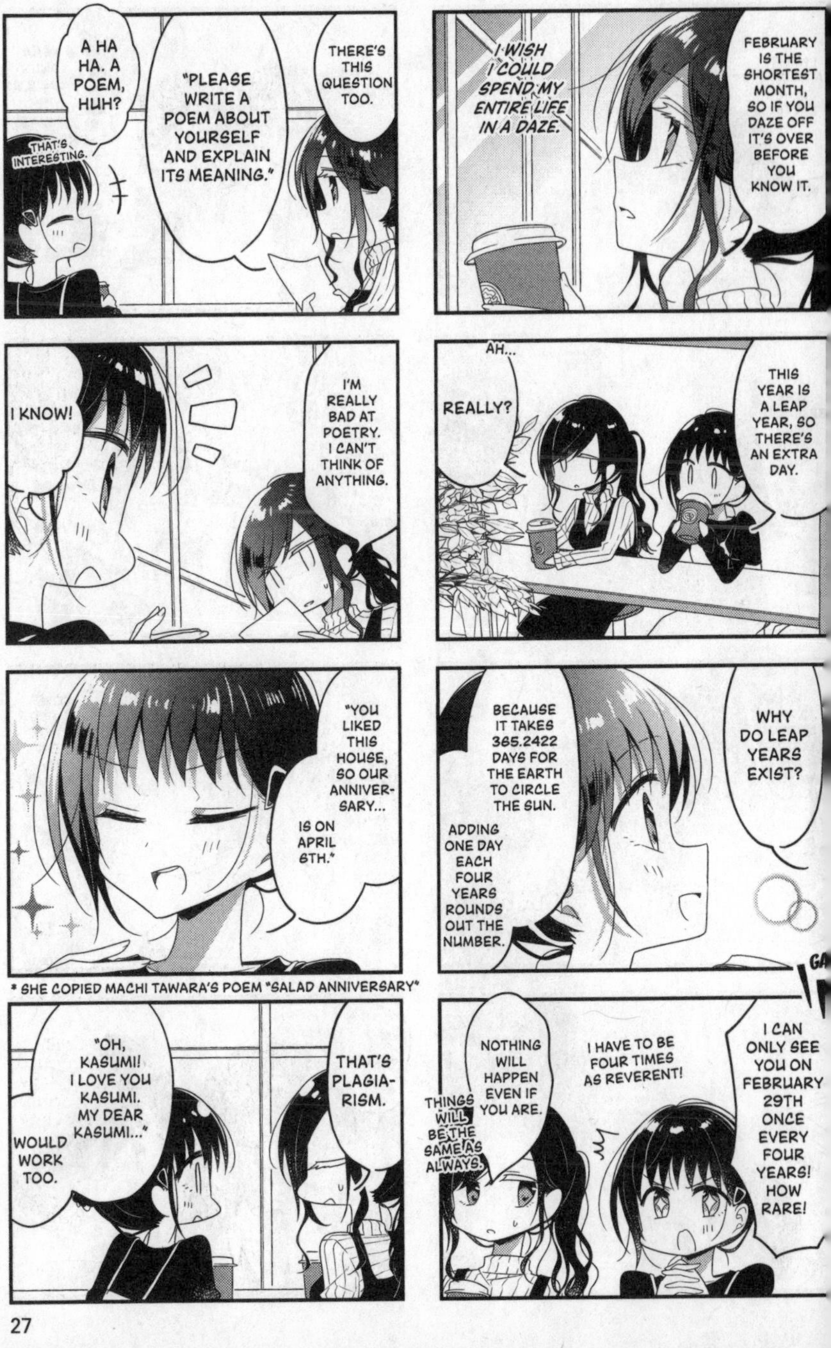
FEBRUARY IS THE SHORTEST MONTH, SO IF YOU DAZE OFF IT'S OVER BEFORE YOU KNOW IT.
I WISH I COULD SPEND MY ENTIRE LIFE IN A DAZE.
THERE'S THIS QUESTION TOO.
"PLEASE WRITE A POEM ABOUT YOURSELF AND EXPLAIN ITS MEANING."
A HA HA. A POEM, HUH?
THAT'S INTERESTING.
THIS YEAR IS A LEAP YEAR, SO THERE'S AN EXTRA DAY.
REALLY?
AH...
I'M REALLY BAD AT POETRY. I CAN'T THINK OF ANYTHING.
I KNOW!
WHY DO LEAP YEARS EXIST?
BECAUSE IT TAKES 365.2422 DAYS FOR THE EARTH TO CIRCLE THE SUN.
ADDING ONE DAY EACH FOUR YEARS ROUNDS OUT THE NUMBER.
"YOU LIKED THIS HOUSE, SO OUR ANNIVERSARY...
IS ON APRIL 6TH."
I CAN ONLY SEE YOU ON FEBRUARY 29TH ONCE EVERY FOUR YEARS! HOW RARE!
I HAVE TO BE FOUR TIMES AS REVERENT!
NOTHING WILL HAPPEN EVEN IF YOU ARE.
THINGS WILL BE THE SAME AS ALWAYS.
THAT'S PLAGIARISM.
"OH, KASUMI! I LOVE YOU KASUMI. MY DEAR KASUMI..."
WOULD WORK TOO.

* SHE COPIED MACHI TAWARA'S POEM "SALAD ANNIVERSARY"

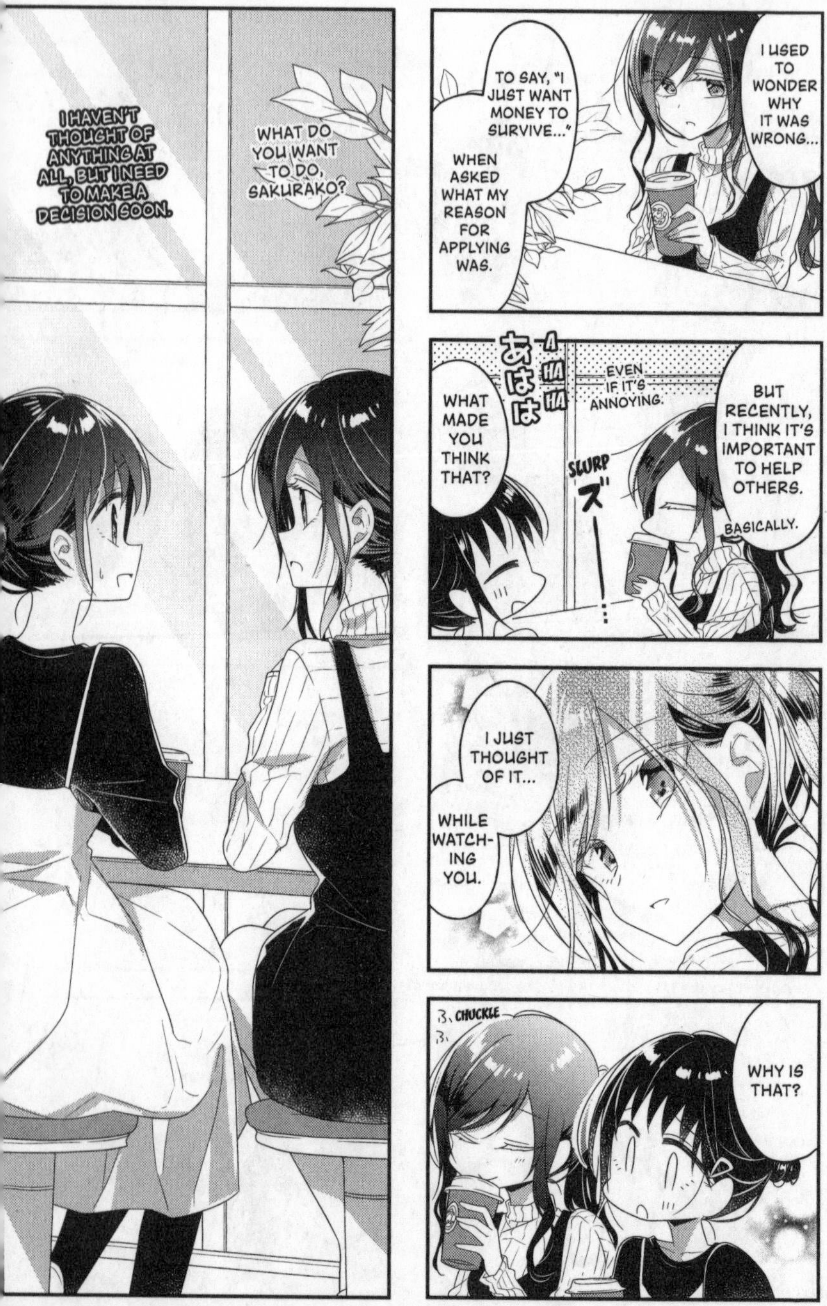

I USED TO WONDER WHY IT WAS WRONG...
TO SAY, "I JUST WANT MONEY TO SURVIVE..."
WHEN ASKED WHAT MY REASON FOR APPLYING WAS.
BUT RECENTLY, I THINK IT'S IMPORTANT TO HELP OTHERS.
BASICALLY.
EVEN IF IT'S ANNOYING.
SLURP
ズー
A HA HA
あはは
WHAT MADE YOU THINK THAT?
I JUST THOUGHT OF IT...
WHILE WATCHING YOU.
WHY IS THAT?
ふふ
CHUCKLE
WHAT DO YOU WANT TO DO, SAKURAKO?
I HAVEN'T THOUGHT OF ANYTHING AT ALL, BUT I NEED TO MAKE A DECISION SOON.

Illustration gallery of Yukiko

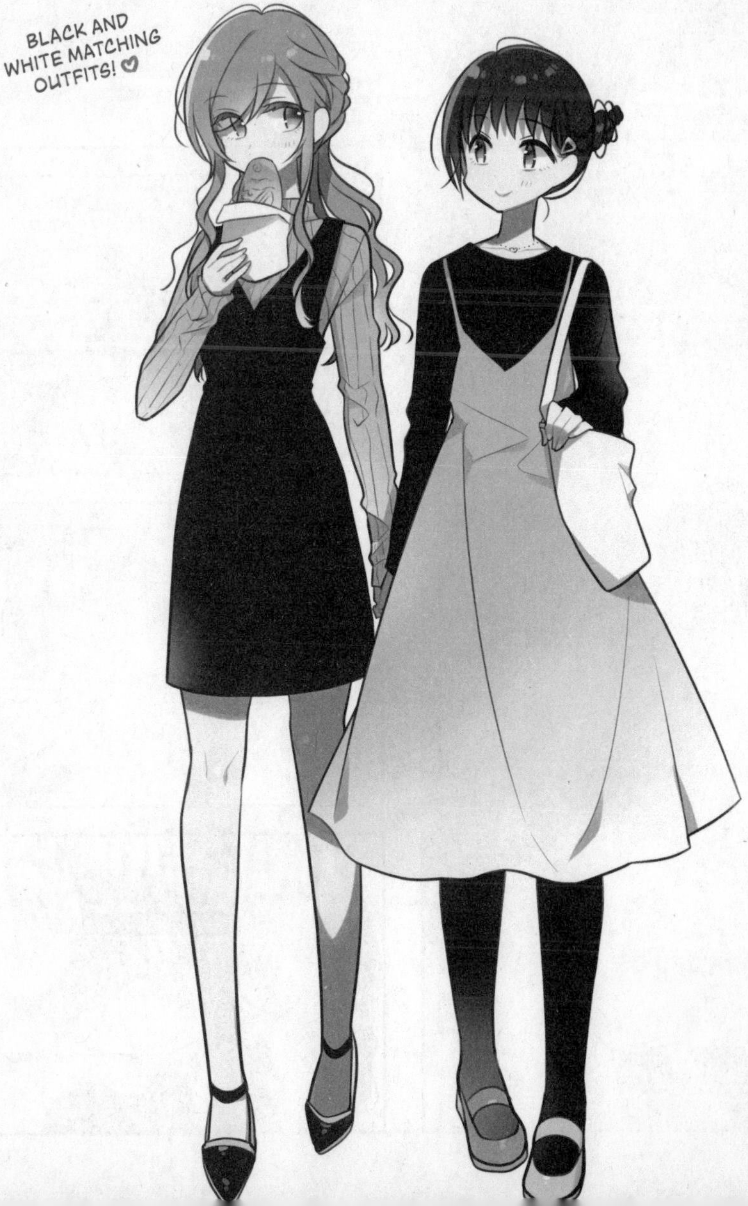
BLACK AND WHITE MATCHING OUTFITS!

Futaribeya
A ROOM FOR TWO

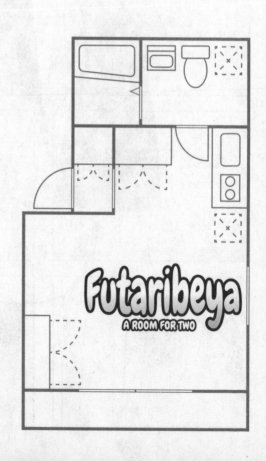

Chapter 63

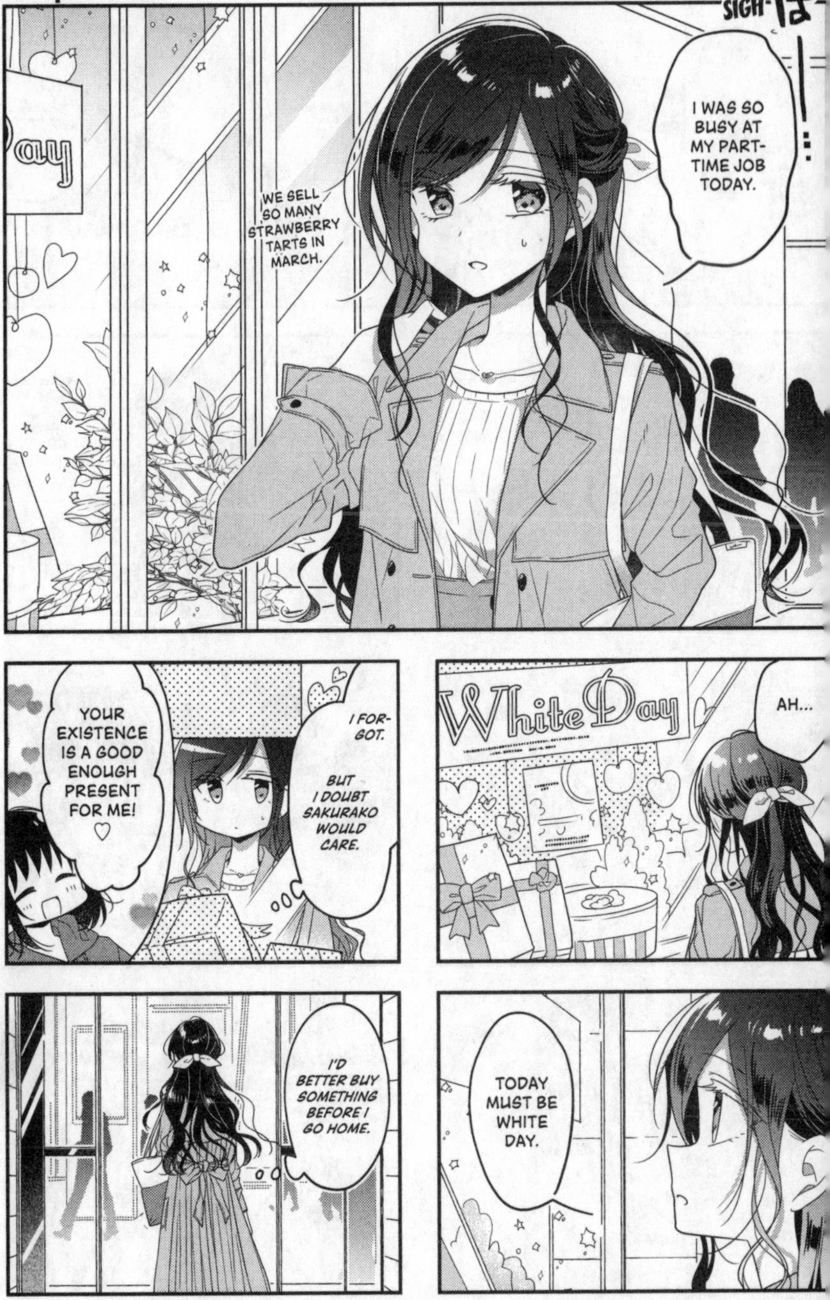
SIGH- は―!!..
I WAS SO BUSY AT MY PART-TIME JOB TODAY.
WE SELL SO MANY STRAWBERRY TARTS IN MARCH.
AH...
White Day
I FORGOT.
BUT I DOUBT SAKURAKO WOULD CARE.
YOUR EXISTENCE IS A GOOD ENOUGH PRESENT FOR ME! ♡
TODAY MUST BE WHITE DAY.
I'D BETTER BUY SOMETHING BEFORE I GO HOME.

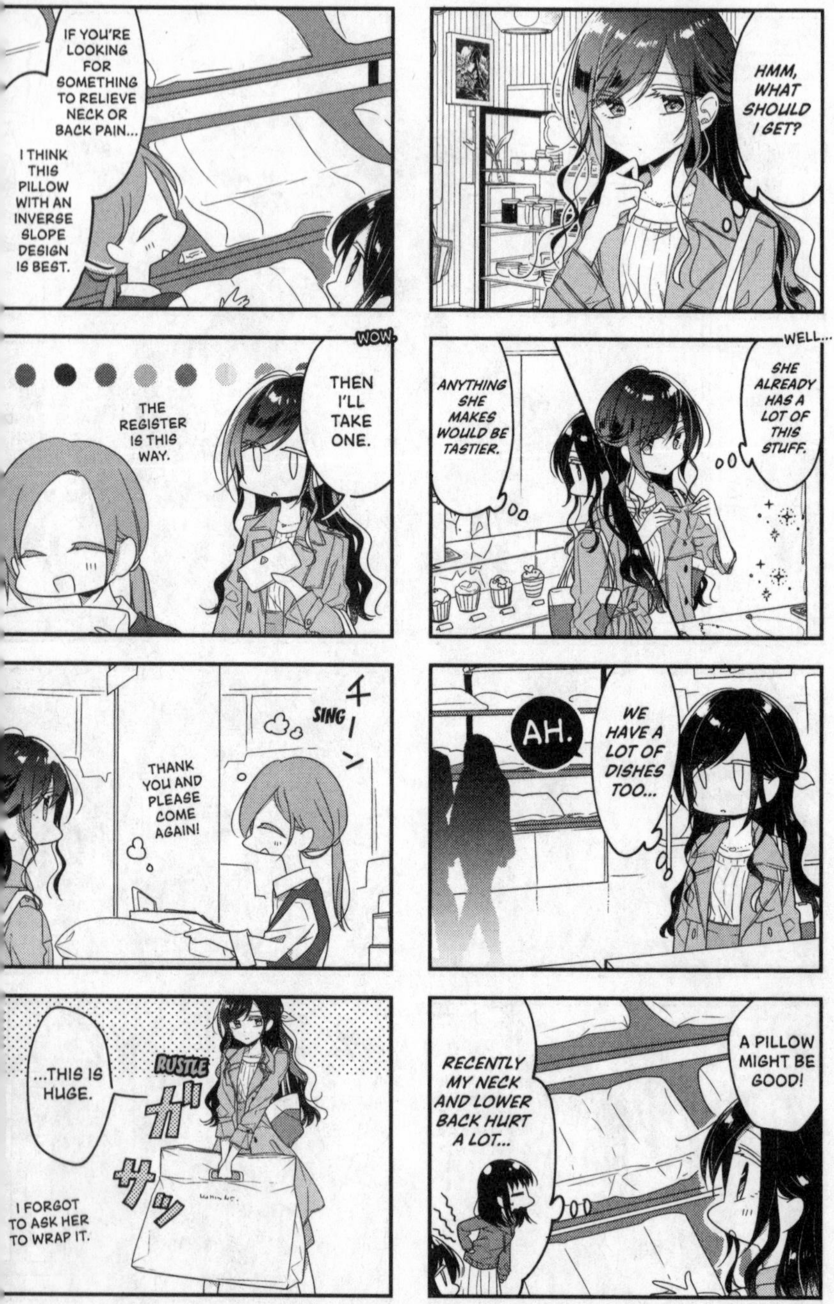
HMM, WHAT SHOULD I GET?
WELL...
SHE ALREADY HAS A LOT OF THIS STUFF.
ANYTHING SHE MAKES WOULD BE TASTIER.
WE HAVE A LOT OF DISHES TOO...
AH.
A PILLOW MIGHT BE GOOD!
RECENTLY MY NECK AND LOWER BACK HURT A LOT...
IF YOU'RE LOOKING FOR SOMETHING TO RELIEVE NECK OR BACK PAIN...
I THINK THIS PILLOW WITH AN INVERSE SLOPE DESIGN IS BEST.
WOW.
THEN I'LL TAKE ONE.
THE REGISTER IS THIS WAY.
SING
THANK YOU AND PLEASE COME AGAIN!
RUSTLE
...THIS IS HUGE.
I FORGOT TO ASK HER TO WRAP IT.

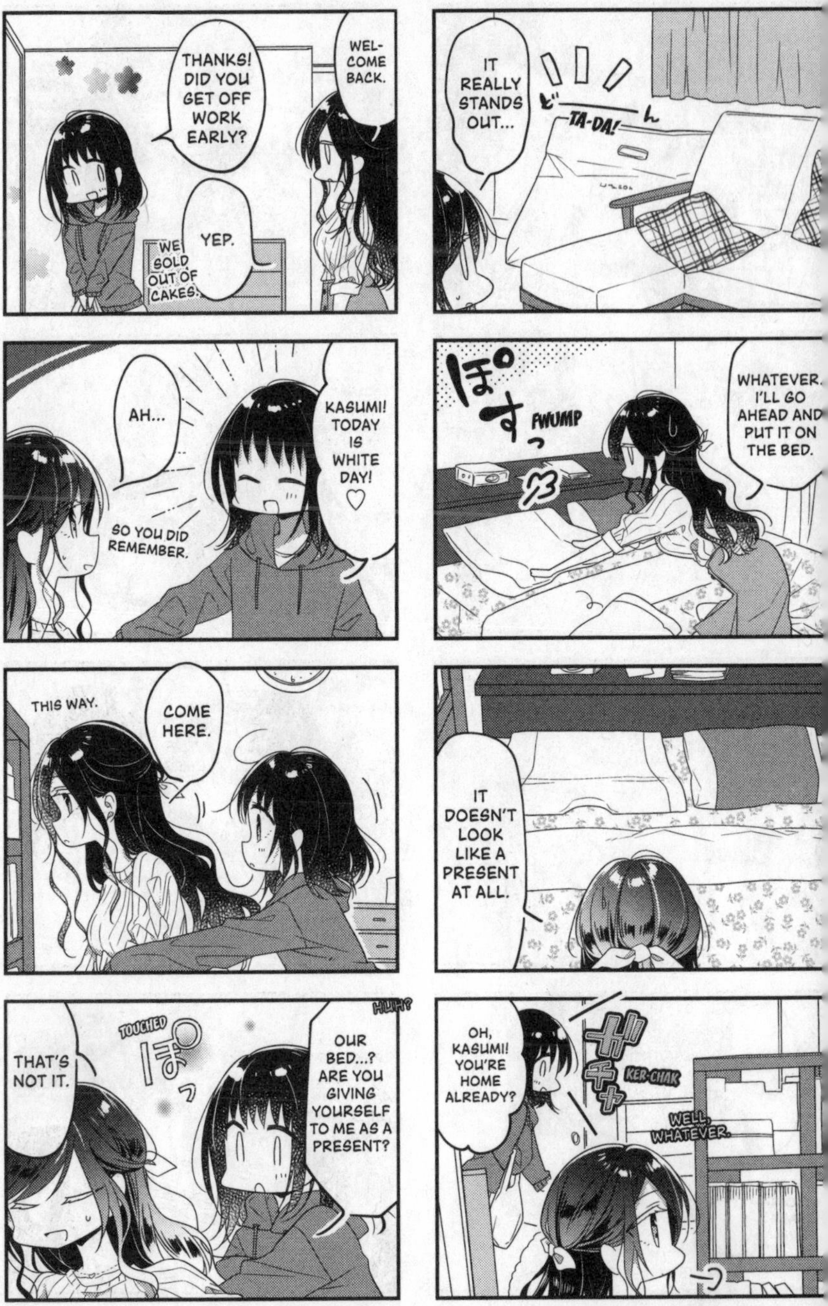
IT REALLY STANDS OUT...
どーん
TA-DA!
WHATEVER. I'LL GO AHEAD AND PUT IT ON THE BED.
ぽすっ
FWUMP
IT DOESN'T LOOK LIKE A PRESENT AT ALL.
ガチャ
KER-CHAK
OH, KASUMI! YOU'RE HOME ALREADY?
WELL, WHATEVER.
WEL-COME BACK.
THANKS! DID YOU GET OFF WORK EARLY?
YEP.
WE SOLD OUT OF CAKES.
KASUMI! TODAY IS WHITE DAY! ♡
AH...
SO YOU DID REMEMBER.
COME HERE.
THIS WAY.
HUH?
OUR BED...? ARE YOU GIVING YOURSELF TO ME AS A PRESENT?
TOUCHED
ぽっ
THAT'S NOT IT.

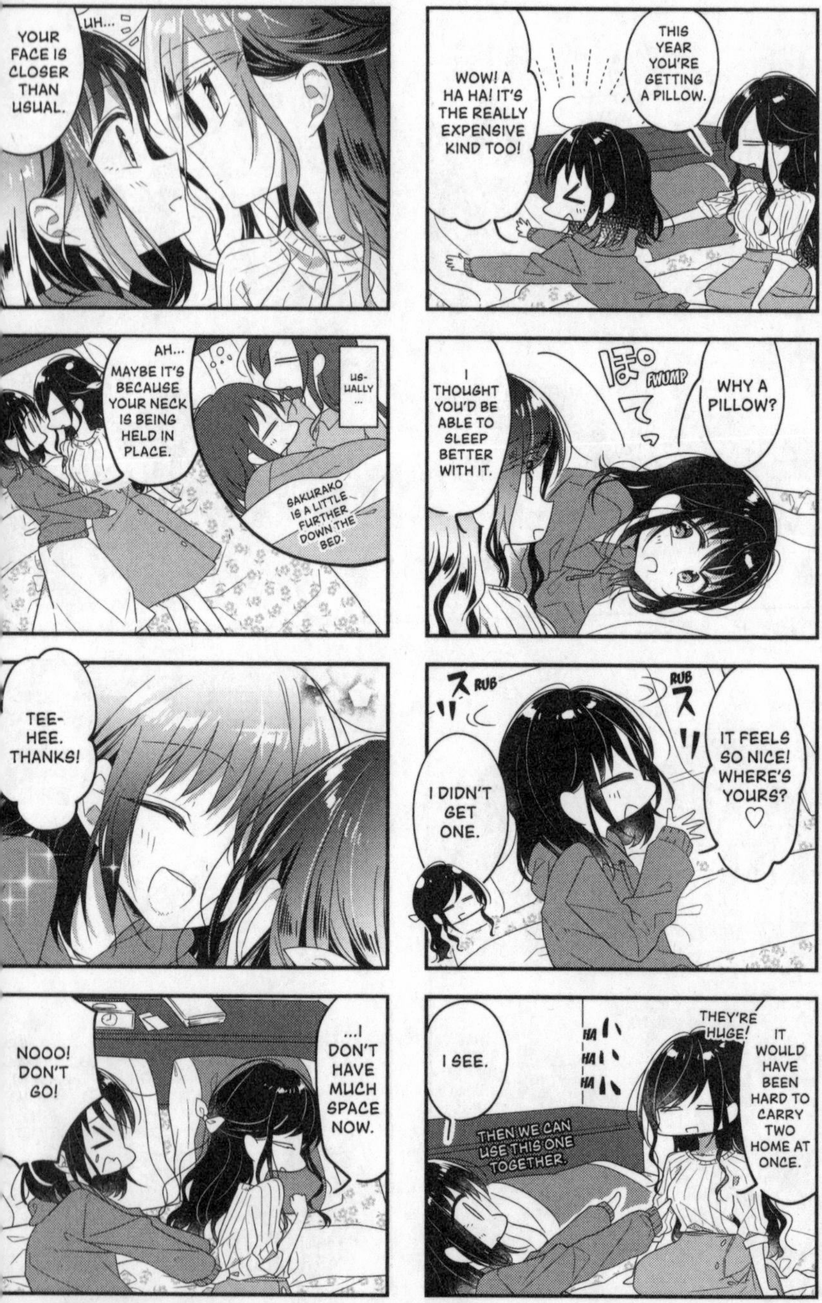
THIS YEAR YOU'RE GETTING A PILLOW.
WOW! A HA HA! IT'S THE REALLY EXPENSIVE KIND TOO!
WHY A PILLOW?
FWUMP
I THOUGHT YOU'D BE ABLE TO SLEEP BETTER WITH IT.
RUB
IT FEELS SO NICE! WHERE'S YOURS? ♡
RUB
I DIDN'T GET ONE.
IT WOULD HAVE BEEN HARD TO CARRY TWO HOME AT ONCE.
THEY'RE HUGE!
HA HA HA
I SEE.
THEN WE CAN USE THIS ONE TOGETHER.
UH...
YOUR FACE IS CLOSER THAN USUAL.
US-UALLY ...
AH... MAYBE IT'S BECAUSE YOUR NECK IS BEING HELD IN PLACE.
SAKURAKO IS A LITTLE FURTHER DOWN THE BED.
TEE-HEE. THANKS!
...I DON'T HAVE MUCH SPACE NOW.
NOOO! DON'T GO!

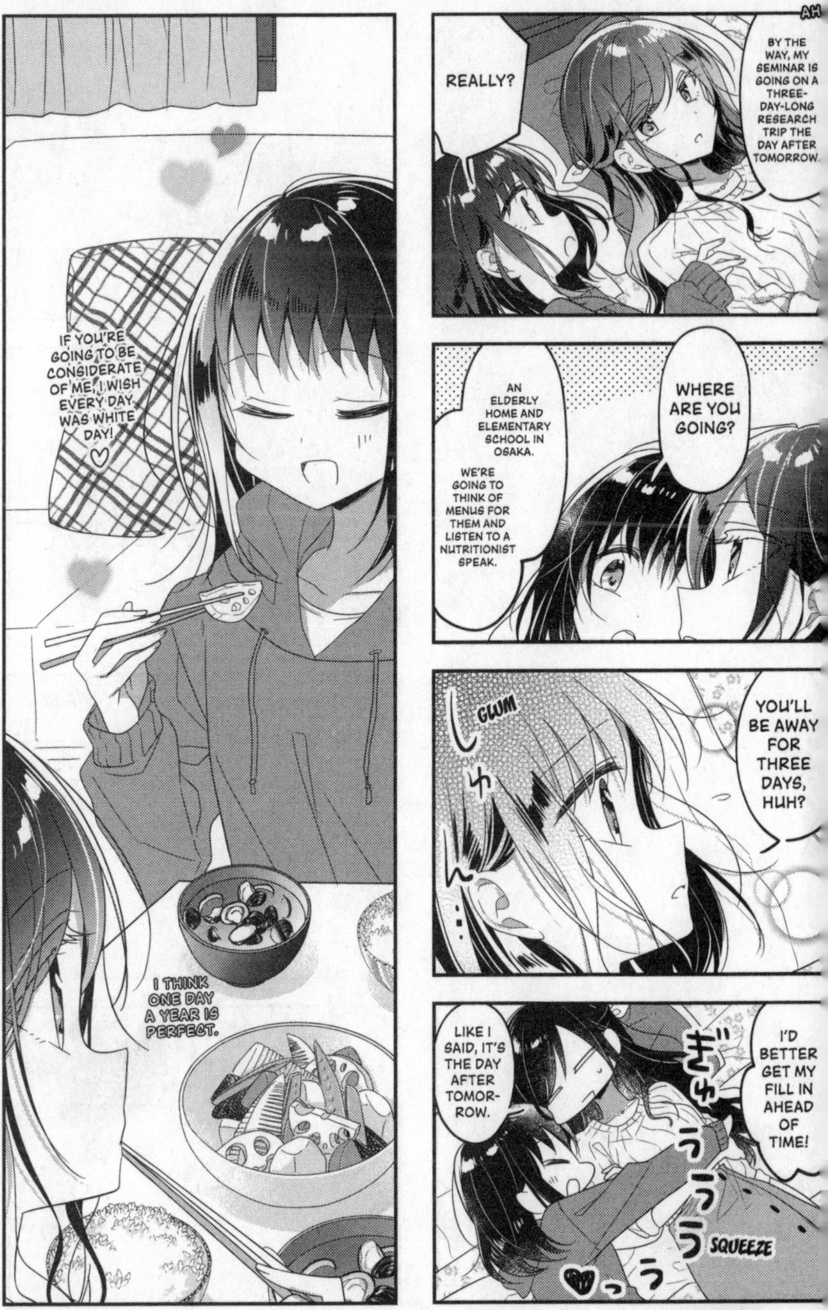
AH
BY THE WAY, MY SEMINAR IS GOING ON A THREE-DAY-LONG RESEARCH TRIP THE DAY AFTER TOMORROW.
REALLY?
WHERE ARE YOU GOING?
AN ELDERLY HOME AND ELEMENTARY SCHOOL IN OSAKA.
WE'RE GOING TO THINK OF MENUS FOR THEM AND LISTEN TO A NUTRITIONIST SPEAK.
YOU'LL BE AWAY FOR THREE DAYS, HUH?
GLUM
しゅん…
I'D BETTER GET MY FILL IN AHEAD OF TIME!
LIKE I SAID, IT'S THE DAY AFTER TOMOR-ROW.
ぎゅううう
SQUEEZE
IF YOU'RE GOING TO BE CONSIDERATE OF ME, I WISH EVERY DAY WAS WHITE DAY!
I THINK ONE DAY A YEAR IS PERFECT.

Futaribeya
A ROOM FOR TWO

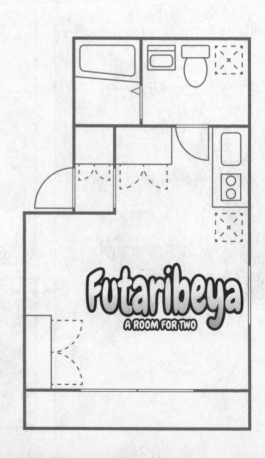

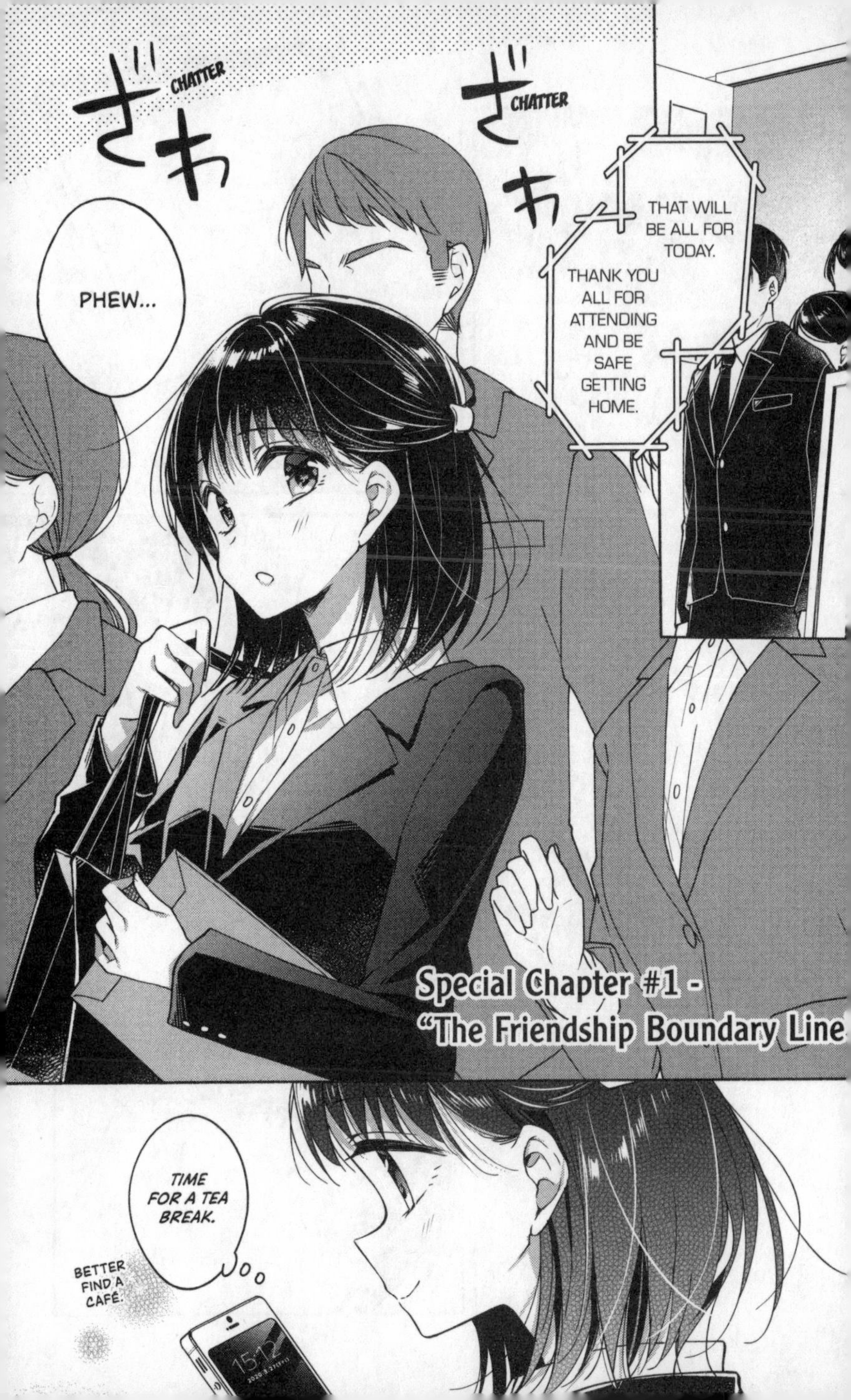
THAT WILL BE ALL FOR TODAY.
THANK YOU ALL FOR ATTENDING AND BE SAFE GETTING HOME.
ざわ CHATTER
ざわ CHATTER
PHEW...
Special Chapter #1 - "The Friendship Boundary Line
TIME FOR A TEA BREAK.
BETTER FIND A CAFÉ.
15:12

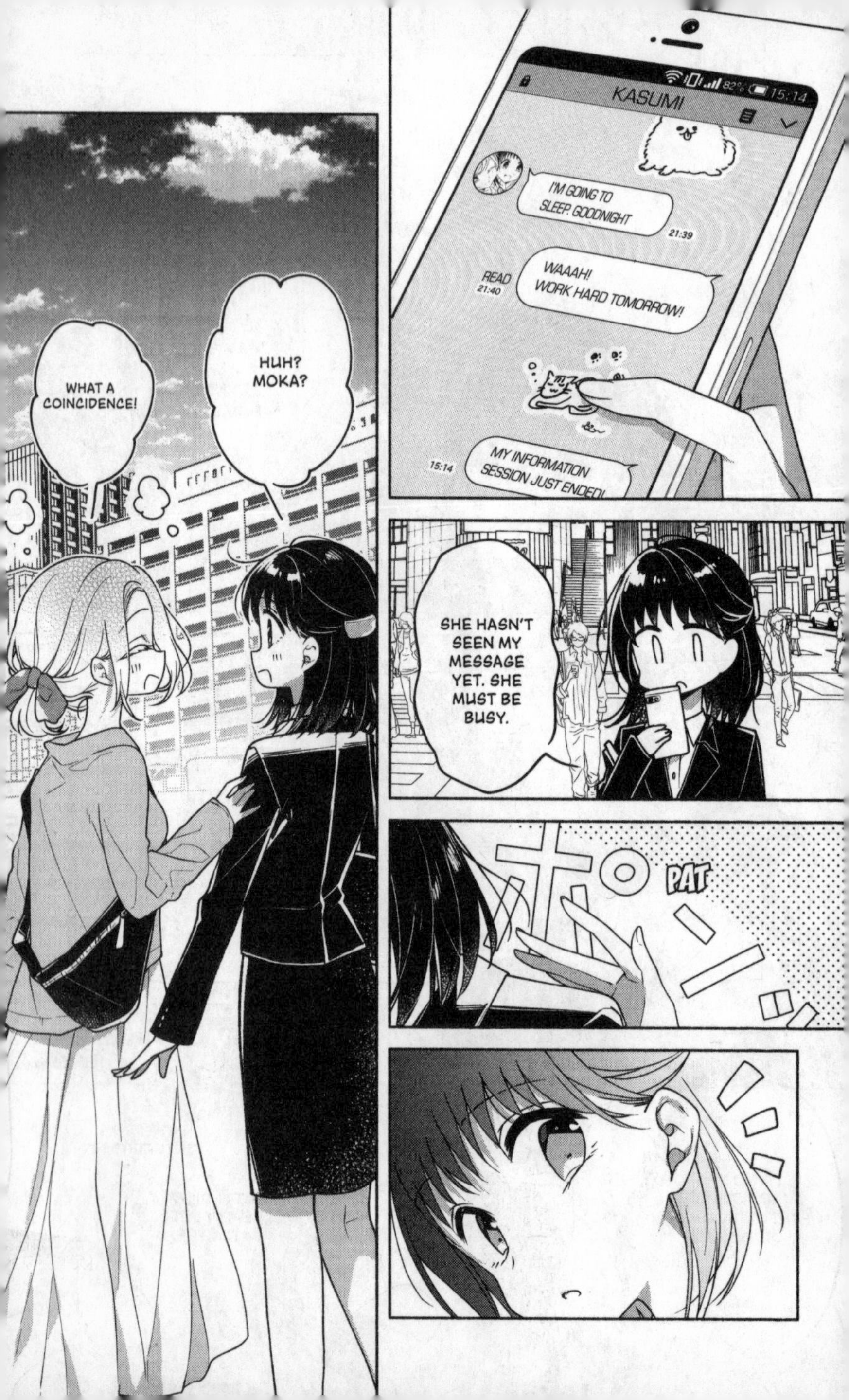
KASUMI
I'M GOING TO SLEEP. GOODNIGHT
21:39
READ 21:40
WAAAH! WORK HARD TOMORROW!
15:14
MY INFORMATION SESSION JUST ENDED!
SHE HASN'T SEEN MY MESSAGE YET. SHE MUST BE BUSY.
PAT
HUH? MOKA?
WHAT A COINCIDENCE!

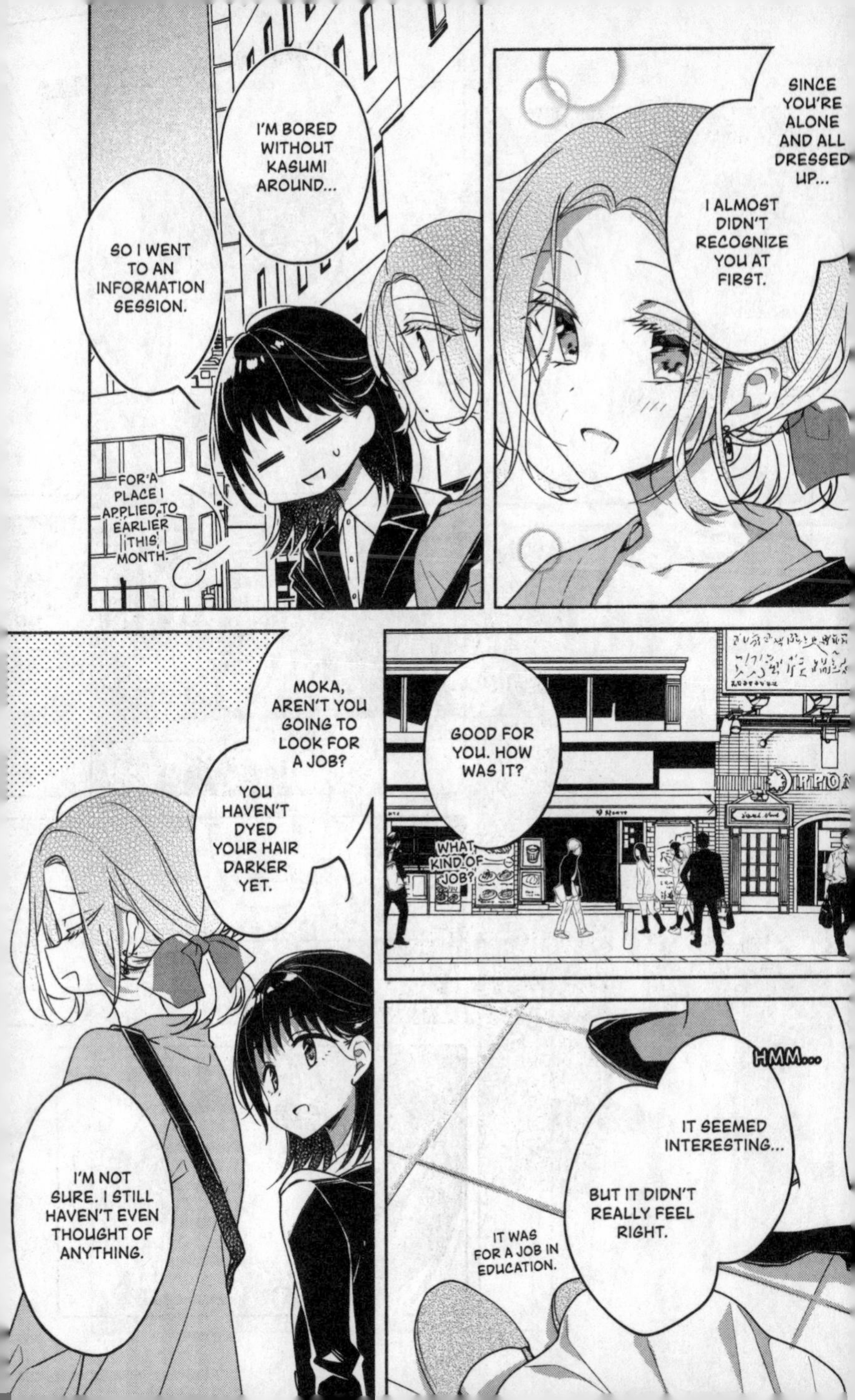
SINCE YOU'RE ALONE AND ALL DRESSED UP...
I ALMOST DIDN'T RECOGNIZE YOU AT FIRST.
I'M BORED WITHOUT KASUMI AROUND...
SO I WENT TO AN INFORMATION SESSION.
FOR A PLACE I APPLIED TO EARLIER THIS MONTH.
GOOD FOR YOU. HOW WAS IT?
WHAT KIND OF JOB?
HMM...
IT SEEMED INTERESTING...
BUT IT DIDN'T REALLY FEEL RIGHT.
IT WAS FOR A JOB IN EDUCATION.
MOKA, AREN'T YOU GOING TO LOOK FOR A JOB?
YOU HAVEN'T DYED YOUR HAIR DARKER YET.
I'M NOT SURE. I STILL HAVEN'T EVEN THOUGHT OF ANYTHING.

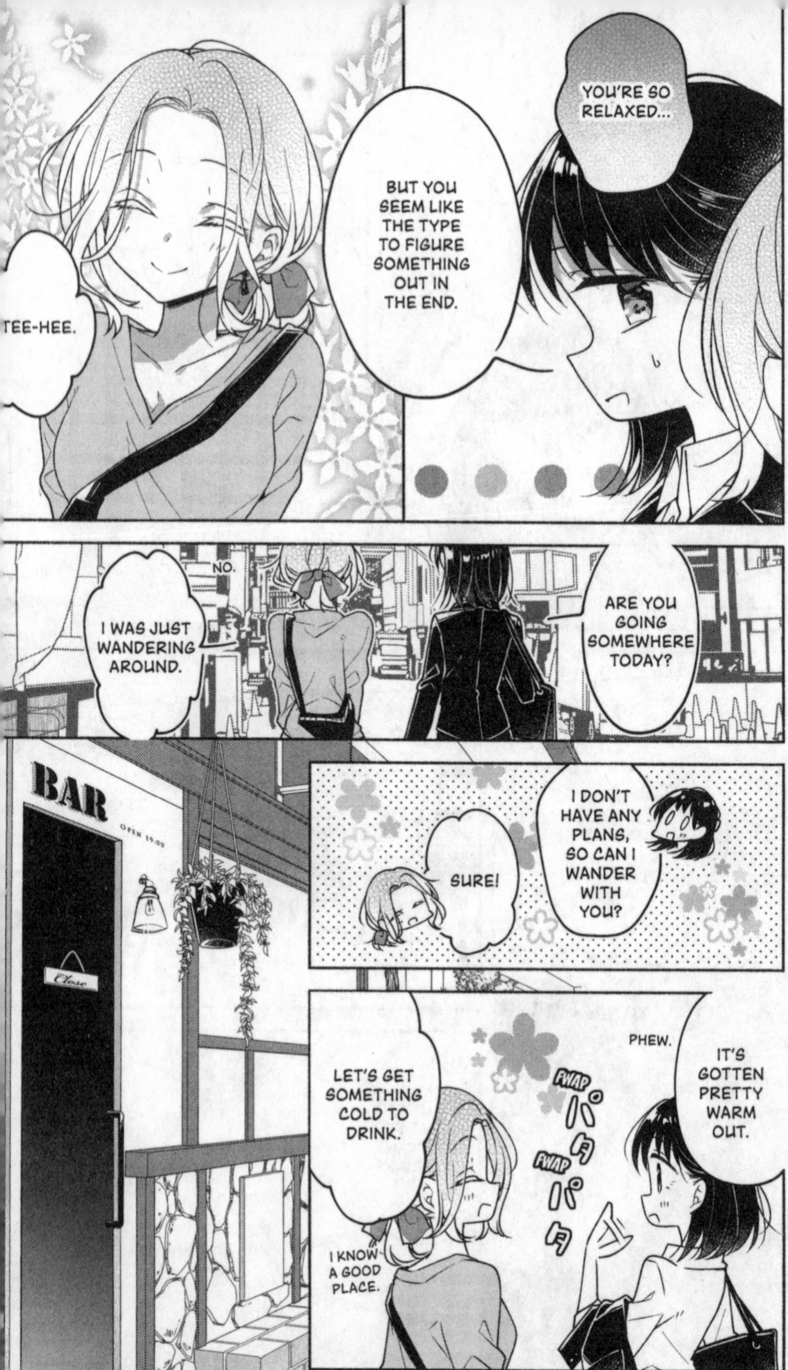
YOU'RE SO RELAXED...
BUT YOU SEEM LIKE THE TYPE TO FIGURE SOMETHING OUT IN THE END.
TEE-HEE.
ARE YOU GOING SOMEWHERE TODAY?
NO.
I WAS JUST WANDERING AROUND.
I DON'T HAVE ANY PLANS, SO CAN I WANDER WITH YOU?
SURE!
IT'S GOTTEN PRETTY WARM OUT.
PHEW.
FWAP パタ
FWAP パタ
LET'S GET SOMETHING COLD TO DRINK.
I KNOW A GOOD PLACE.
BAR
OPEN 19:00
Close

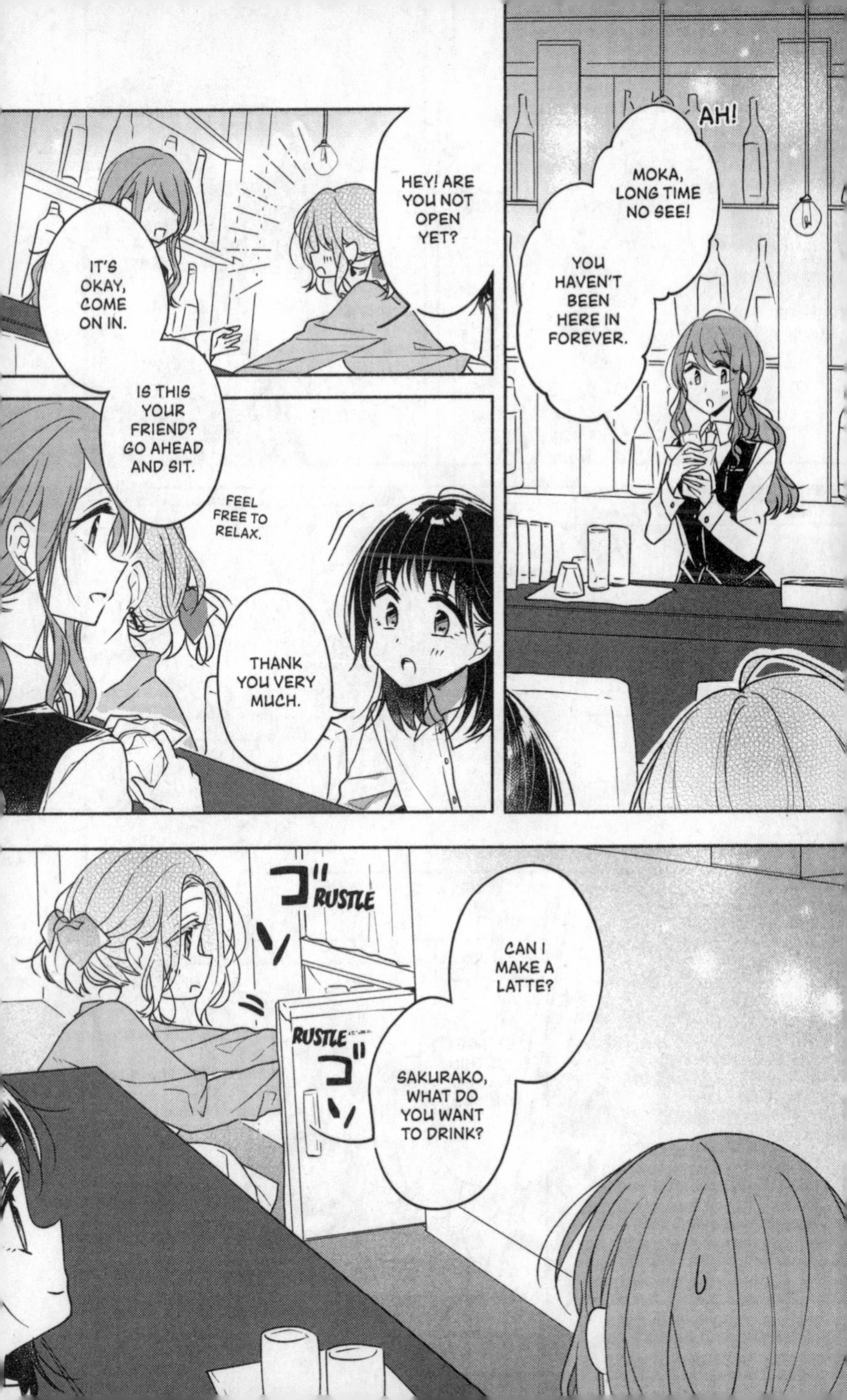
AH!
MOKA, LONG TIME NO SEE!
YOU HAVEN'T BEEN HERE IN FOREVER.
HEY! ARE YOU NOT OPEN YET?
IT'S OKAY, COME ON IN.
IS THIS YOUR FRIEND? GO AHEAD AND SIT.
FEEL FREE TO RELAX.
THANK YOU VERY MUCH.
ゴソ RUSTLE
CAN I MAKE A LATTE?
SAKURAKO, WHAT DO YOU WANT TO DRINK?
RUSTLE ゴソ

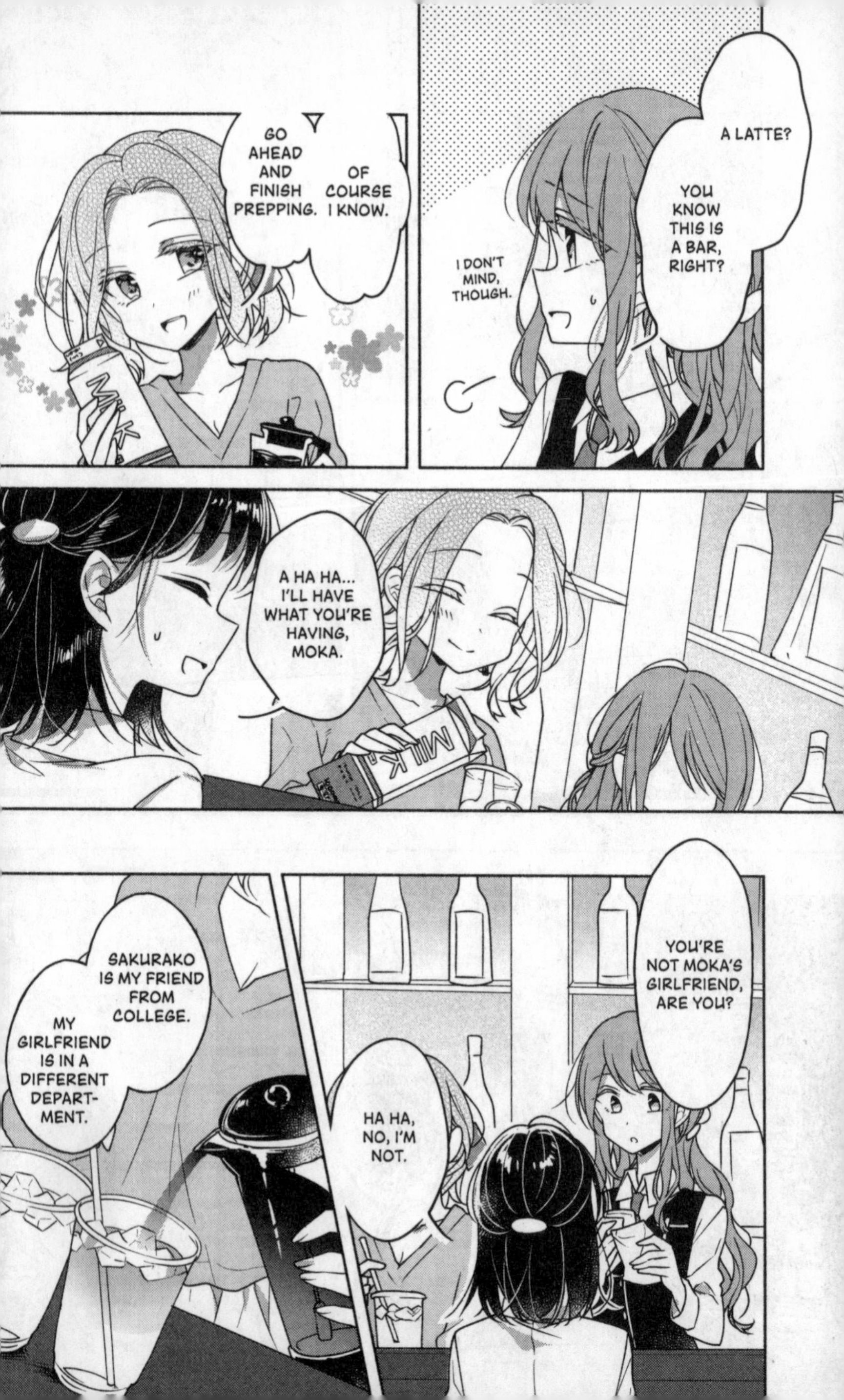
A LATTE?
YOU KNOW THIS IS A BAR, RIGHT?
I DON'T MIND, THOUGH.
OF COURSE I KNOW.
GO AHEAD AND FINISH PREPPING.
A HA HA... I'LL HAVE WHAT YOU'RE HAVING, MOKA.
YOU'RE NOT MOKA'S GIRLFRIEND, ARE YOU?
HA HA, NO, I'M NOT.
SAKURAKO IS MY FRIEND FROM COLLEGE.
MY GIRLFRIEND IS IN A DIFFERENT DEPARTMENT.

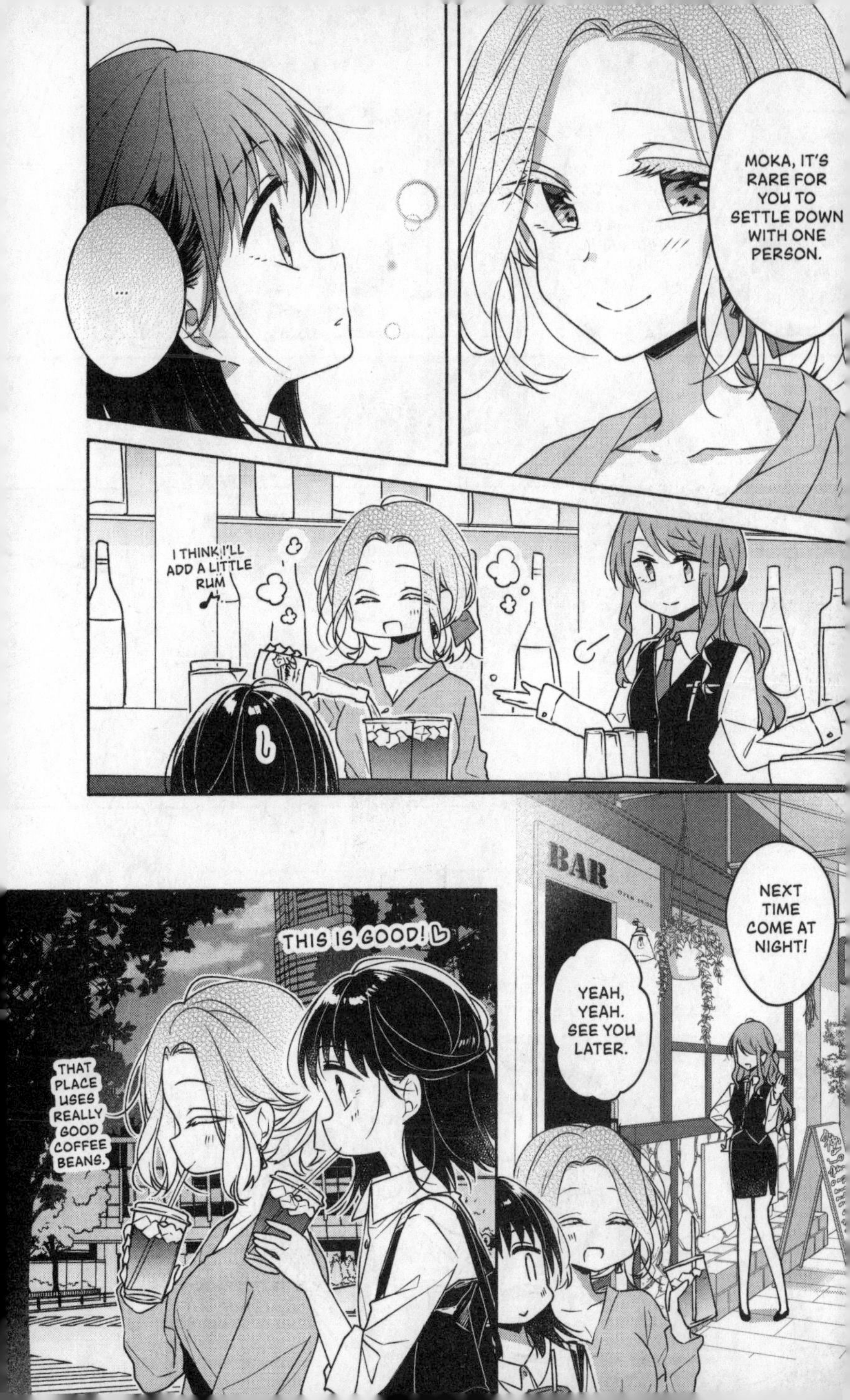
MOKA, IT'S RARE FOR YOU TO SETTLE DOWN WITH ONE PERSON.
...
I THINK I'LL ADD A LITTLE RUM ♪
BAR
NEXT TIME COME AT NIGHT!
YEAH, YEAH. SEE YOU LATER.
THIS IS GOOD! ♥
THAT PLACE USES REALLY GOOD COFFEE BEANS.

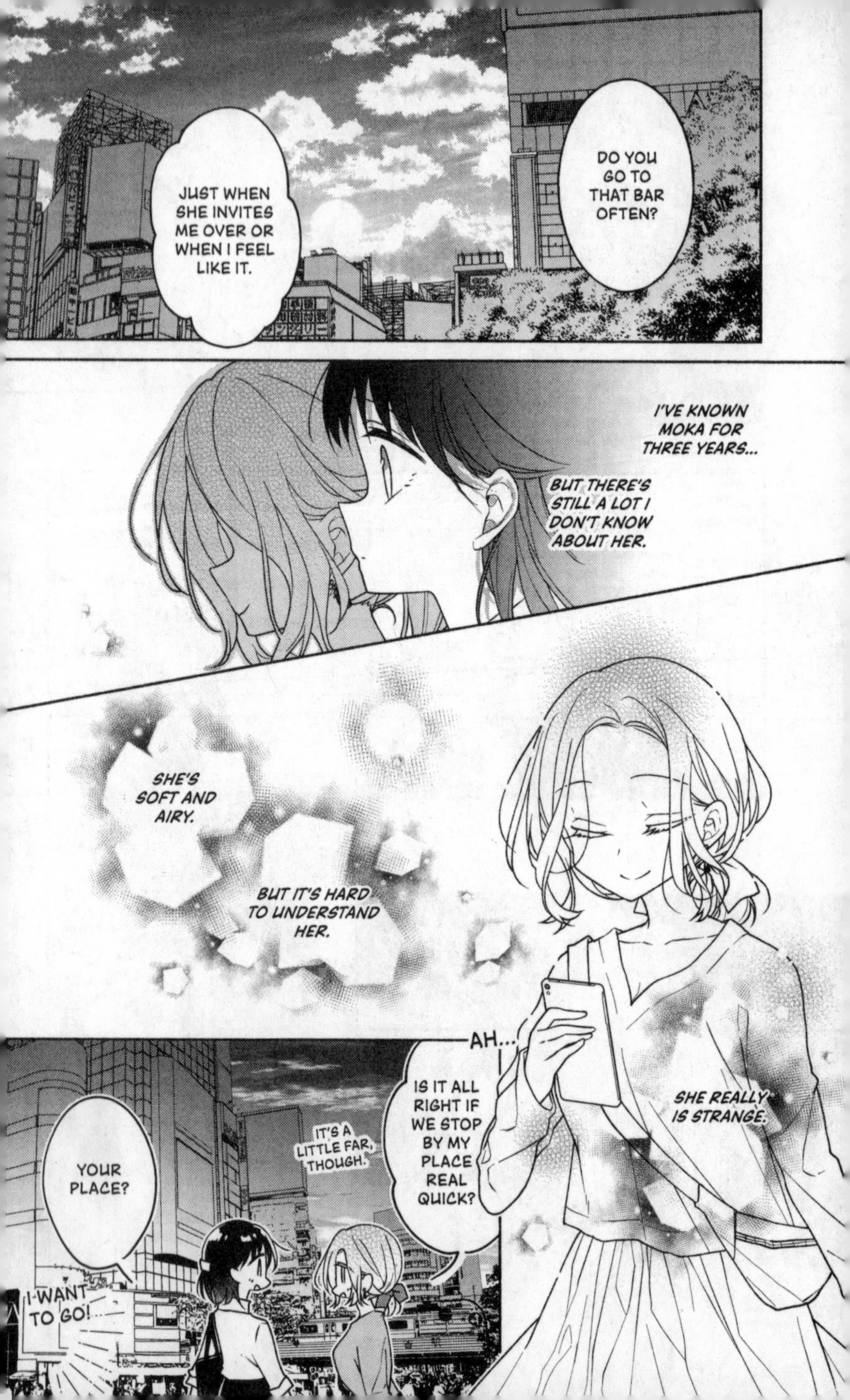
DO YOU GO TO THAT BAR OFTEN?
JUST WHEN SHE INVITES ME OVER OR WHEN I FEEL LIKE IT.
I'VE KNOWN MOKA FOR THREE YEARS...
BUT THERE'S STILL A LOT I DON'T KNOW ABOUT HER.
SHE'S SOFT AND AIRY.
BUT IT'S HARD TO UNDERSTAND HER.
AH...
SHE REALLY IS STRANGE.
IS IT ALL RIGHT IF WE STOP BY MY PLACE REAL QUICK?
IT'S A LITTLE FAR, THOUGH.
YOUR PLACE?
I-WANT TO GO!...

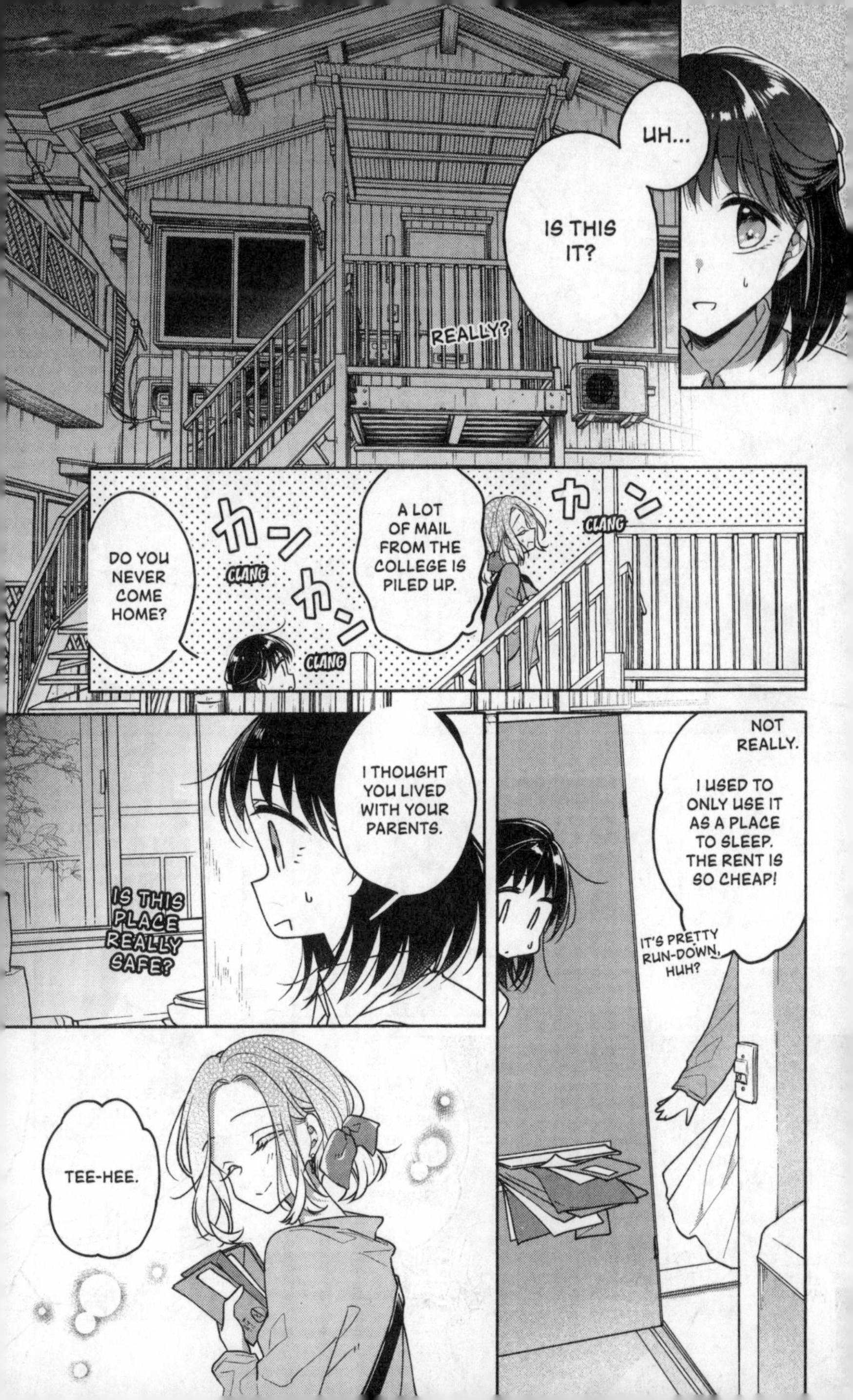
UH...
IS THIS IT?
REALLY?
CLANG
A LOT OF MAIL FROM THE COLLEGE IS PILED UP.
CLANG
CLANG
DO YOU NEVER COME HOME?
NOT REALLY.
I USED TO ONLY USE IT AS A PLACE TO SLEEP. THE RENT IS SO CHEAP!
IT'S PRETTY RUN-DOWN, HUH?
I THOUGHT YOU LIVED WITH YOUR PARENTS.
IS THIS PLACE REALLY SAFE?
TEE-HEE.

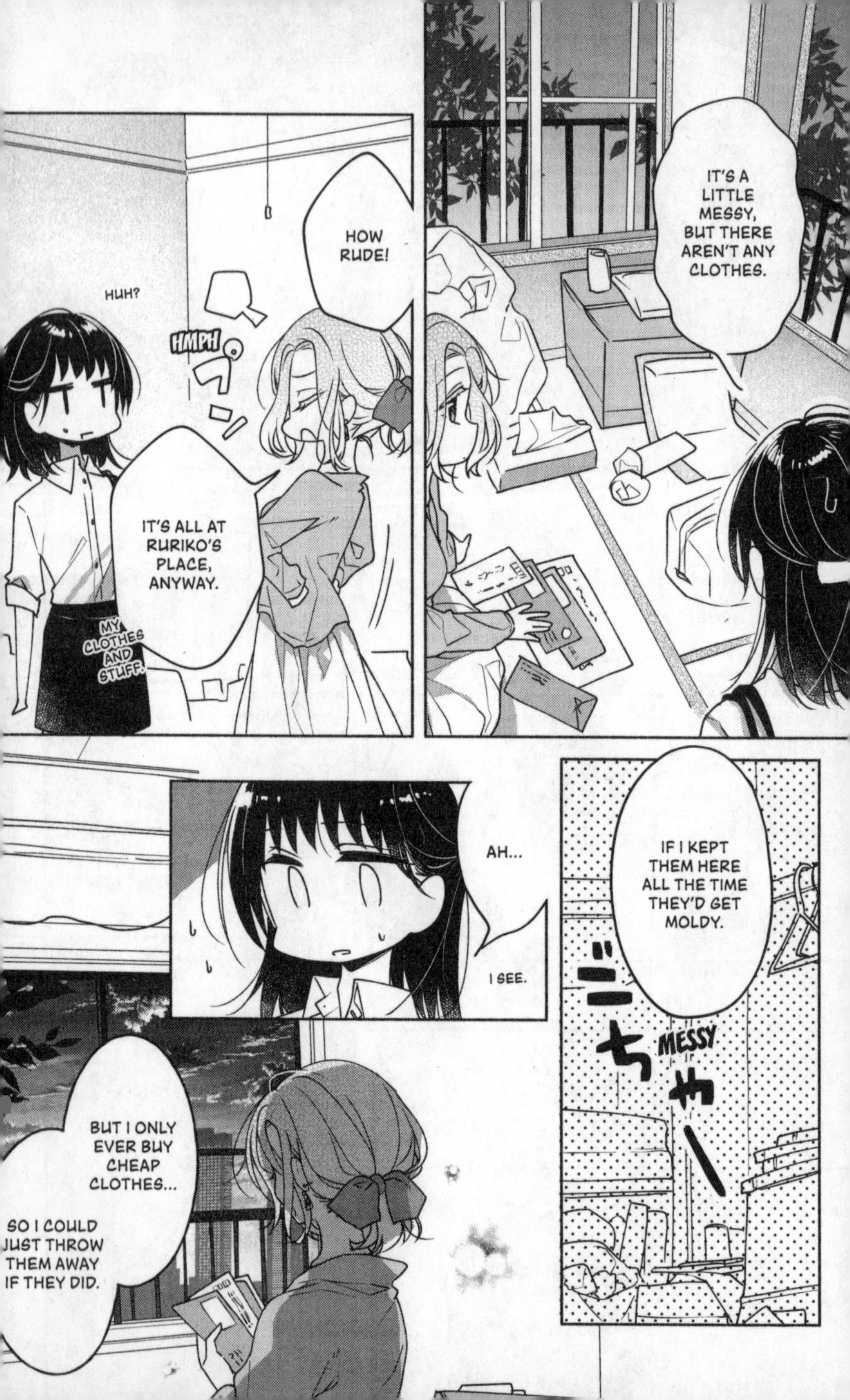
IT'S A LITTLE MESSY, BUT THERE AREN'T ANY CLOTHES.
HOW RUDE!
HMPH
HUH?
IT'S ALL AT RURIKO'S PLACE, ANYWAY.
MY CLOTHES AND STUFF.
IF I KEPT THEM HERE ALL THE TIME THEY'D GET MOLDY.
MESSY
AH...
I SEE.
BUT I ONLY EVER BUY CHEAP CLOTHES...
SO I COULD JUST THROW THEM AWAY IF THEY DID.

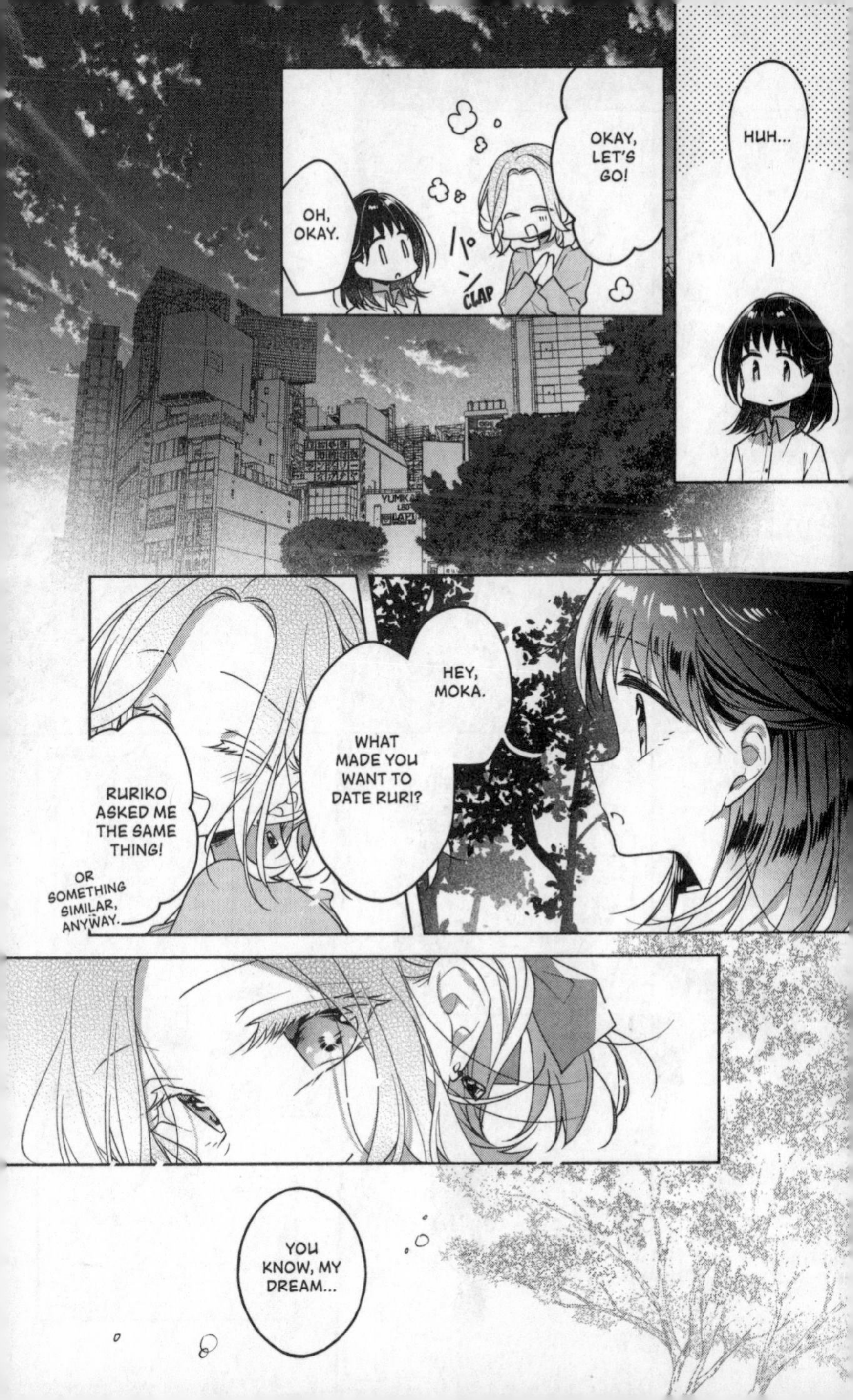
HUH...
OKAY, LET'S GO!
OH, OKAY.
CLAP
HEY, MOKA.
WHAT MADE YOU WANT TO DATE RURI?
RURIKO ASKED ME THE SAME THING!
OR SOMETHING SIMILAR, ANYWAY.
YOU KNOW, MY DREAM...

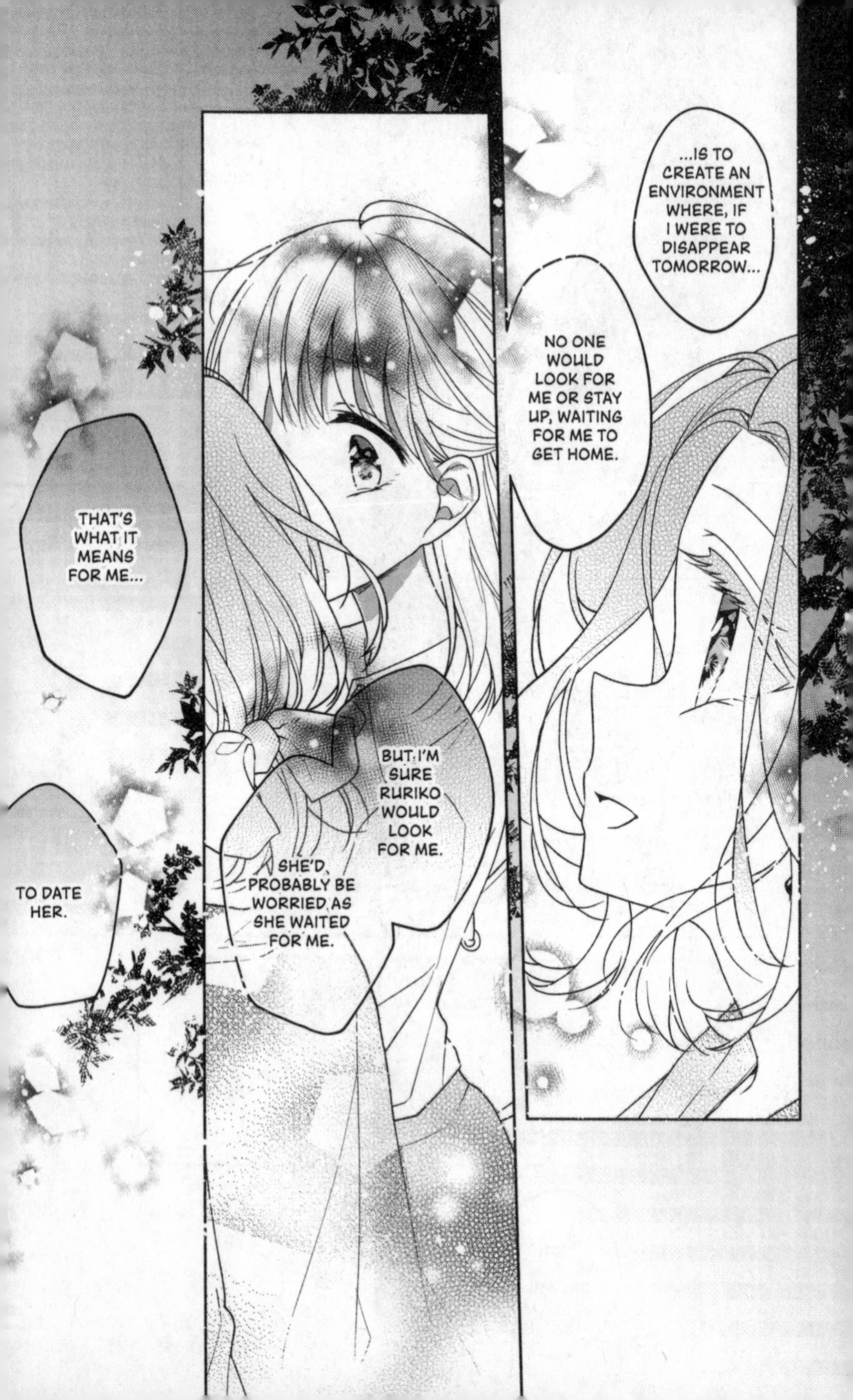
...IS TO CREATE AN ENVIRONMENT WHERE, IF I WERE TO DISAPPEAR TOMORROW...
NO ONE WOULD LOOK FOR ME OR STAY UP, WAITING FOR ME TO GET HOME.
BUT I'M SURE RURIKO WOULD LOOK FOR ME.
SHE'D PROBABLY BE WORRIED AS SHE WAITED FOR ME.
THAT'S WHAT IT MEANS FOR ME...
TO DATE HER.

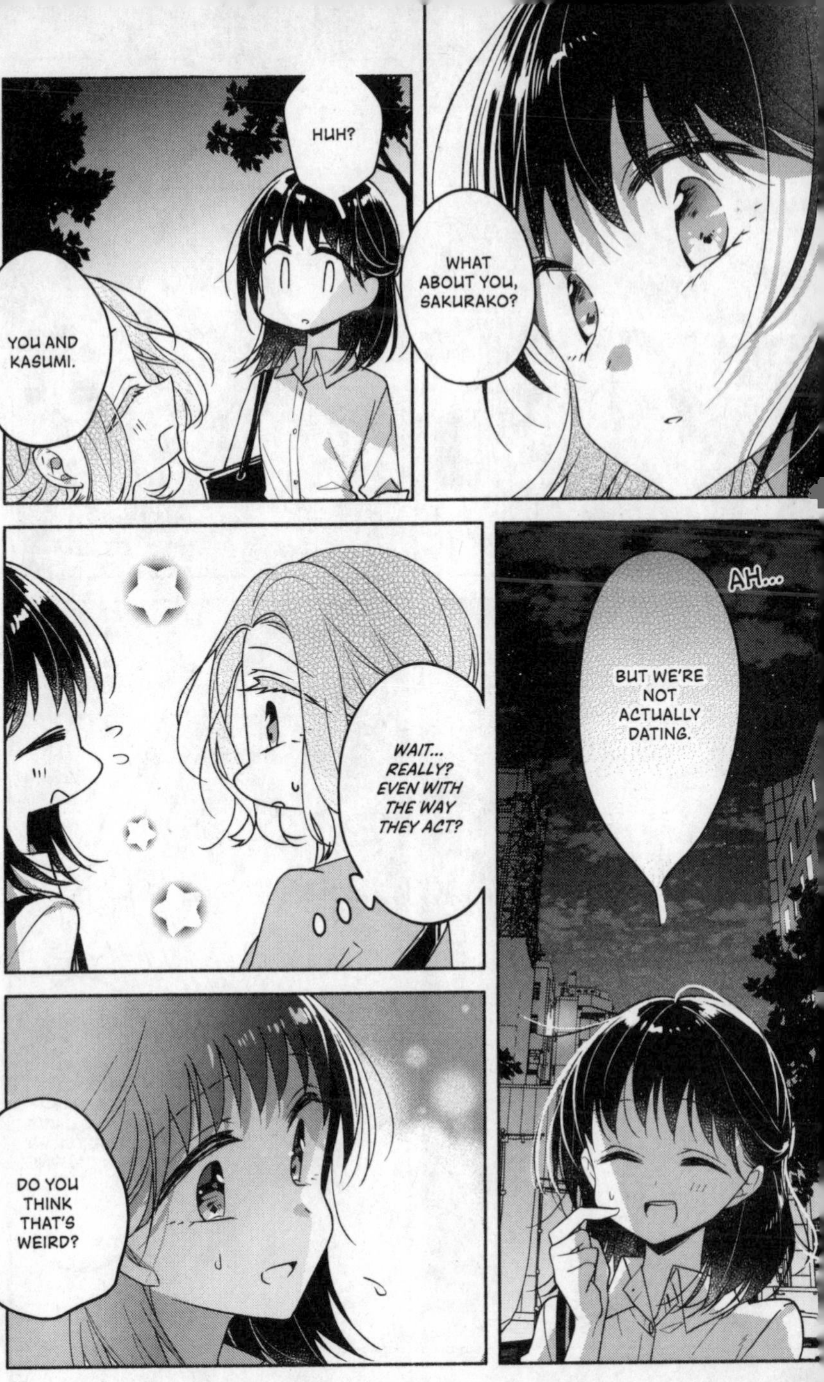
WHAT ABOUT YOU, SAKURAKO?
HUH?
YOU AND KASUMI.
AH...
BUT WE'RE NOT ACTUALLY DATING.
WAIT... REALLY? EVEN WITH THE WAY THEY ACT?
DO YOU THINK THAT'S WEIRD?

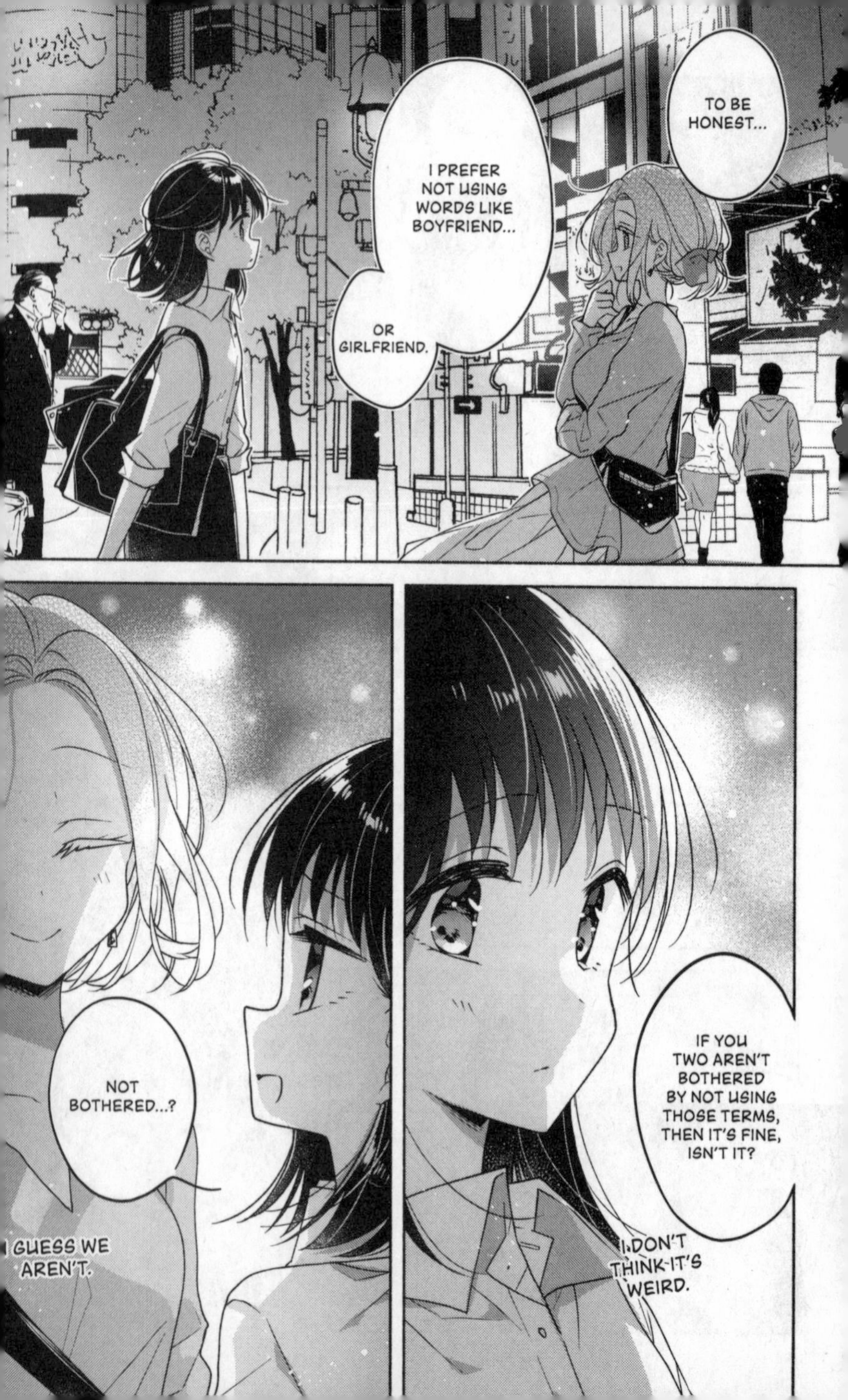
TO BE HONEST...
I PREFER NOT USING WORDS LIKE BOYFRIEND...
OR GIRLFRIEND.
IF YOU TWO AREN'T BOTHERED BY NOT USING THOSE TERMS, THEN IT'S FINE, ISN'T IT?
I DON'T THINK IT'S WEIRD.
NOT BOTHERED...?
I GUESS WE AREN'T.

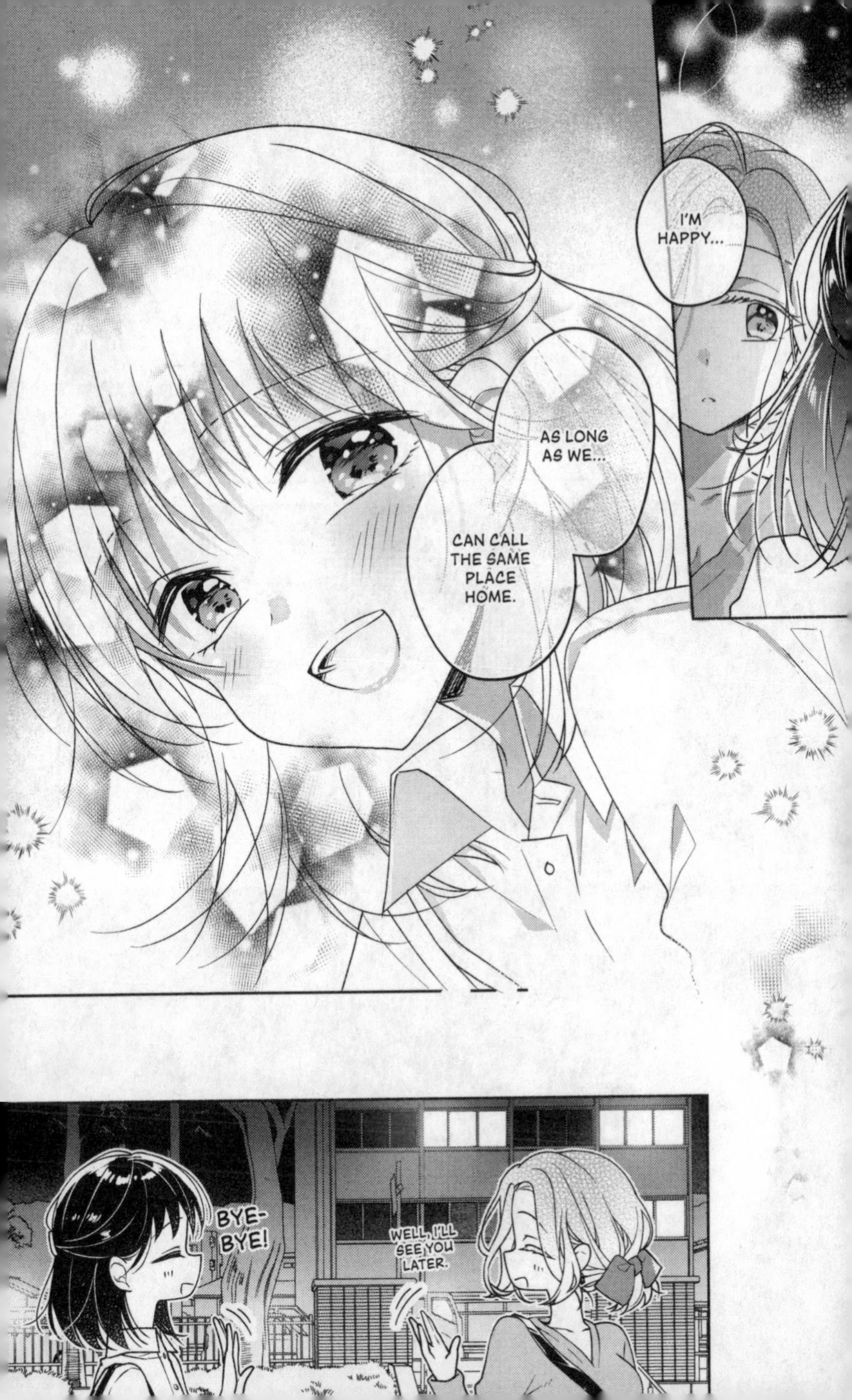
I'M HAPPY...
AS LONG AS WE...
CAN CALL THE SAME PLACE HOME.
WELL, I'LL SEE YOU LATER.
BYE-BYE!

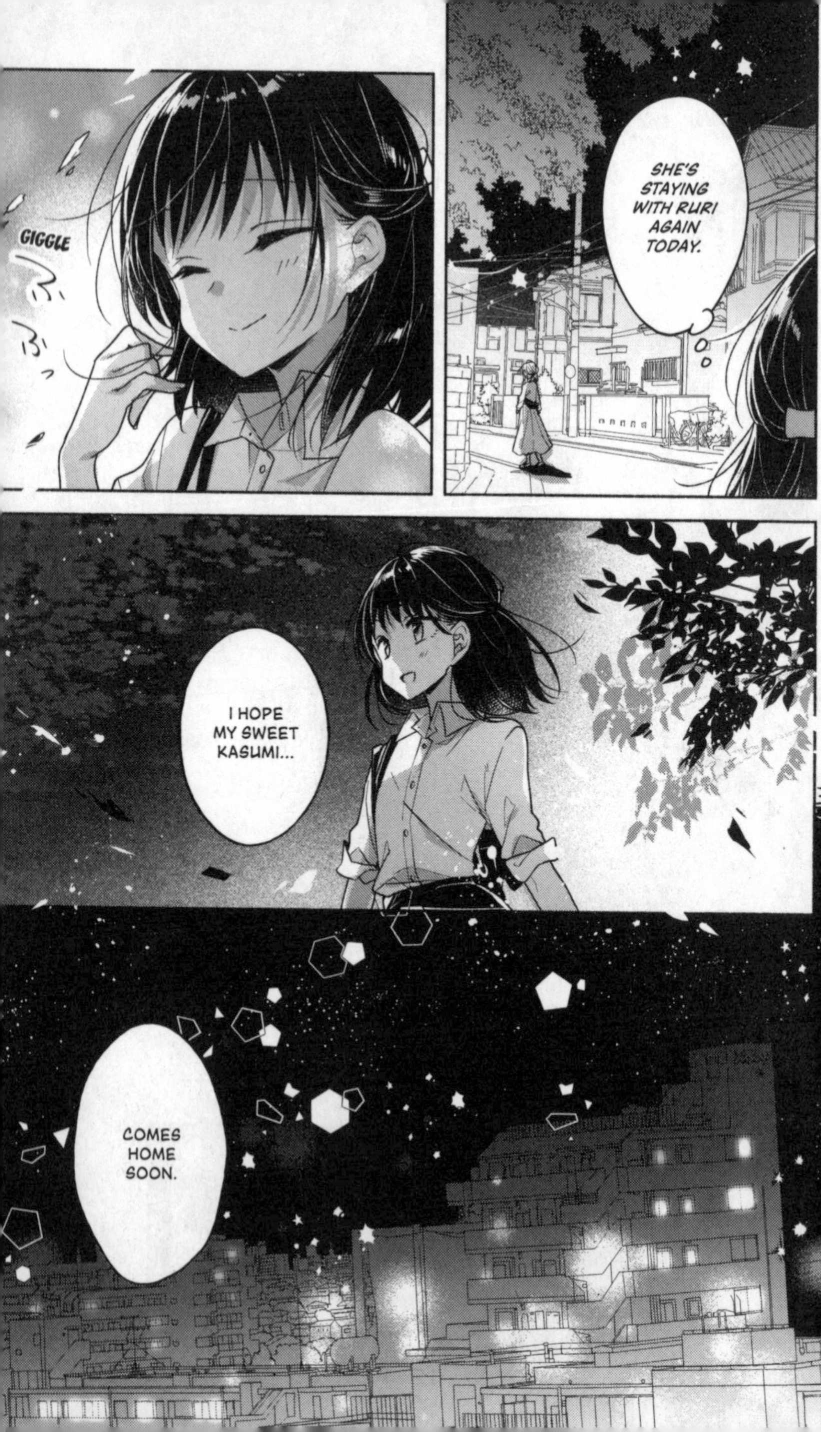
SHE'S STAYING WITH RURI AGAIN TODAY.
GIGGLE
ふふっ
I HOPE MY SWEET KASUMI...
COMES HOME SOON.

Illustration gallery of Yukik

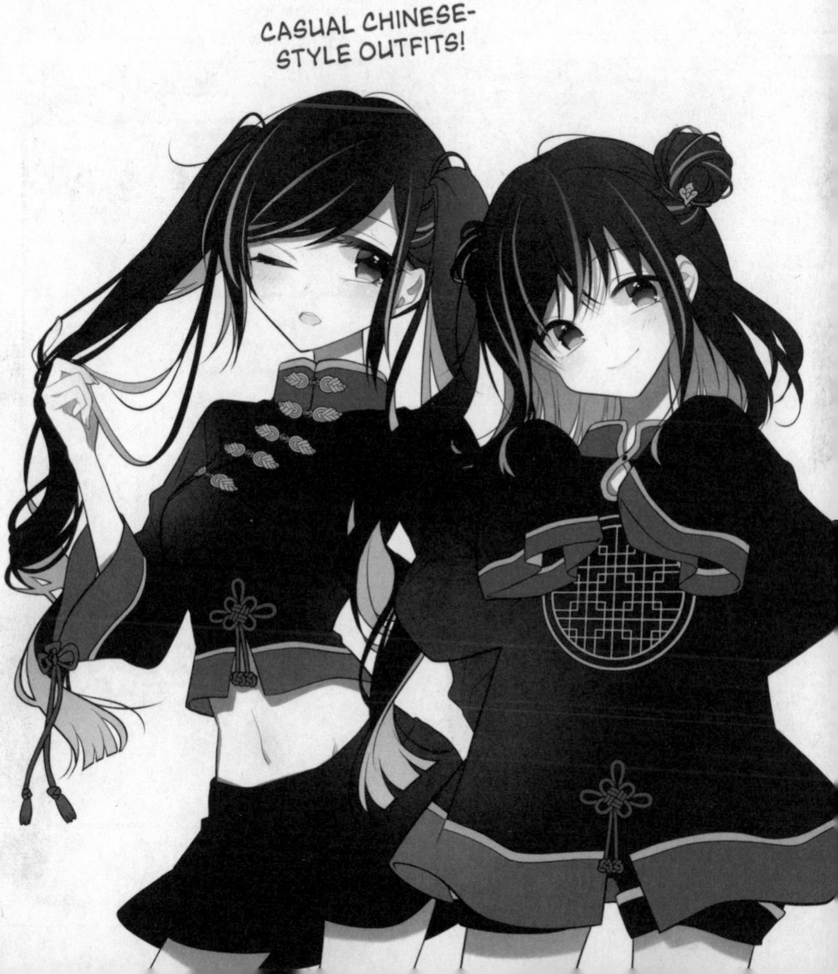
CASUAL CHINESE-
STYLE OUTFITS!

Futaribeya
A ROOM FOR TWO

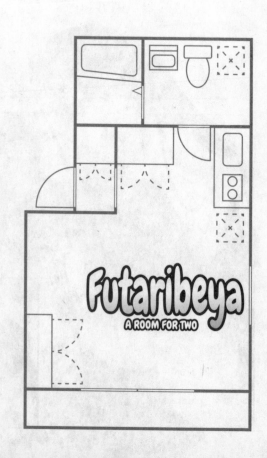

Chapter 64

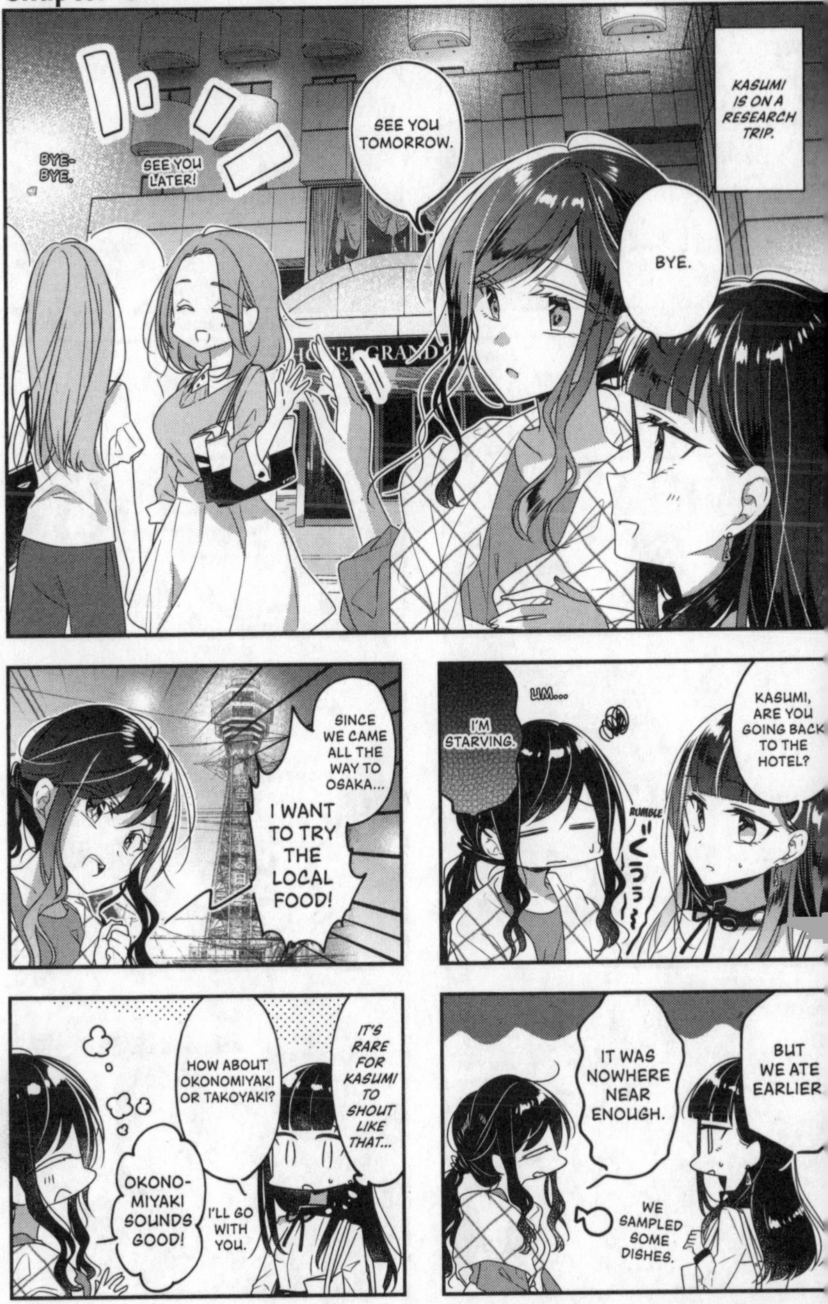
KASUMI IS ON A RESEARCH TRIP.
BYE.
SEE YOU TOMORROW.
SEE YOU LATER!
BYE-BYE.
KASUMI, ARE YOU GOING BACK TO THE HOTEL?
UM...
RUMBLE
I'M STARVING.
SINCE WE CAME ALL THE WAY TO OSAKA...
I WANT TO TRY THE LOCAL FOOD!
BUT WE ATE EARLIER.
IT WAS NOWHERE NEAR ENOUGH.
WE SAMPLED SOME DISHES.
IT'S RARE FOR KASUMI TO SHOUT LIKE THAT...
HOW ABOUT OKONOMIYAKI OR TAKOYAKI?
I'LL GO WITH YOU.
OKONOMIYAKI SOUNDS GOOD!

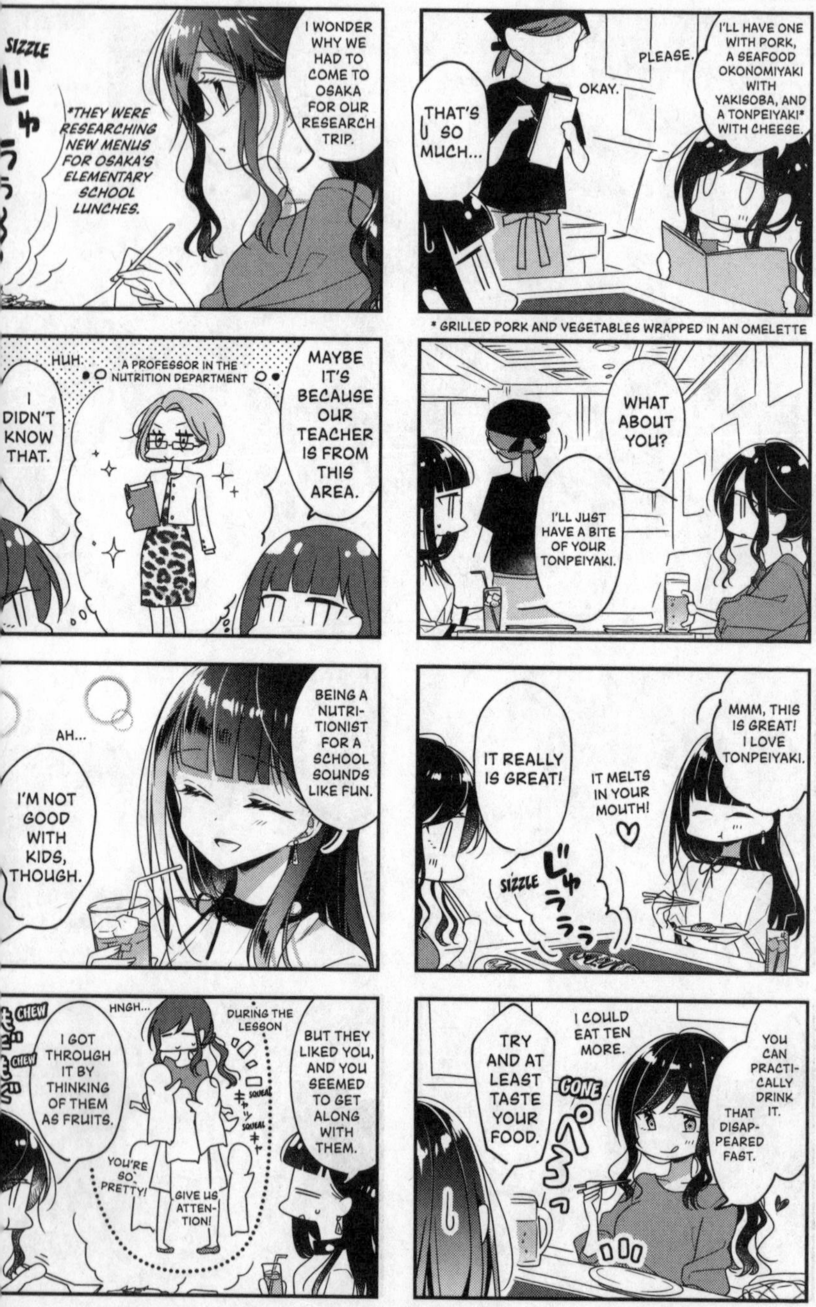
I'LL HAVE ONE WITH PORK, A SEAFOOD OKONOMIYAKI WITH YAKISOBA, AND A TONPEIYAKI* WITH CHEESE.
PLEASE.
OKAY.
THAT'S SO MUCH...
* GRILLED PORK AND VEGETABLES WRAPPED IN AN OMELETTE
I WONDER WHY WE HAD TO COME TO OSAKA FOR OUR RESEARCH TRIP.
*THEY WERE RESEARCHING NEW MENUS FOR OSAKA'S ELEMENTARY SCHOOL LUNCHES.
SIZZLE
WHAT ABOUT YOU?
I'LL JUST HAVE A BITE OF YOUR TONPEIYAKI.
MAYBE IT'S BECAUSE OUR TEACHER IS FROM THIS AREA.
A PROFESSOR IN THE NUTRITION DEPARTMENT
HUH.
I DIDN'T KNOW THAT.
MMM, THIS IS GREAT! I LOVE TONPEIYAKI.
IT MELTS IN YOUR MOUTH!
IT REALLY IS GREAT!
SIZZLE
BEING A NUTRI-TIONIST FOR A SCHOOL SOUNDS LIKE FUN.
AH...
I'M NOT GOOD WITH KIDS, THOUGH.
YOU CAN PRACTI-CALLY DRINK IT.
THAT DISAP-PEARED FAST.
I COULD EAT TEN MORE.
GONE
TRY AND AT LEAST TASTE YOUR FOOD.
BUT THEY LIKED YOU, AND YOU SEEMED TO GET ALONG WITH THEM.
DURING THE LESSON
SQUEAL
SQUEAL
HNGH...
I GOT THROUGH IT BY THINKING OF THEM AS FRUITS.
YOU'RE SO PRETTY!
GIVE US ATTEN-TION!
CHEW
CHEW

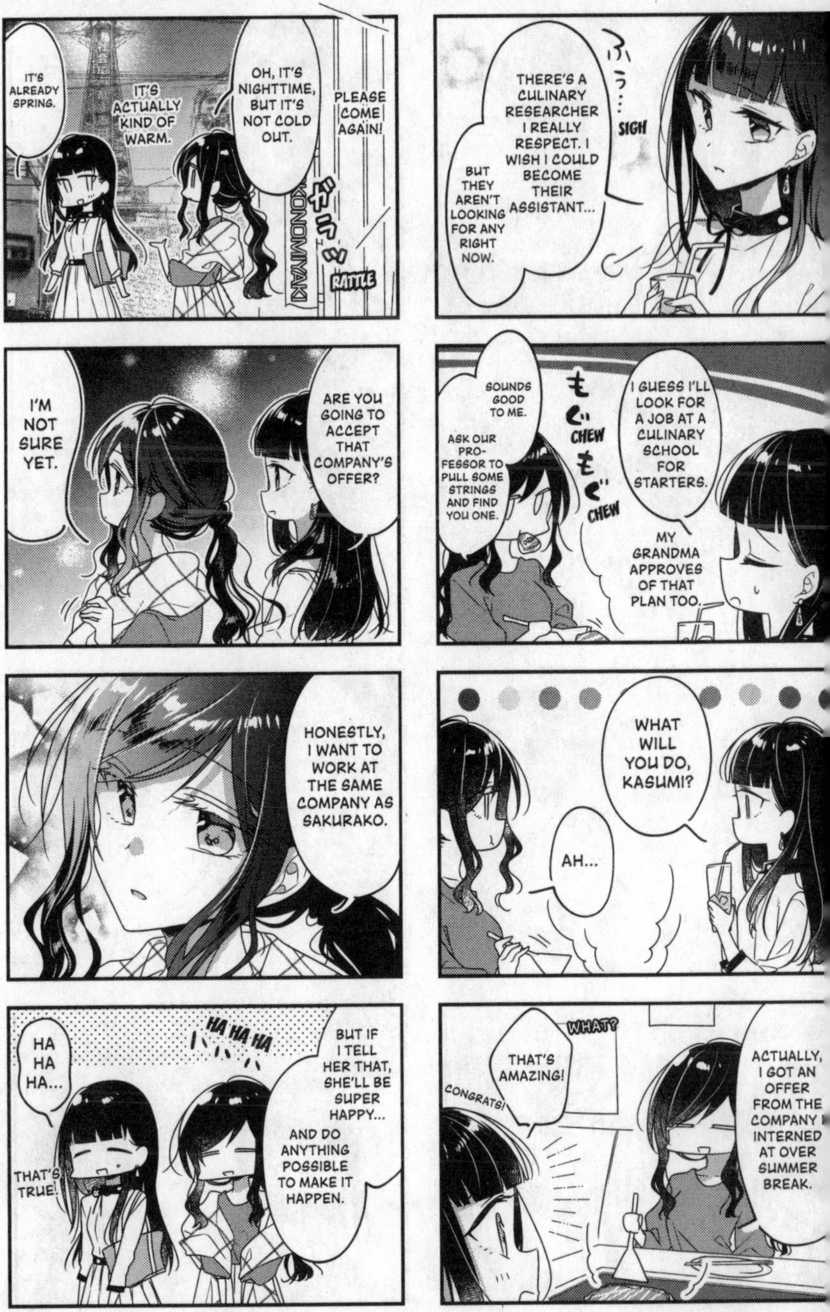
ふう…
SIGH
THERE'S A CULINARY RESEARCHER I REALLY RESPECT. I WISH I COULD BECOME THEIR ASSISTANT...
BUT THEY AREN'T LOOKING FOR ANY RIGHT NOW.
I GUESS I'LL LOOK FOR A JOB AT A CULINARY SCHOOL FOR STARTERS.
MY GRANDMA APPROVES OF THAT PLAN TOO.
もぐ CHEW もぐ CHEW
SOUNDS GOOD TO ME.
ASK OUR PRO-FESSOR TO PULL SOME STRINGS AND FIND YOU ONE.
WHAT WILL YOU DO, KASUMI?
AH...
ACTUALLY, I GOT AN OFFER FROM THE COMPANY I INTERNED AT OVER SUMMER BREAK.
WHAT?
THAT'S AMAZING!
CONGRATS!
PLEASE COME AGAIN!
OKONOMIYAKI
ガラッ
RATTLE
OH, IT'S NIGHTTIME, BUT IT'S NOT COLD OUT.
IT'S ACTUALLY KIND OF WARM.
IT'S ALREADY SPRING.
ARE YOU GOING TO ACCEPT THAT COMPANY'S OFFER?
I'M NOT SURE YET.
HONESTLY, I WANT TO WORK AT THE SAME COMPANY AS SAKURAKO.
BUT IF I TELL HER THAT, SHE'LL BE SUPER HAPPY...
AND DO ANYTHING POSSIBLE TO MAKE IT HAPPEN.
ハハハ
HA HA HA
HA HA HA...
THAT'S TRUE!

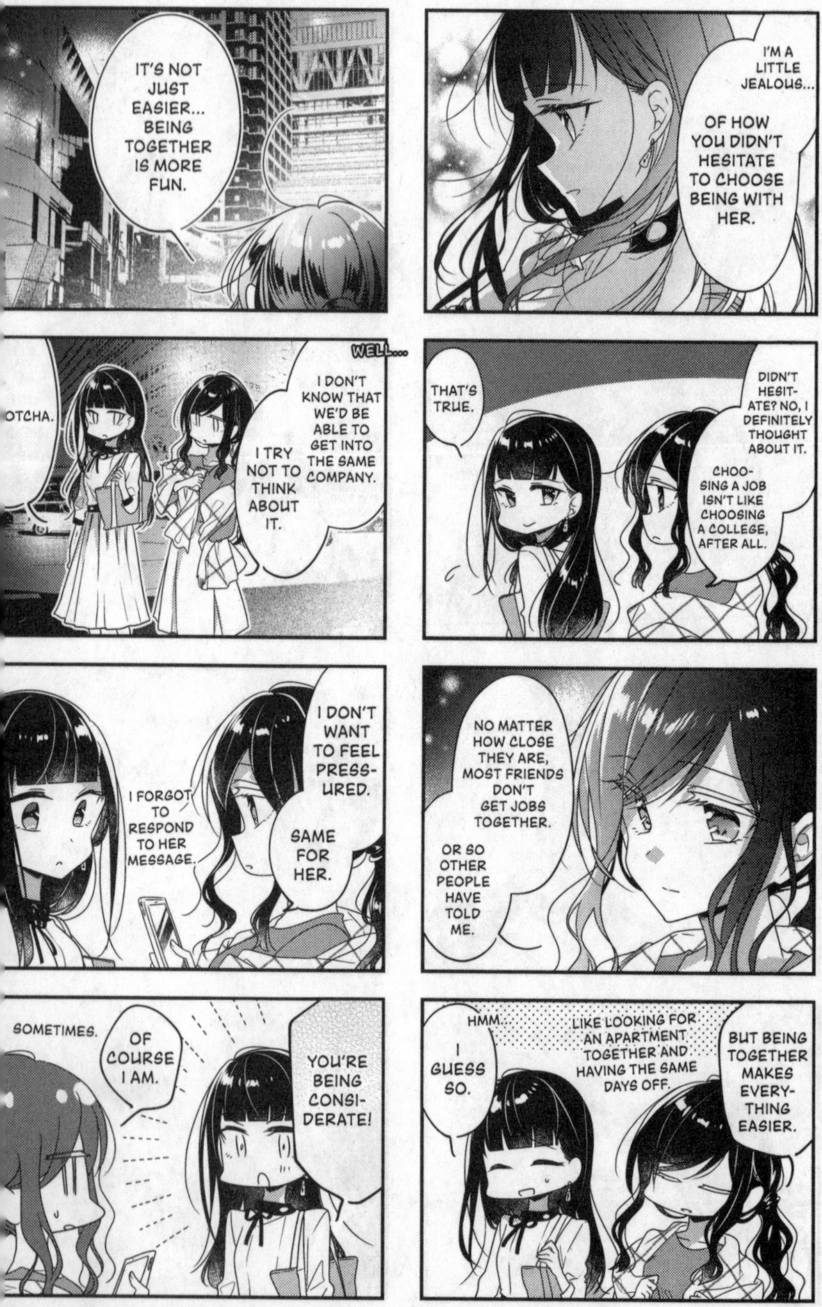
I'M A LITTLE JEALOUS...
OF HOW YOU DIDN'T HESITATE TO CHOOSE BEING WITH HER.
DIDN'T HESITATE? NO, I DEFINITELY THOUGHT ABOUT IT.
CHOOSING A JOB ISN'T LIKE CHOOSING A COLLEGE, AFTER ALL.
THAT'S TRUE.
NO MATTER HOW CLOSE THEY ARE, MOST FRIENDS DON'T GET JOBS TOGETHER.
OR SO OTHER PEOPLE HAVE TOLD ME.
BUT BEING TOGETHER MAKES EVERYTHING EASIER.
LIKE LOOKING FOR AN APARTMENT TOGETHER AND HAVING THE SAME DAYS OFF.
HMM...
I GUESS SO.
IT'S NOT JUST EASIER... BEING TOGETHER IS MORE FUN.
WELL...
I DON'T KNOW THAT WE'D BE ABLE TO GET INTO THE SAME COMPANY.
I TRY NOT TO THINK ABOUT IT.
OTCHA.
I DON'T WANT TO FEEL PRESSURED.
SAME FOR HER.
I FORGOT TO RESPOND TO HER MESSAGE.
YOU'RE BEING CONSIDERATE!
OF COURSE I AM.
SOMETIMES.

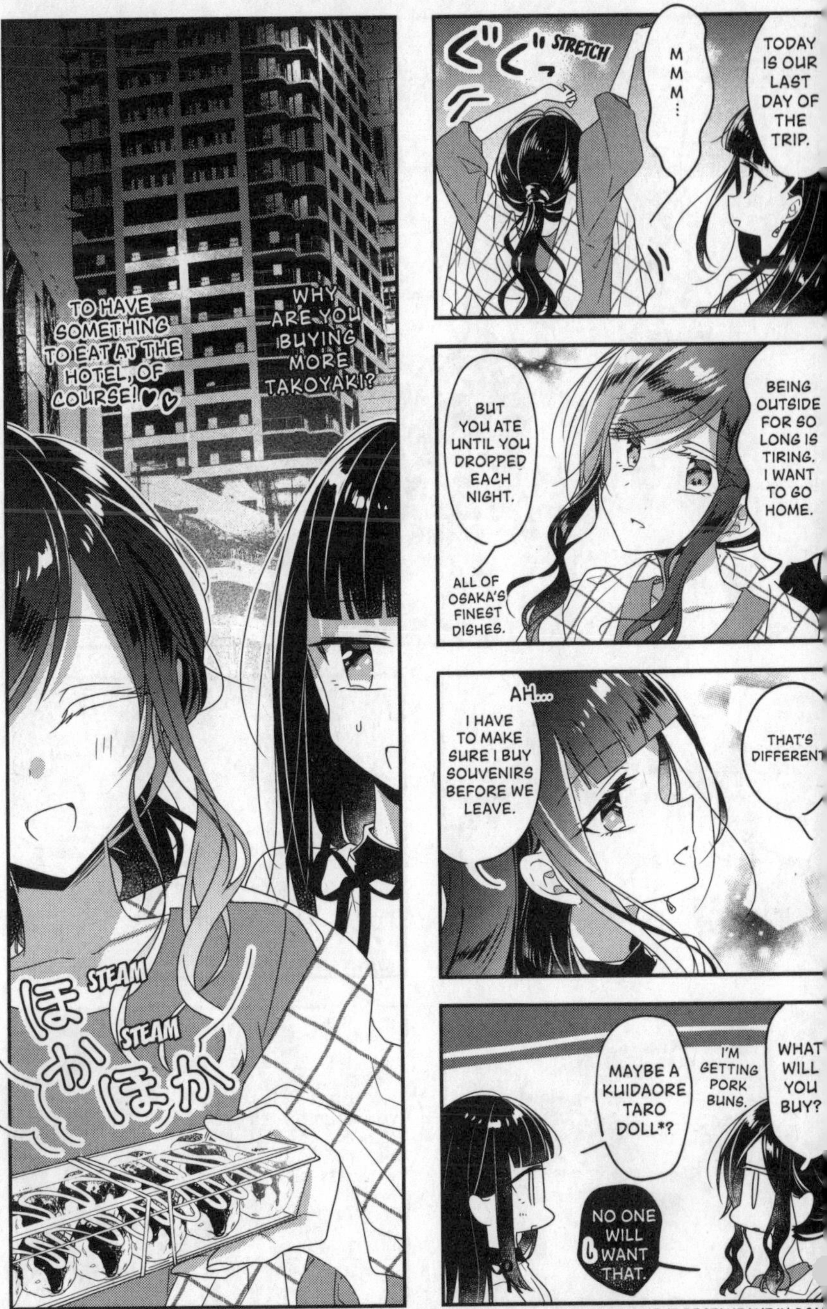
TODAY IS OUR LAST DAY OF THE TRIP.
MMM...
ぐぐっ STRETCH
BEING OUTSIDE FOR SO LONG IS TIRING. I WANT TO GO HOME.
BUT YOU ATE UNTIL YOU DROPPED EACH NIGHT.
ALL OF OSAKA'S FINEST DISHES.
THAT'S DIFFERENT
AH...
I HAVE TO MAKE SURE I BUY SOUVENIRS BEFORE WE LEAVE.
WHAT WILL YOU BUY?
I'M GETTING PORK BUNS.
MAYBE A KUIDAORE TARO DOLL*?
NO ONE WILL WANT THAT.
WHY ARE YOU BUYING MORE TAKOYAKI?
TO HAVE SOMETHING TO EAT AT THE HOTEL, OF COURSE! ♥♥
ほかほか STEAM STEAM

* FAMOUS CLOWN MASCOT FROM A PROMINENT RESTAURANT IN OSA

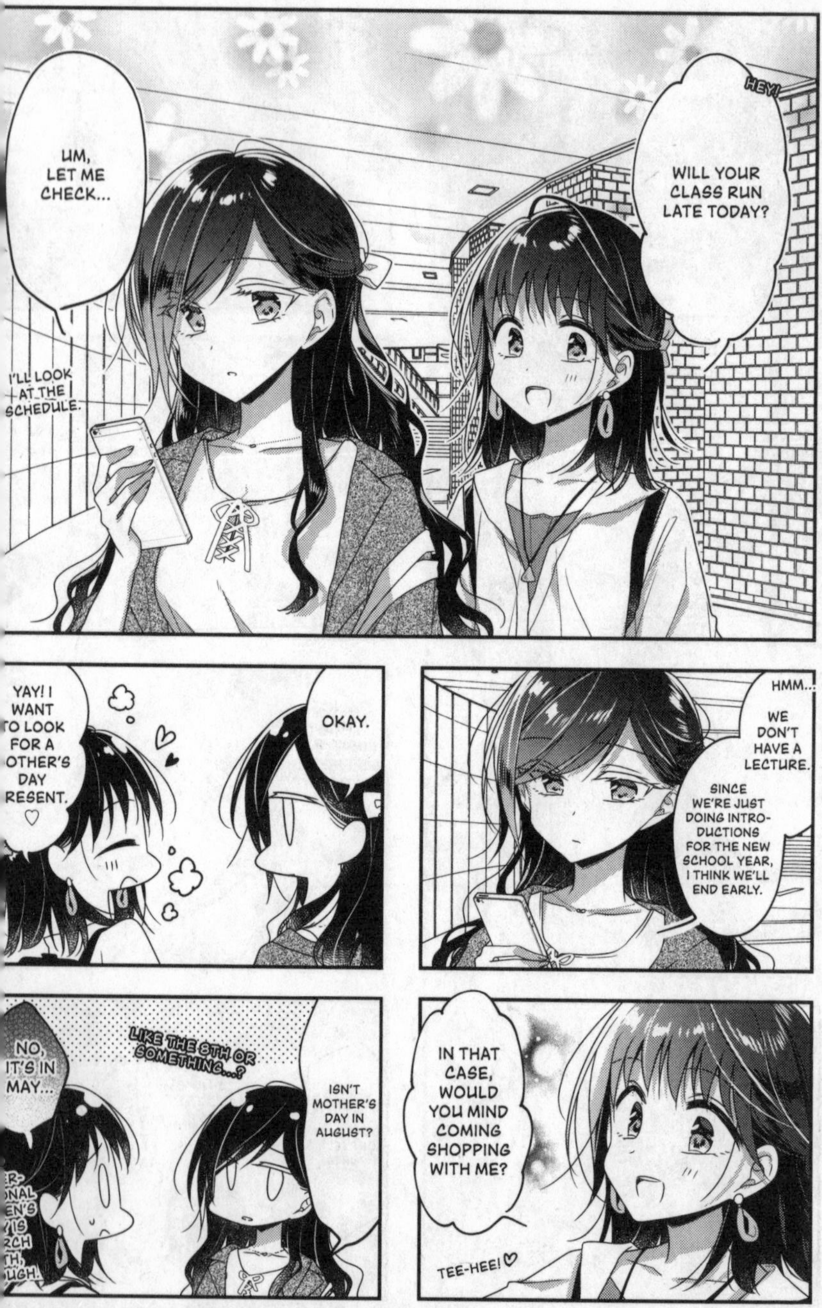
HEY!
WILL YOUR CLASS RUN LATE TODAY?
UM, LET ME CHECK...
I'LL LOOK AT THE SCHEDULE.
HMM...
WE DON'T HAVE A LECTURE.
SINCE WE'RE JUST DOING INTRO-DUCTIONS FOR THE NEW SCHOOL YEAR, I THINK WE'LL END EARLY.
OKAY.
YAY! I WANT TO LOOK FOR A OTHER'S DAY RESENT. ♡
IN THAT CASE, WOULD YOU MIND COMING SHOPPING WITH ME?
TEE-HEE! ♡
ISN'T MOTHER'S DAY IN AUGUST?
LIKE THE 8TH OR SOMETHING...?
NO, IT'S IN MAY...

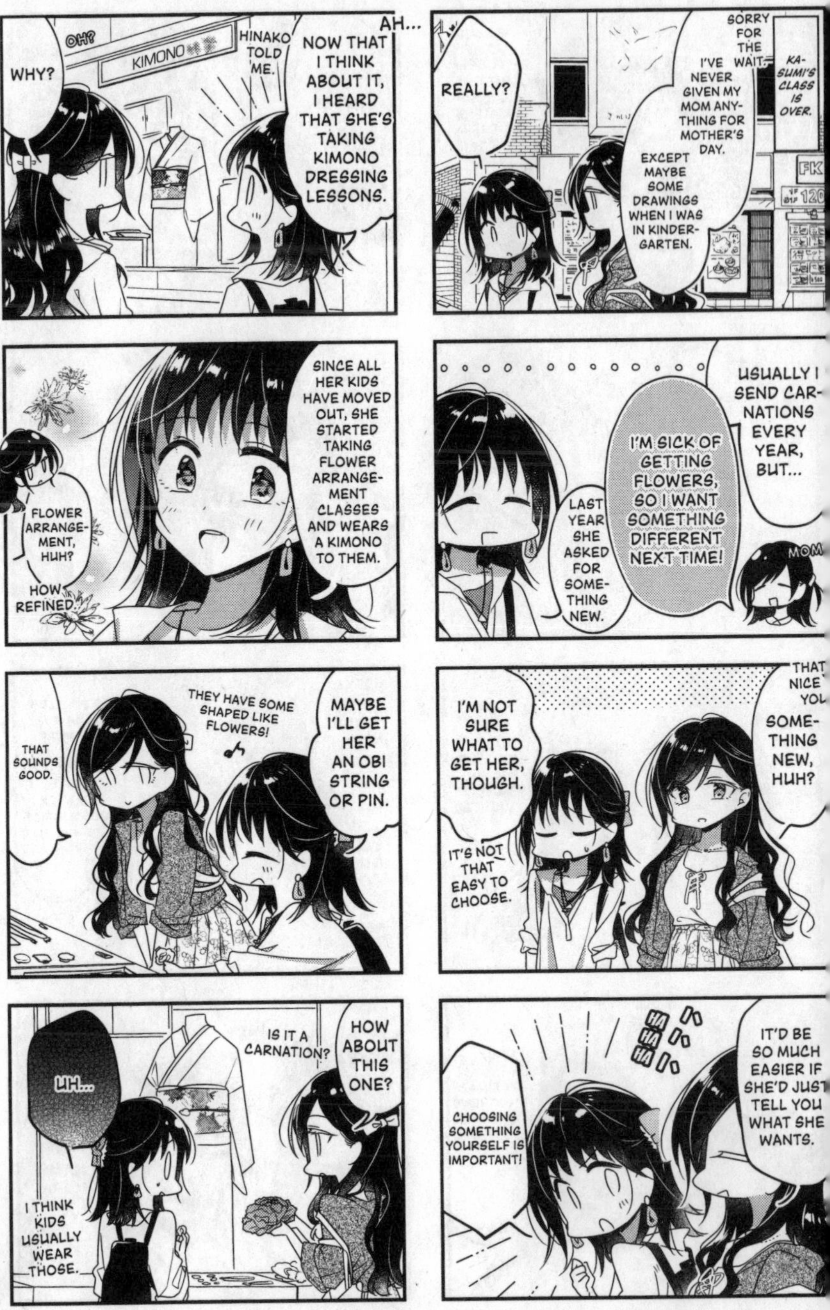

SORRY FOR THE WAIT.
KASUMI'S CLASS IS OVER.
I'VE NEVER GIVEN MY MOM ANYTHING FOR MOTHER'S DAY.
EXCEPT MAYBE SOME DRAWINGS WHEN I WAS IN KINDERGARTEN.
REALLY?
USUALLY I SEND CARNATIONS EVERY YEAR, BUT...
MOM
I'M SICK OF GETTING FLOWERS, SO I WANT SOMETHING DIFFERENT NEXT TIME!
LAST YEAR SHE ASKED FOR SOMETHING NEW.
....
THAT NICE YOU
SOMETHING NEW, HUH?
I'M NOT SURE WHAT TO GET HER, THOUGH.
IT'S NOT THAT EASY TO CHOOSE.
IT'D BE SO MUCH EASIER IF SHE'D JUST TELL YOU WHAT SHE WANTS.
HA HA HA
CHOOSING SOMETHING YOURSELF IS IMPORTANT!
AH...
NOW THAT I THINK ABOUT IT, I HEARD THAT SHE'S TAKING KIMONO DRESSING LESSONS.
HINAKO TOLD ME.
KIMONO
OH?
WHY?
SINCE ALL HER KIDS HAVE MOVED OUT, SHE STARTED TAKING FLOWER ARRANGEMENT CLASSES AND WEARS A KIMONO TO THEM.
FLOWER ARRANGEMENT, HUH?
HOW REFINED.
MAYBE I'LL GET HER AN OBI STRING OR PIN.
THEY HAVE SOME SHAPED LIKE FLOWERS!
THAT SOUNDS GOOD.
HOW ABOUT THIS ONE?
IS IT A CARNATION?
UH...
I THINK KIDS USUALLY WEAR THOSE.

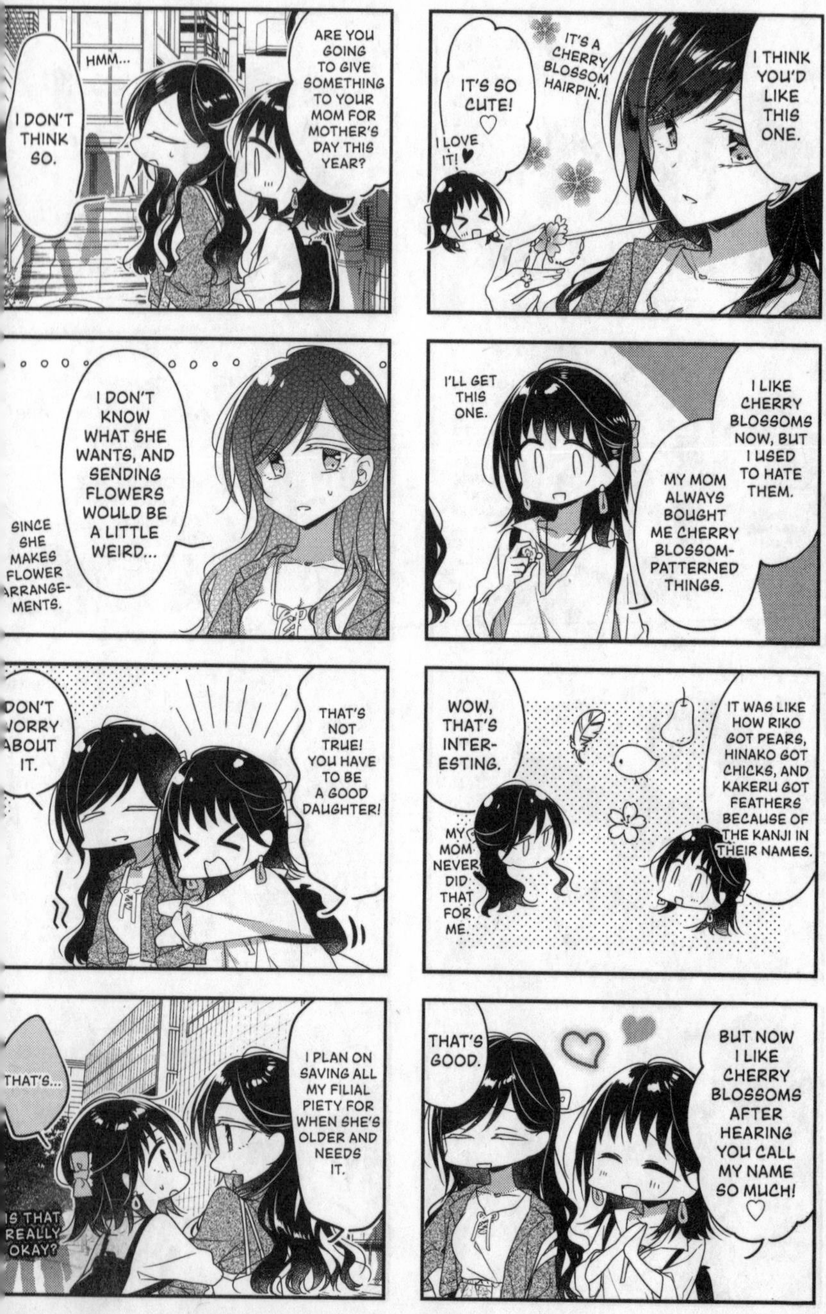
I THINK YOU'D LIKE THIS ONE.
IT'S A CHERRY BLOSSOM HAIRPIN.
IT'S SO CUTE! ♡
I LOVE IT! ♥
I LIKE CHERRY BLOSSOMS NOW, BUT I USED TO HATE THEM.
MY MOM ALWAYS BOUGHT ME CHERRY BLOSSOM-PATTERNED THINGS.
I'LL GET THIS ONE.
IT WAS LIKE HOW RIKO GOT PEARS, HINAKO GOT CHICKS, AND KAKERU GOT FEATHERS BECAUSE OF THE KANJI IN THEIR NAMES.
WOW, THAT'S INTERESTING.
MY MOM NEVER DID THAT FOR ME.
BUT NOW I LIKE CHERRY BLOSSOMS AFTER HEARING YOU CALL MY NAME SO MUCH! ♡
THAT'S GOOD.
ARE YOU GOING TO GIVE SOMETHING TO YOUR MOM FOR MOTHER'S DAY THIS YEAR?
HMM...
I DON'T THINK SO.
I DON'T KNOW WHAT SHE WANTS, AND SENDING FLOWERS WOULD BE A LITTLE WEIRD...
SINCE SHE MAKES FLOWER ARRANGEMENTS.
THAT'S NOT TRUE! YOU HAVE TO BE A GOOD DAUGHTER!
DON'T WORRY ABOUT IT.
I PLAN ON SAVING ALL MY FILIAL PIETY FOR WHEN SHE'S OLDER AND NEEDS IT.
THAT'S...
IS THAT REALLY OKAY?

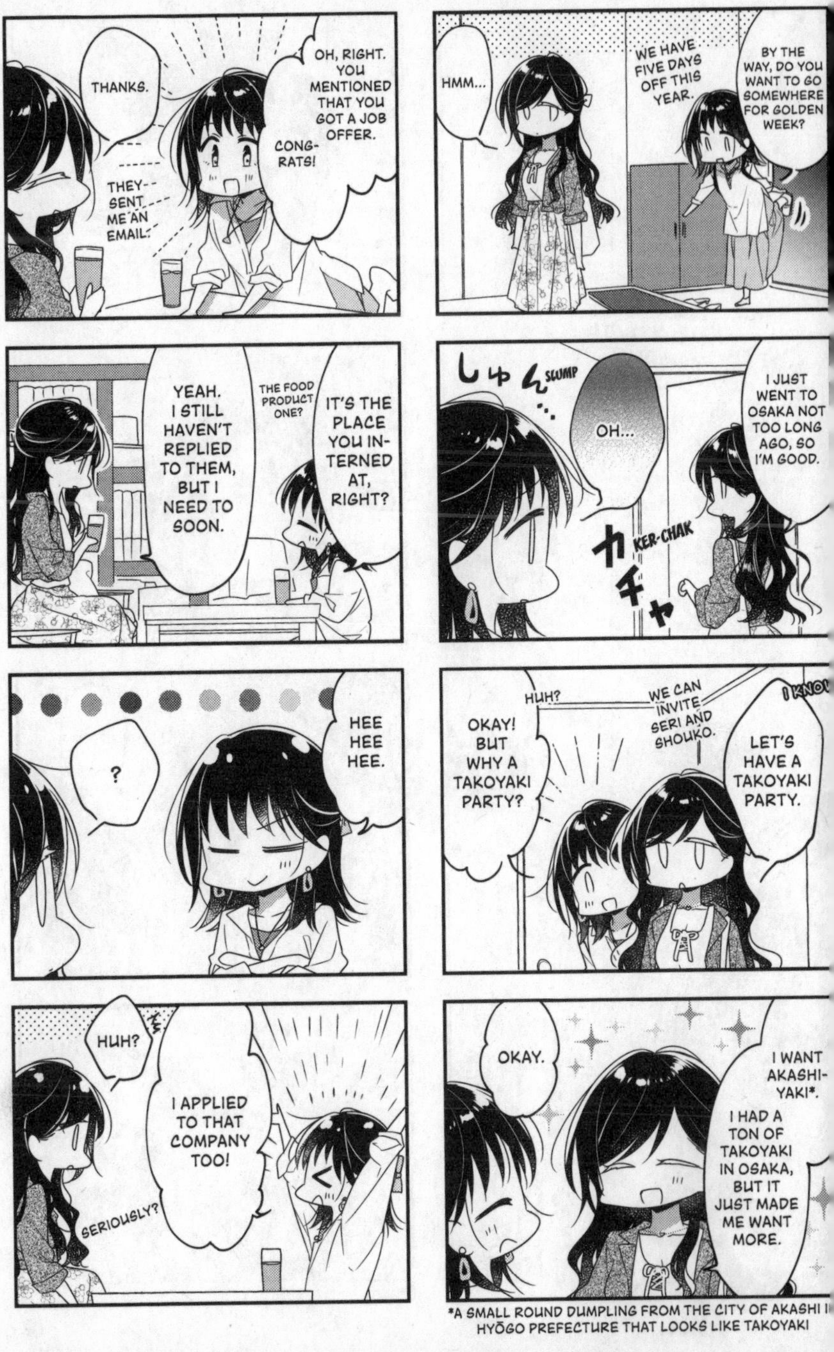
BY THE WAY, DO YOU WANT TO GO SOMEWHERE FOR GOLDEN WEEK?
WE HAVE FIVE DAYS OFF THIS YEAR.
HMM...
I JUST WENT TO OSAKA NOT TOO LONG AGO, SO I'M GOOD.
しゅん SLUMP
OH...
カチャ KER-CHAK
I KNOW
LET'S HAVE A TAKOYAKI PARTY.
WE CAN INVITE SERI AND SHOUKO.
HUH?
OKAY! BUT WHY A TAKOYAKI PARTY?
I WANT AKASHI-YAKI*.
I HAD A TON OF TAKOYAKI IN OSAKA, BUT IT JUST MADE ME WANT MORE.
OKAY.
OH, RIGHT. YOU MENTIONED THAT YOU GOT A JOB OFFER.
CONGRATS!
THANKS.
THEY SENT ME AN EMAIL.
IT'S THE PLACE YOU INTERNED AT, RIGHT?
THE FOOD PRODUCT ONE?
YEAH. I STILL HAVEN'T REPLIED TO THEM, BUT I NEED TO SOON.
HEE HEE HEE.
?
I APPLIED TO THAT COMPANY TOO!
HUH?
SERIOUSLY?

*A SMALL ROUND DUMPLING FROM THE CITY OF AKASHI I
HYŌGO PREFECTURE THAT LOOKS LIKE TAKOYAKI

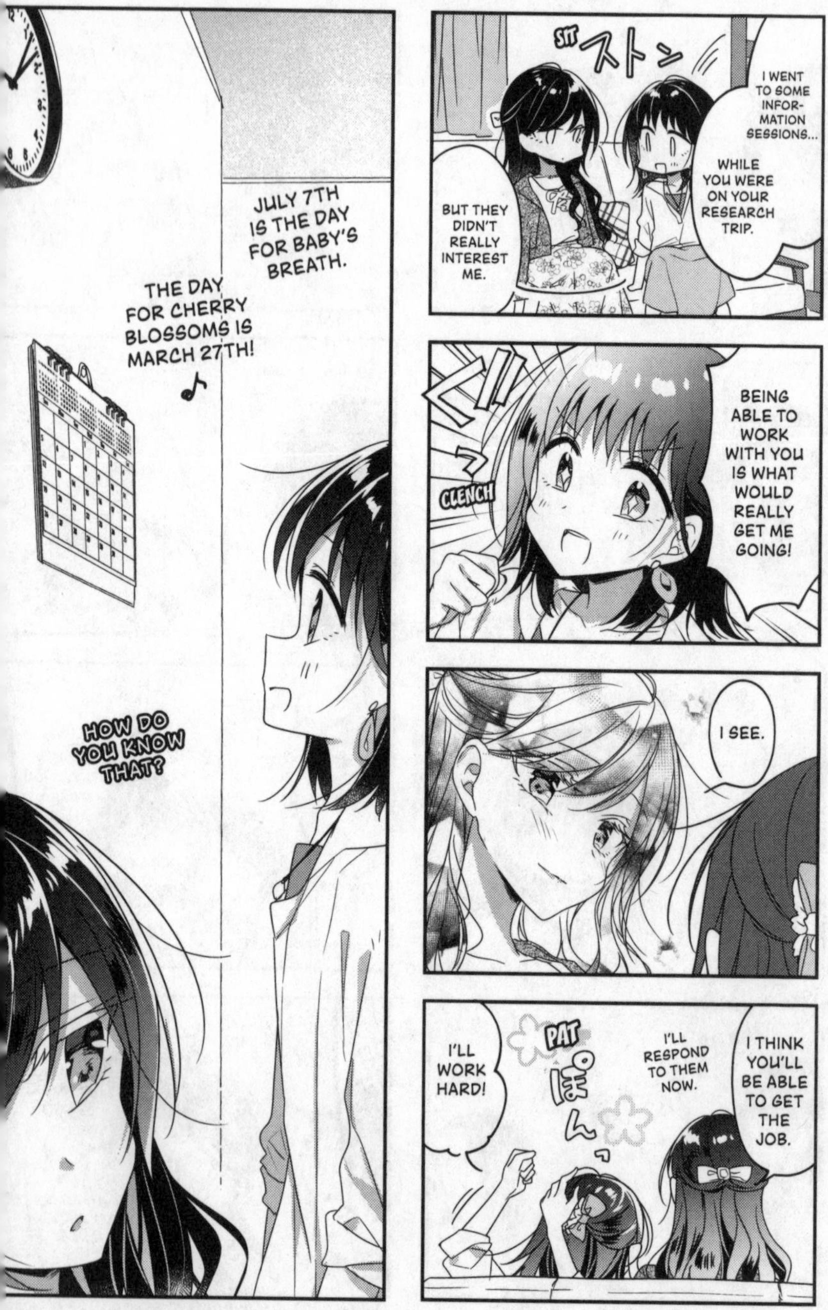
SIT ストン
I WENT TO SOME INFOR-MATION SESSIONS...
WHILE YOU WERE ON YOUR RESEARCH TRIP.
BUT THEY DIDN'T REALLY INTEREST ME.
BEING ABLE TO WORK WITH YOU IS WHAT WOULD REALLY GET ME GOING!
CLENCH
I SEE.
I THINK YOU'LL BE ABLE TO GET THE JOB.
I'LL RESPOND TO THEM NOW.
PAT ぽん
I'LL WORK HARD!
JULY 7TH IS THE DAY FOR BABY'S BREATH.
THE DAY FOR CHERRY BLOSSOMS IS MARCH 27TH! ♪
HOW DO YOU KNOW THAT?

Illustration gallery of Yukiko

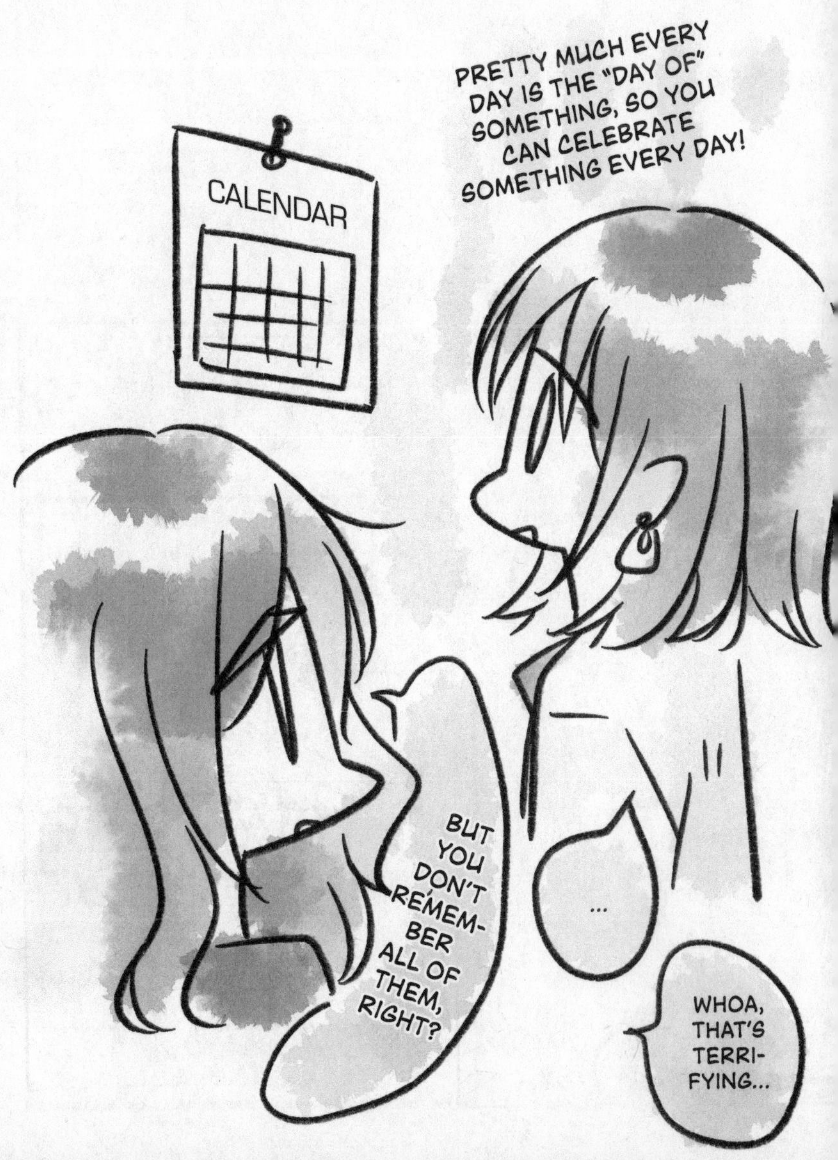
PRETTY MUCH EVERY DAY IS THE "DAY OF" SOMETHING, SO YOU CAN CELEBRATE SOMETHING EVERY DAY!
CALENDAR
BUT YOU DON'T REMEMBER ALL OF THEM, RIGHT?
...
WHOA, THAT'S TERRIFYING...

Futaribeya
A ROOM FOR TWO

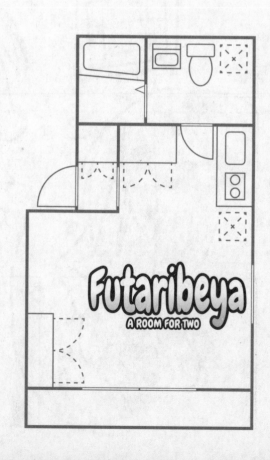

Special Chapter #2 - "Let's Have a Takoyaki Party!"

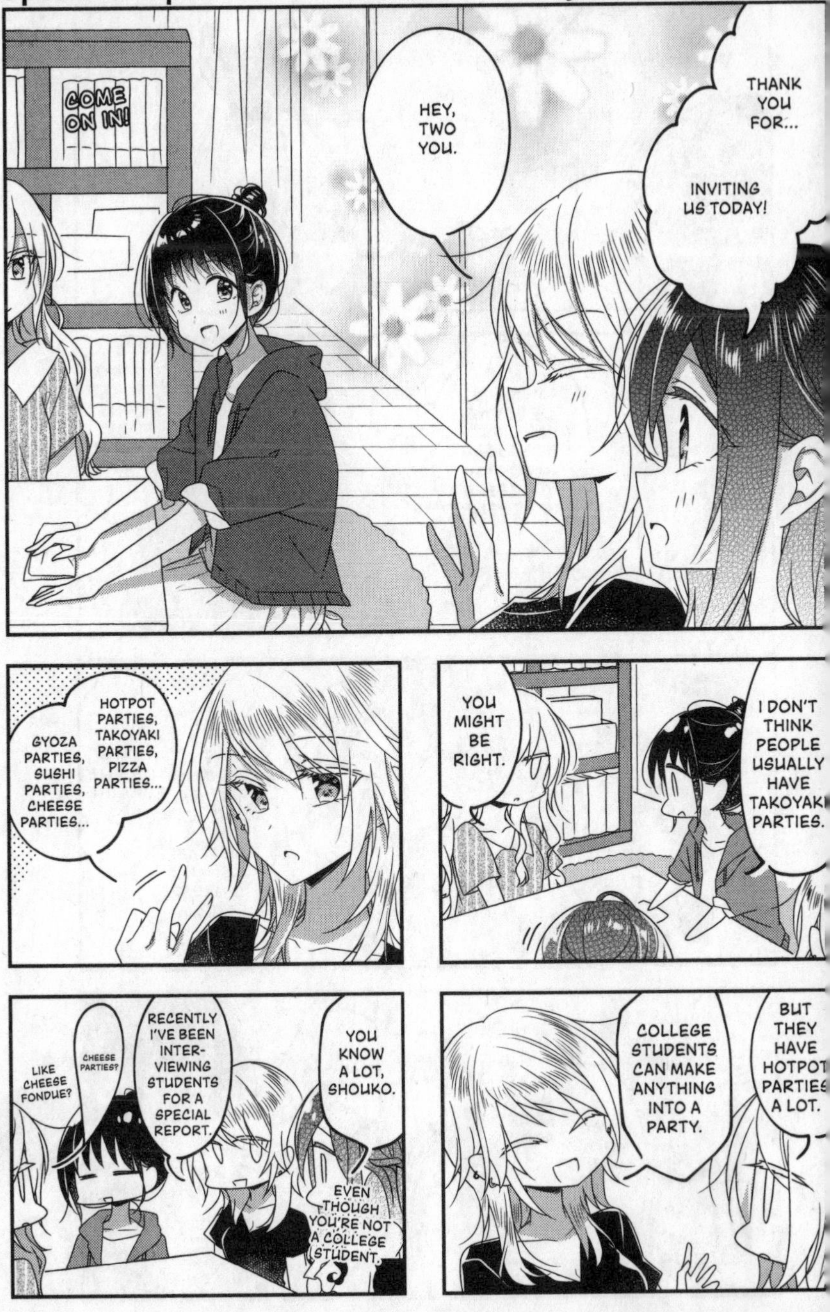
THANK YOU FOR... INVITING US TODAY!
HEY, TWO YOU.
COME ON IN!
I DON'T THINK PEOPLE USUALLY HAVE TAKOYAKI PARTIES.
YOU MIGHT BE RIGHT.
HOTPOT PARTIES, TAKOYAKI PARTIES, PIZZA PARTIES...
GYOZA PARTIES, SUSHI PARTIES, CHEESE PARTIES...
BUT THEY HAVE HOTPOT PARTIES A LOT.
COLLEGE STUDENTS CAN MAKE ANYTHING INTO A PARTY.
YOU KNOW A LOT, SHOUKO.
RECENTLY I'VE BEEN INTER-VIEWING STUDENTS FOR A SPECIAL REPORT.
EVEN THOUGH YOU'RE NOT A COLLEGE STUDENT.
CHEESE PARTIES?
LIKE CHEESE FONDUE?

PLEASE ACCEPT THIS

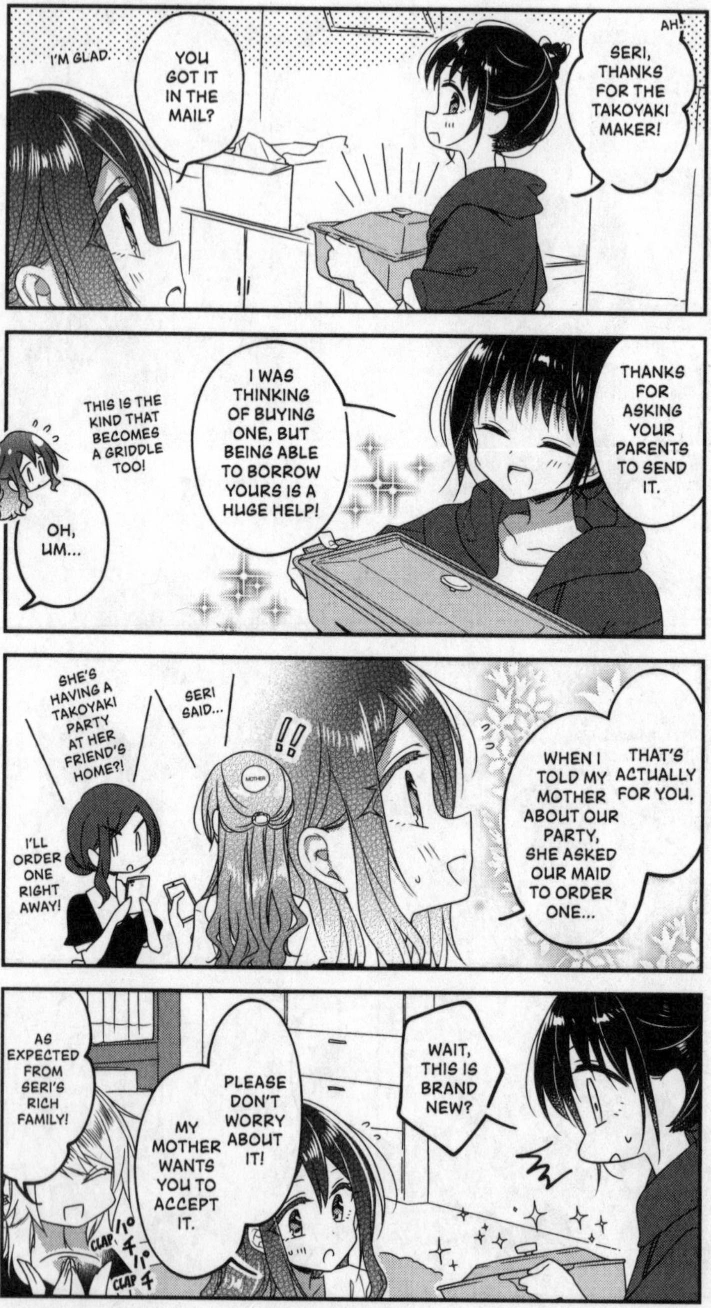
AH...
SERI, THANKS FOR THE TAKOYAKI MAKER!
YOU GOT IT IN THE MAIL?
I'M GLAD.
THANKS FOR ASKING YOUR PARENTS TO SEND IT.
I WAS THINKING OF BUYING ONE, BUT BEING ABLE TO BORROW YOURS IS A HUGE HELP!
THIS IS THE KIND THAT BECOMES A GRIDDLE TOO!
OH, UM...
THAT'S ACTUALLY FOR YOU.
WHEN I TOLD MY MOTHER ABOUT OUR PARTY, SHE ASKED OUR MAID TO ORDER ONE...
!!
SERI SAID...
SHE'S HAVING A TAKOYAKI PARTY AT HER FRIEND'S HOME?!
MOTHER
I'LL ORDER ONE RIGHT AWAY!
WAIT, THIS IS BRAND NEW?
PLEASE DON'T WORRY ABOUT IT!
MY MOTHER WANTS YOU TO ACCEPT IT.
AS EXPECTED FROM SERI'S RICH FAMILY!
パチパチ
CLAP CLAP

GREED

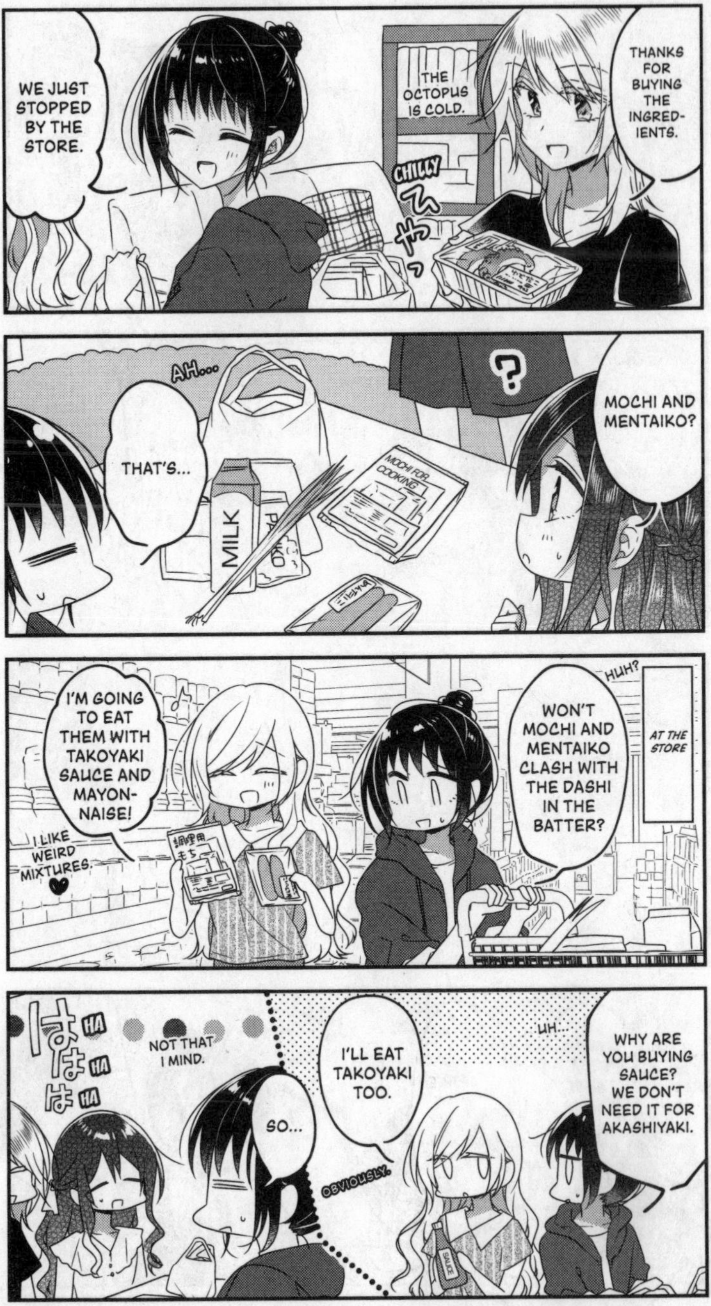
THANKS FOR BUYING THE INGREDIENTS.
THE OCTOPUS IS COLD.
CHILLY
WE JUST STOPPED BY THE STORE.
MOCHI AND MENTAIKO?
?
MOCHI FOR COOKING
MILK
AH...
THAT'S...
AT THE STORE
HUH?
WON'T MOCHI AND MENTAIKO CLASH WITH THE DASHI IN THE BATTER?
I'M GOING TO EAT THEM WITH TAKOYAKI SAUCE AND MAYONNAISE!
調理用もち
I LIKE WEIRD MIXTURES.
WHY ARE YOU BUYING SAUCE? WE DON'T NEED IT FOR AKASHIYAKI.
UH...
SAUCE
OBVIOUSLY.
I'LL EAT TAKOYAKI TOO.
SO...
NOT THAT I MIND.
は HA は HA は HA

SAME-COLORED BATTER

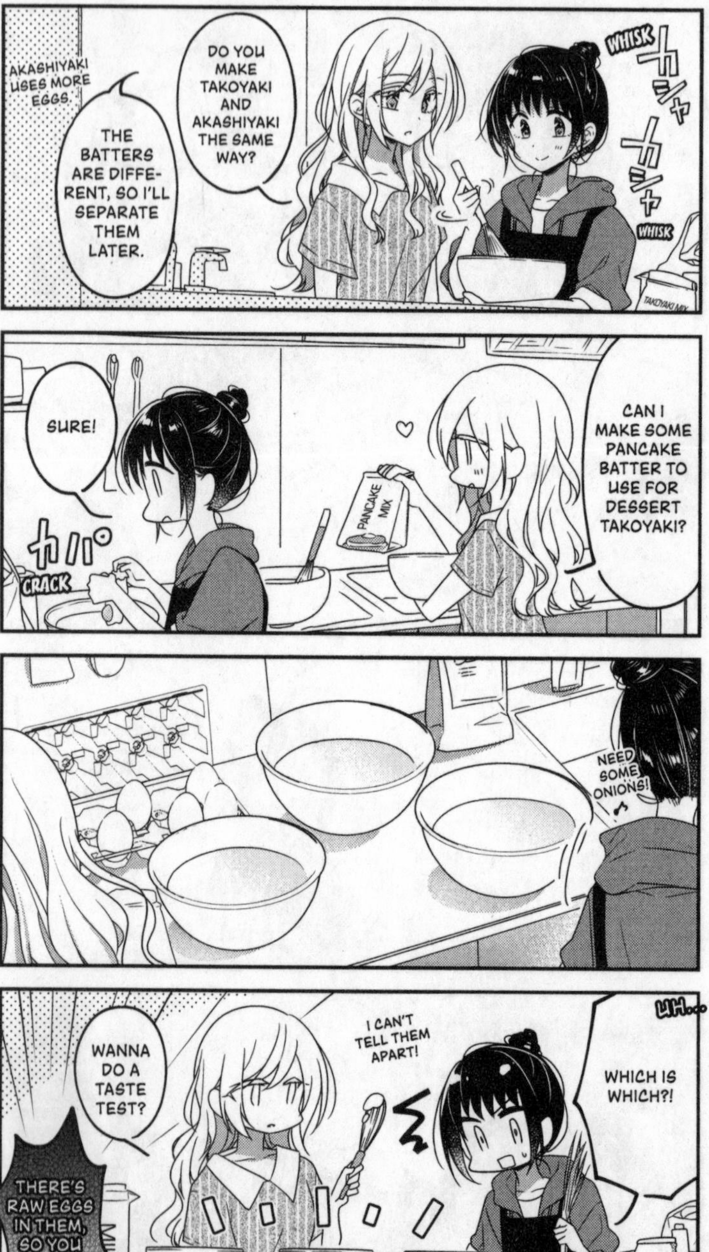
WHISK
DO YOU MAKE TAKOYAKI AND AKASHIYAKI THE SAME WAY?
THE BATTERS ARE DIFFERENT, SO I'LL SEPARATE THEM LATER.
AKASHIYAKI USES MORE EGGS.
WHISK
TAKOYAKI MIX
CAN I MAKE SOME PANCAKE BATTER TO USE FOR DESSERT TAKOYAKI?
PANCAKE MIX
SURE!
CRACK
NEED SOME ONIONS!
UH...
WHICH IS WHICH?!
I CAN'T TELL THEM APART!
WANNA DO A TASTE TEST?
THERE'S RAW EGGS IN THEM, SO YOU CAN'T!
MILK

HOW TO ENJOY TAKOYAKI PARTIES

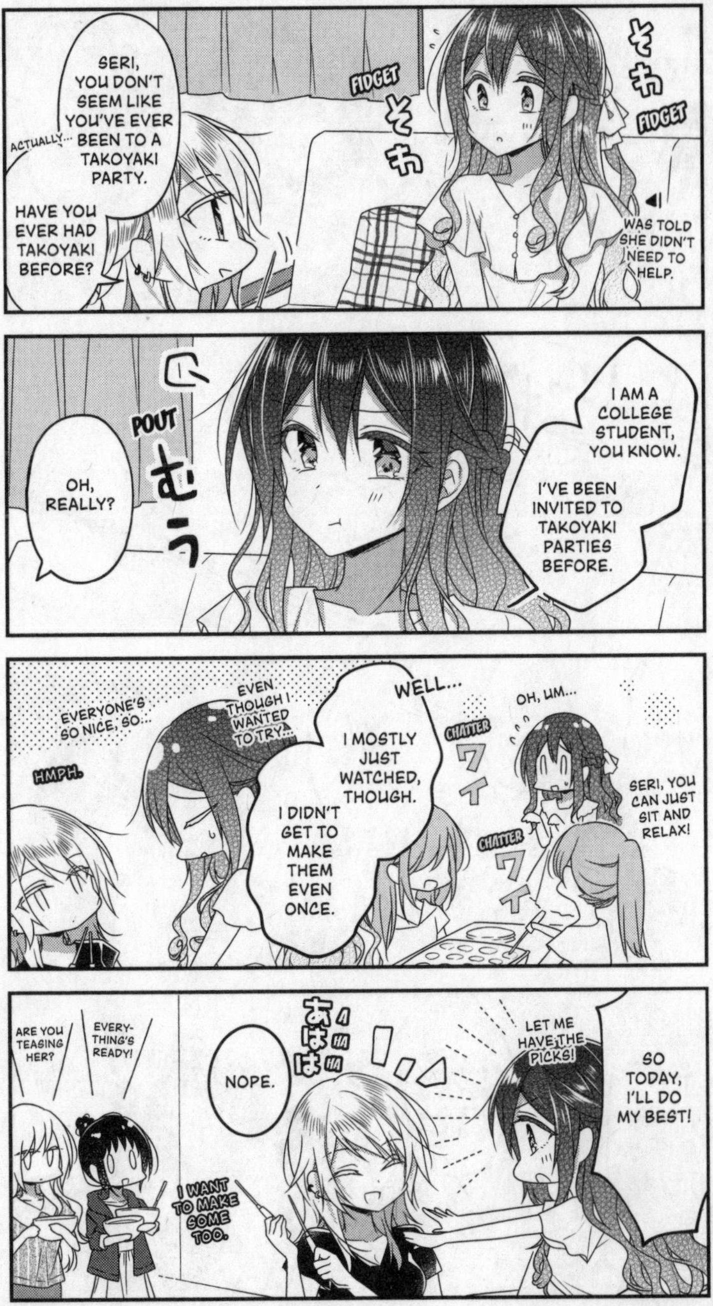

FIDGET
そわ
WAS TOLD SHE DIDN'T NEED TO HELP.
FIDGET
そわ
SERI, YOU DON'T SEEM LIKE YOU'VE EVER BEEN TO A TAKOYAKI PARTY.
HAVE YOU EVER HAD TAKOYAKI BEFORE?
ACTUALLY...
I AM A COLLEGE STUDENT, YOU KNOW.
I'VE BEEN INVITED TO TAKOYAKI PARTIES BEFORE.
POUT
むう
OH, REALLY?
OH, UM...
SERI, YOU CAN JUST SIT AND RELAX!
CHATTER
ワイ
CHATTER
ワイ
WELL...
I MOSTLY JUST WATCHED, THOUGH.
I DIDN'T GET TO MAKE THEM EVEN ONCE.
EVEN THOUGH I WANTED TO TRY...
EVERYONE'S SO NICE, SO...
HMPH.
SO TODAY, I'LL DO MY BEST!
LET ME HAVE THE PICKS!
!!
あはは
A HA HA
NOPE.
I WANT TO MAKE SOME TOO.
EVERY-THING'S READY!
ARE YOU TEASING HER?

A SILLY MISTAKE

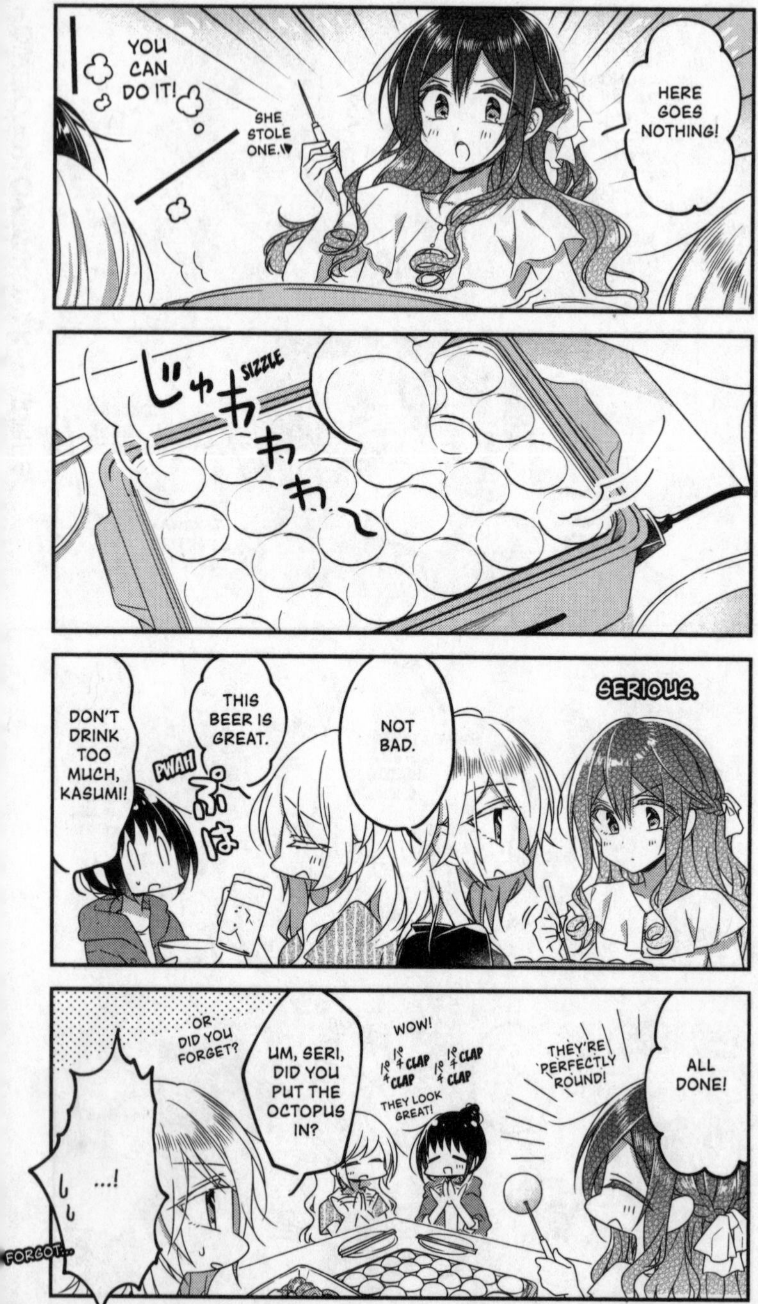
HERE GOES NOTHING!
SHE STOLE ONE.♥
YOU CAN DO IT!
じゅわわわ〜
SIZZLE
SERIOUS.
NOT BAD.
THIS BEER IS GREAT.
ぷは
PWAH
DON'T DRINK TOO MUCH, KASUMI!
ALL DONE!
THEY'RE PERFECTLY ROUND!
パチパチ CLAP CLAP
パチパチ CLAP CLAP
WOW!
THEY LOOK GREAT!
UM, SERI, DID YOU PUT THE OCTOPUS IN?
OR DID YOU FORGET?
...!
しし
FORGOT...

CHEEK POUCHES

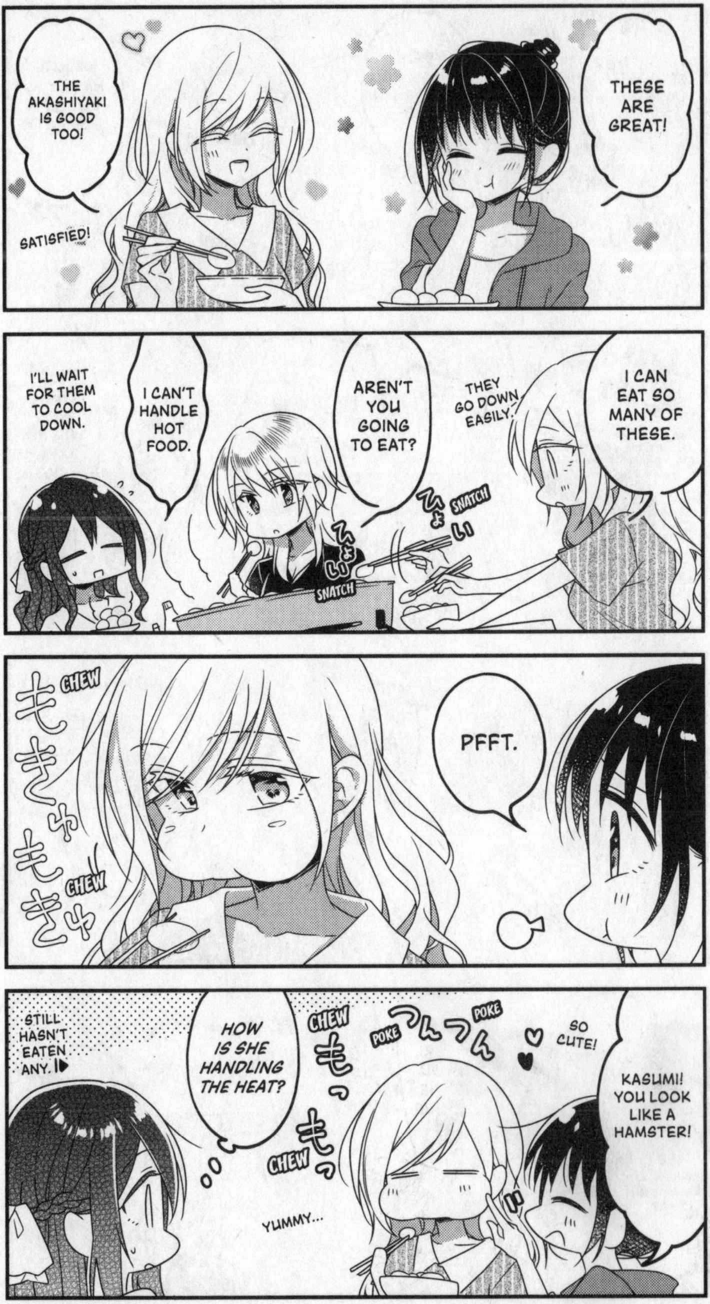
THESE ARE GREAT!
THE AKASHIYAKI IS GOOD TOO!
SATISFIED!
I CAN EAT SO MANY OF THESE.
THEY GO DOWN EASILY.
ひょい SNATCH
ひょい SNATCH
AREN'T YOU GOING TO EAT?
I CAN'T HANDLE HOT FOOD.
I'LL WAIT FOR THEM TO COOL DOWN.
PFFT.
もきゅ CHEW
もきゅ CHEW
KASUMI! YOU LOOK LIKE A HAMSTER!
SO CUTE!
つんつん POKE POKE
もっ CHEW
もっ CHEW
YUMMY...
HOW IS SHE HANDLING THE HEAT?
STILL HASN'T EATEN ANY.

THE SAME PATH

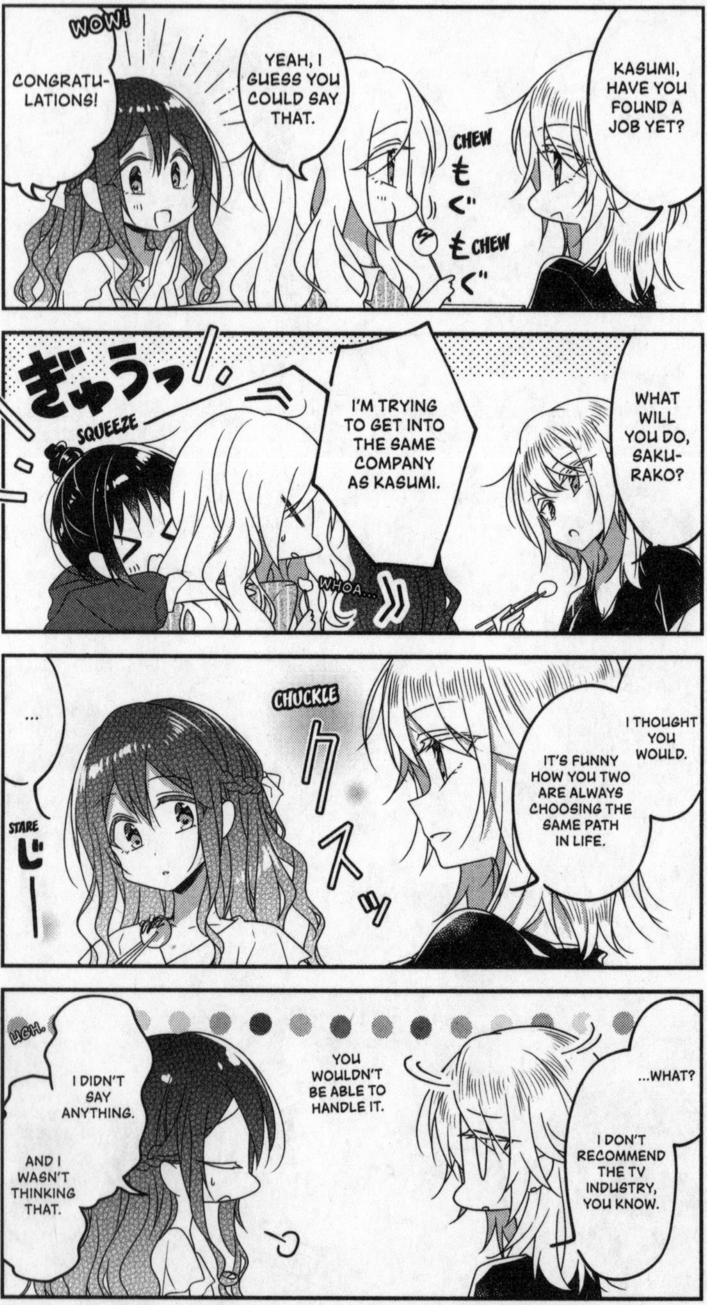
KASUMI, HAVE YOU FOUND A JOB YET?
CHEW もぐ
もぐ CHEW
YEAH, I GUESS YOU COULD SAY THAT.
WOW!
CONGRATULATIONS!
WHAT WILL YOU DO, SAKURAKO?
I'M TRYING TO GET INTO THE SAME COMPANY AS KASUMI.
ぎゅうっ
SQUEEZE
WHOA...
I THOUGHT YOU WOULD.
IT'S FUNNY HOW YOU TWO ARE ALWAYS CHOOSING THE SAME PATH IN LIFE.
CHUCKLE
クスッ
STARE
じー
...
...WHAT?
I DON'T RECOMMEND THE TV INDUSTRY, YOU KNOW.
YOU WOULDN'T BE ABLE TO HANDLE IT.
UGH.
I DIDN'T SAY ANYTHING.
AND I WASN'T THINKING THAT.

WHY?

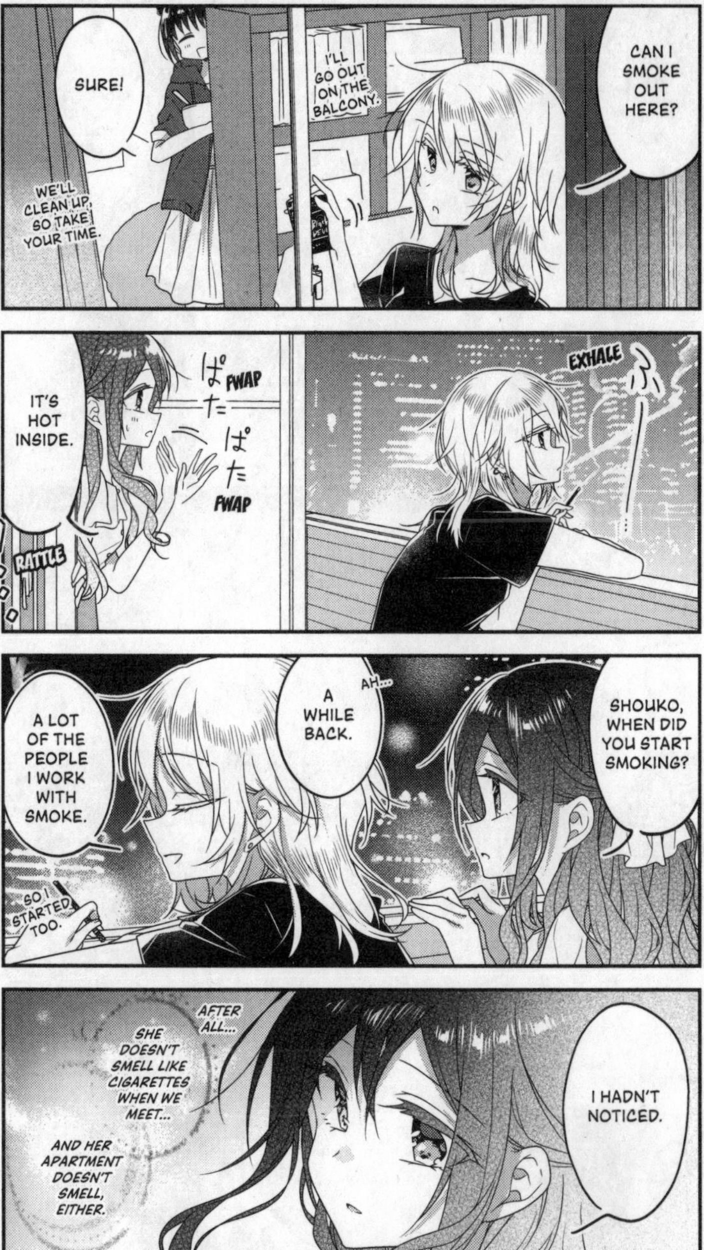
CAN I SMOKE OUT HERE?
I'LL GO OUT ON THE BALCONY.
SURE!
WE'LL CLEAN UP, SO TAKE YOUR TIME.
ふー
EXHALE
IT'S HOT INSIDE.
ぱた FWAP
ぱた FWAP
RATTLE
SHOUKO, WHEN DID YOU START SMOKING?
AH...
A WHILE BACK.
A LOT OF THE PEOPLE I WORK WITH SMOKE.
SO I STARTED TOO.
I HADN'T NOTICED.
AFTER ALL...
SHE DOESN'T SMELL LIKE CIGARETTES WHEN WE MEET...
AND HER APARTMENT DOESN'T SMELL, EITHER.

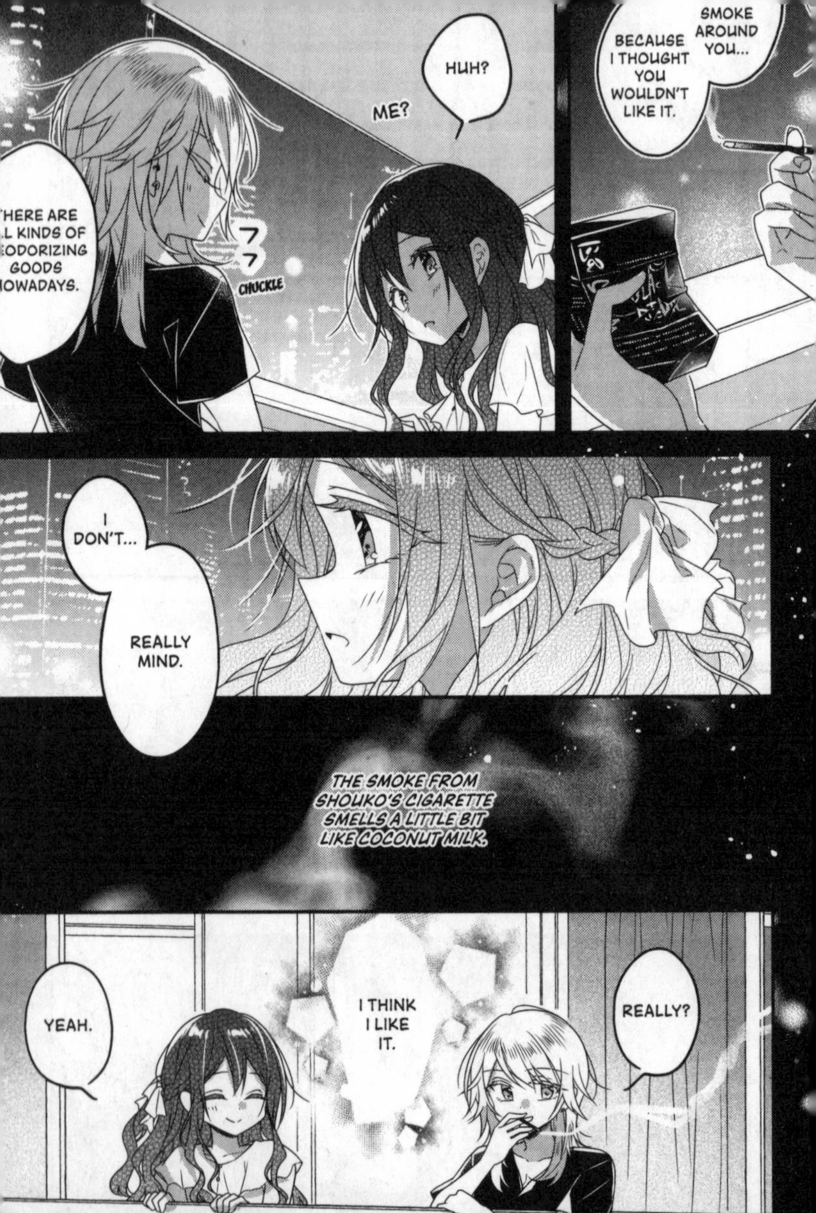
SMOKE AROUND YOU...
BECAUSE I THOUGHT YOU WOULDN'T LIKE IT.
HUH?
ME?
CHUCKLE
THERE ARE L KINDS OF EODORIZING GOODS OWADAYS.
I DON'T...
REALLY MIND.
THE SMOKE FROM SHOUKO'S CIGARETTE SMELLS A LITTLE BIT LIKE COCONUT MILK.
REALLY?
I THINK I LIKE IT.
YEAH.

Illustration gallery of Yukik

GETTING ALONG
IN SCHOOL
UNIFORMS!

Futaribeya
A ROOM FOR TWO

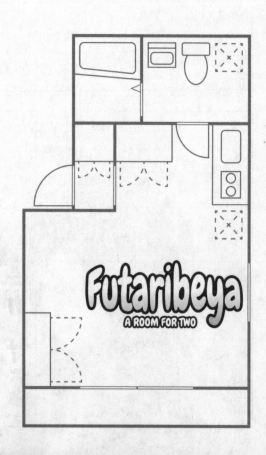

Chapter 65

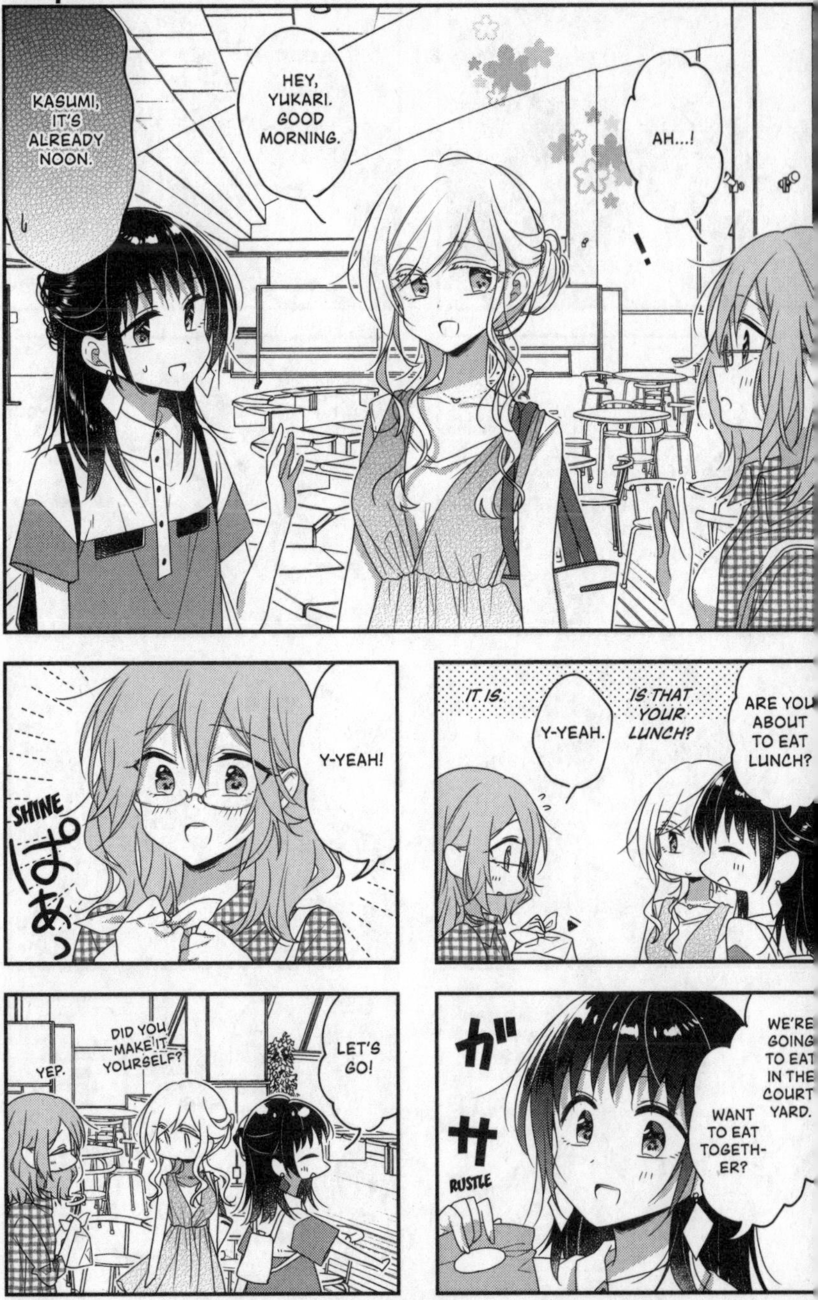
AH...!
!
HEY, YUKARI. GOOD MORNING.
KASUMI, IT'S ALREADY NOON.
ARE YOU ABOUT TO EAT LUNCH?
IS THAT YOUR LUNCH?
Y-YEAH.
IT IS.
Y-YEAH!
SHINE
ぱあっ
WE'RE GOING TO EAT IN THE COURTYARD.
WANT TO EAT TOGETH-ER?
ガサ
RUSTLE
LET'S GO!
DID YOU MAKE IT YOURSELF?
YEP.

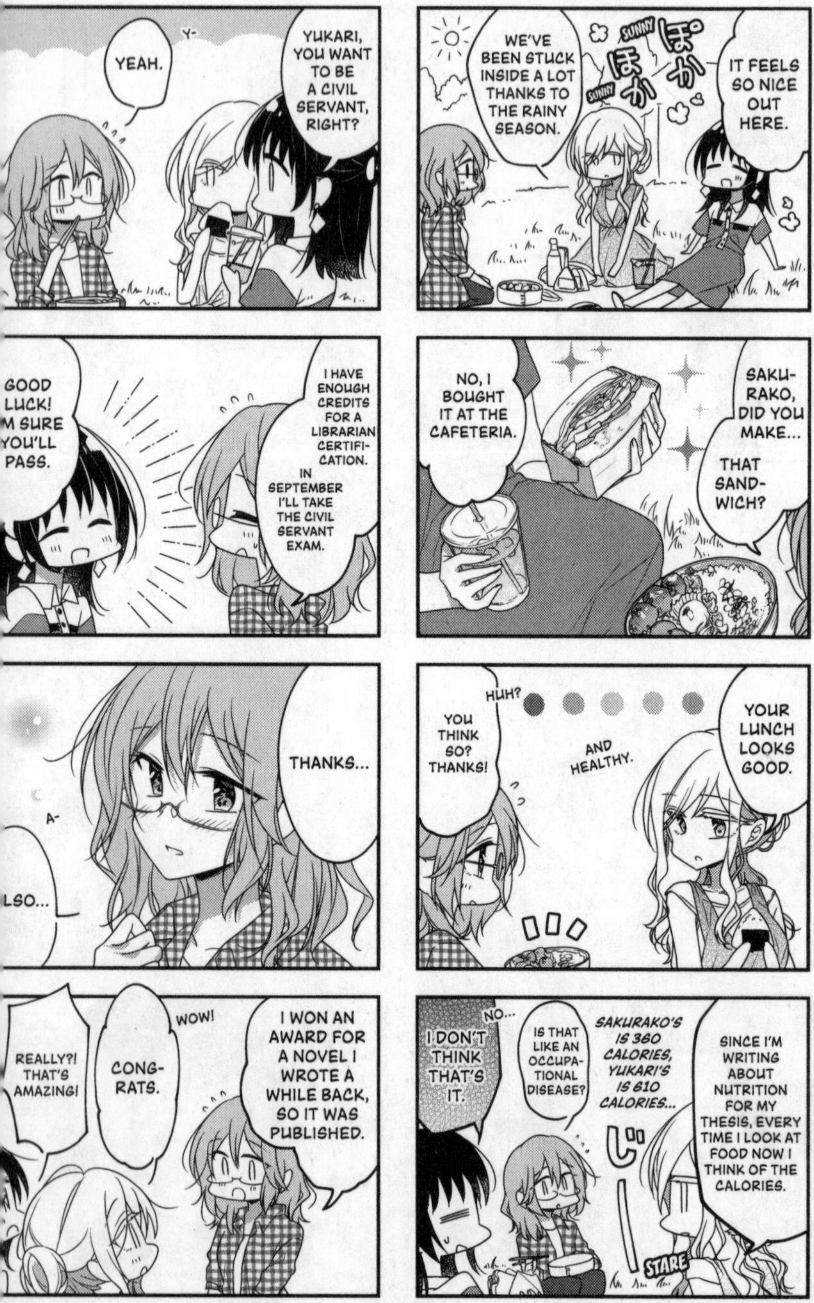
IT FEELS SO NICE OUT HERE.
ぽか ぽか
SUNNY
SUNNY
WE'VE BEEN STUCK INSIDE A LOT THANKS TO THE RAINY SEASON.
SAKU-RAKO, DID YOU MAKE... THAT SAND-WICH?
NO, I BOUGHT IT AT THE CAFETERIA.
YOUR LUNCH LOOKS GOOD.
AND HEALTHY.
HUH?
YOU THINK SO? THANKS!
SINCE I'M WRITING ABOUT NUTRITION FOR MY THESIS, EVERY TIME I LOOK AT FOOD NOW I THINK OF THE CALORIES.
SAKURAKO'S IS 360 CALORIES, YUKARI'S IS 610 CALORIES...
じー
STARE
IS THAT LIKE AN OCCUPA-TIONAL DISEASE?
NO...
I DON'T THINK THAT'S IT.
YUKARI, YOU WANT TO BE A CIVIL SERVANT, RIGHT?
Y-
YEAH.
I HAVE ENOUGH CREDITS FOR A LIBRARIAN CERTIFI-CATION.
IN SEPTEMBER I'LL TAKE THE CIVIL SERVANT EXAM.
GOOD LUCK! M SURE YOU'LL PASS.
THANKS...
A-
LSO...
I WON AN AWARD FOR A NOVEL I WROTE A WHILE BACK, SO IT WAS PUBLISHED.
WOW!
CONG-RATS.
REALLY?! THAT'S AMAZING!

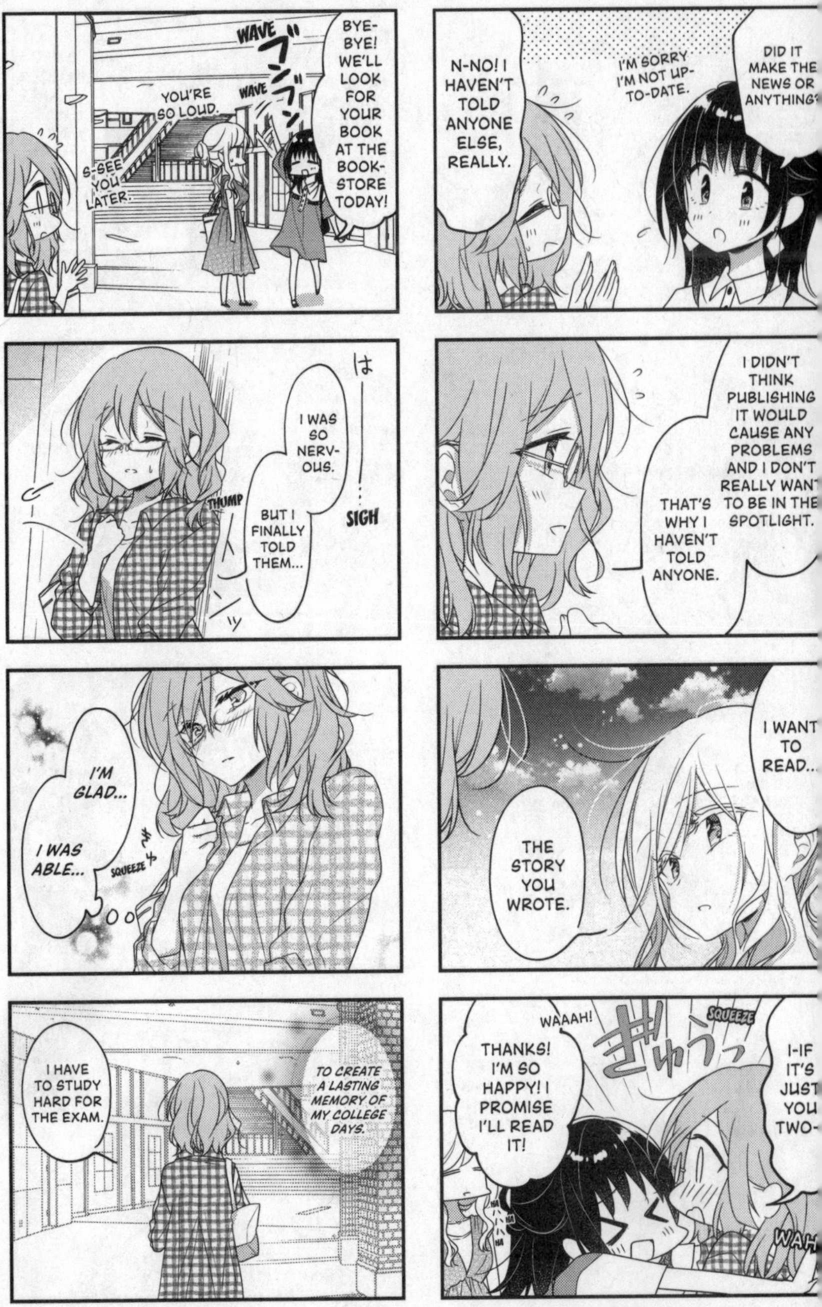
DID IT MAKE THE NEWS OR ANYTHING?
I'M SORRY I'M NOT UP-TO-DATE.
N-NO! I HAVEN'T TOLD ANYONE ELSE, REALLY.
I DIDN'T THINK PUBLISHING IT WOULD CAUSE ANY PROBLEMS AND I DON'T REALLY WANT TO BE IN THE SPOTLIGHT.
THAT'S WHY I HAVEN'T TOLD ANYONE.
I WANT TO READ...
THE STORY YOU WROTE.
I-IF IT'S JUST YOU TWO-
SQUEEZE
WAAAH!
THANKS! I'M SO HAPPY! I PROMISE I'LL READ IT!
BYE-BYE! WE'LL LOOK FOR YOUR BOOK AT THE BOOKSTORE TODAY!
WAVE
WAVE
YOU'RE SO LOUD.
S-SEE YOU LATER.
SIGH
I WAS SO NERVOUS.
BUT I FINALLY TOLD THEM...
THUMP
I'M GLAD...
I WAS ABLE...
SQUEEZE
TO CREATE A LASTING MEMORY OF MY COLLEGE DAYS.
I HAVE TO STUDY HARD FOR THE EXAM.

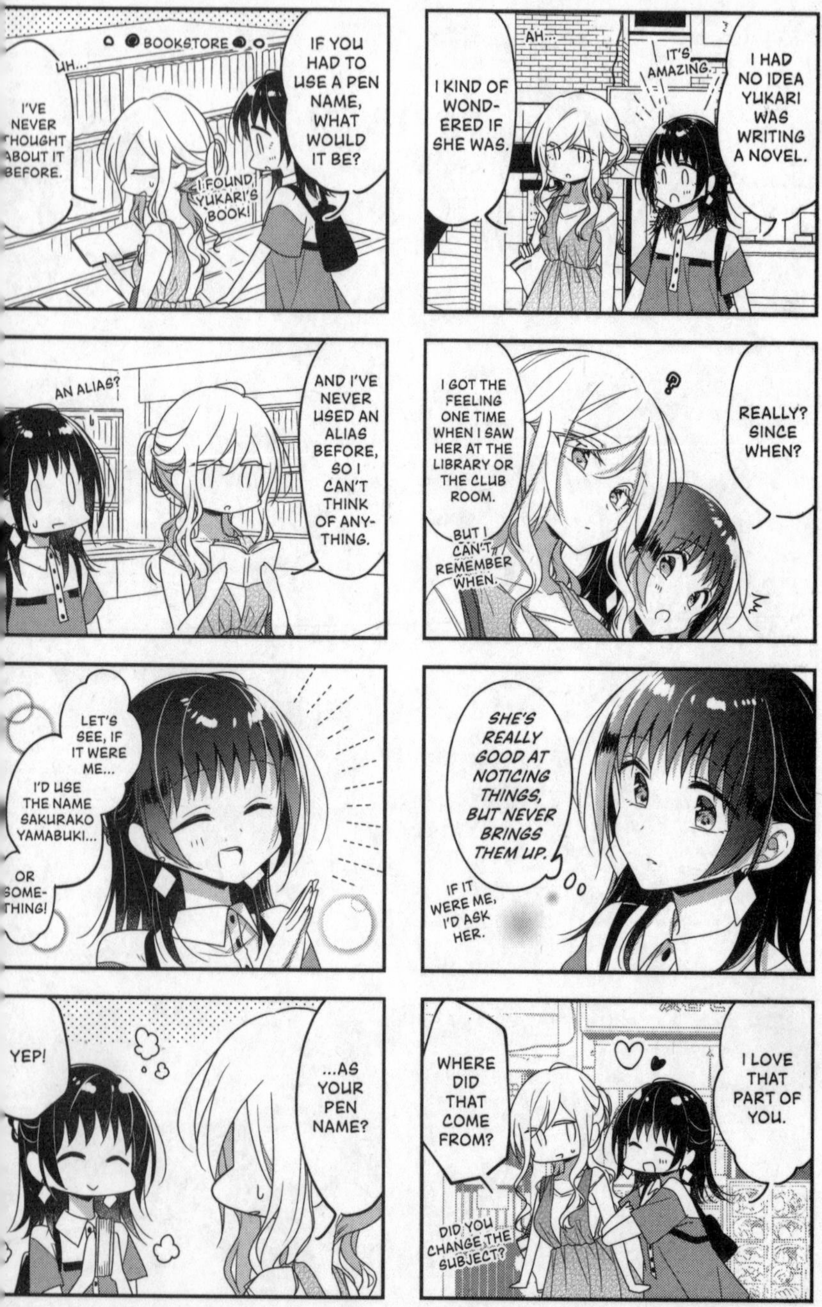
I HAD NO IDEA YUKARI WAS WRITING A NOVEL.
IT'S AMAZING.
AH...
I KIND OF WONDERED IF SHE WAS.
REALLY? SINCE WHEN?
?
I GOT THE FEELING ONE TIME WHEN I SAW HER AT THE LIBRARY OR THE CLUB ROOM.
BUT I CAN'T REMEMBER WHEN.
SHE'S REALLY GOOD AT NOTICING THINGS, BUT NEVER BRINGS THEM UP.
IF IT WERE ME, I'D ASK HER.
I LOVE THAT PART OF YOU.
WHERE DID THAT COME FROM?
DID YOU CHANGE THE SUBJECT?
BOOKSTORE
IF YOU HAD TO USE A PEN NAME, WHAT WOULD IT BE?
I FOUND YUKARI'S BOOK!
UH...
I'VE NEVER THOUGHT ABOUT IT BEFORE.
AND I'VE NEVER USED AN ALIAS BEFORE, SO I CAN'T THINK OF ANY-THING.
AN ALIAS?
LET'S SEE, IF IT WERE ME...
I'D USE THE NAME SAKURAKO YAMABUKI...
OR SOME-THING!
...AS YOUR PEN NAME?
YEP!

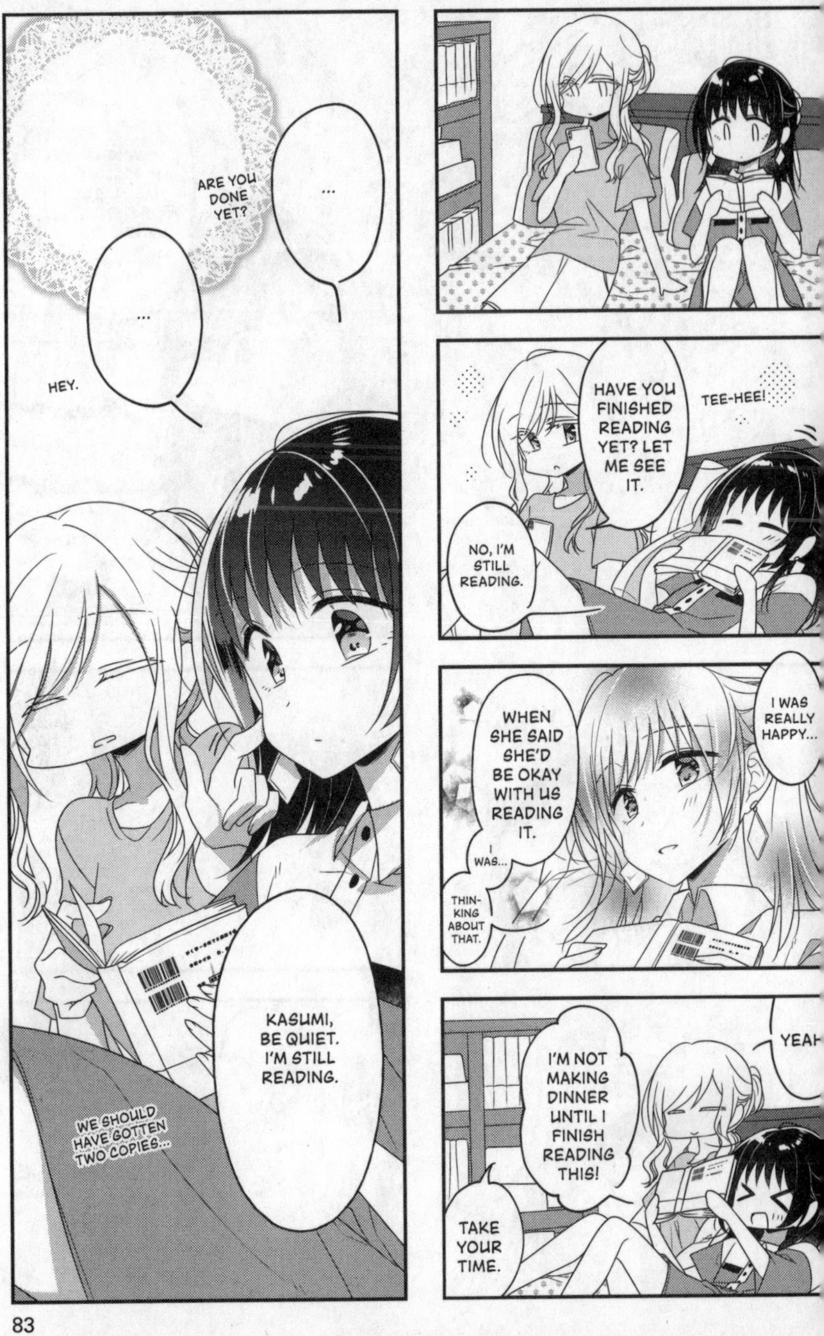
HAVE YOU FINISHED READING YET? LET ME SEE IT.
TEE-HEE!
NO, I'M STILL READING.
I WAS REALLY HAPPY...
WHEN SHE SAID SHE'D BE OKAY WITH US READING IT.
I WAS...
THIN-KING ABOUT THAT.
YEAH
I'M NOT MAKING DINNER UNTIL I FINISH READING THIS!
TAKE YOUR TIME.
...
ARE YOU DONE YET?
...
HEY.
KASUMI, BE QUIET. I'M STILL READING.
WE SHOULD HAVE GOTTEN TWO COPIES...

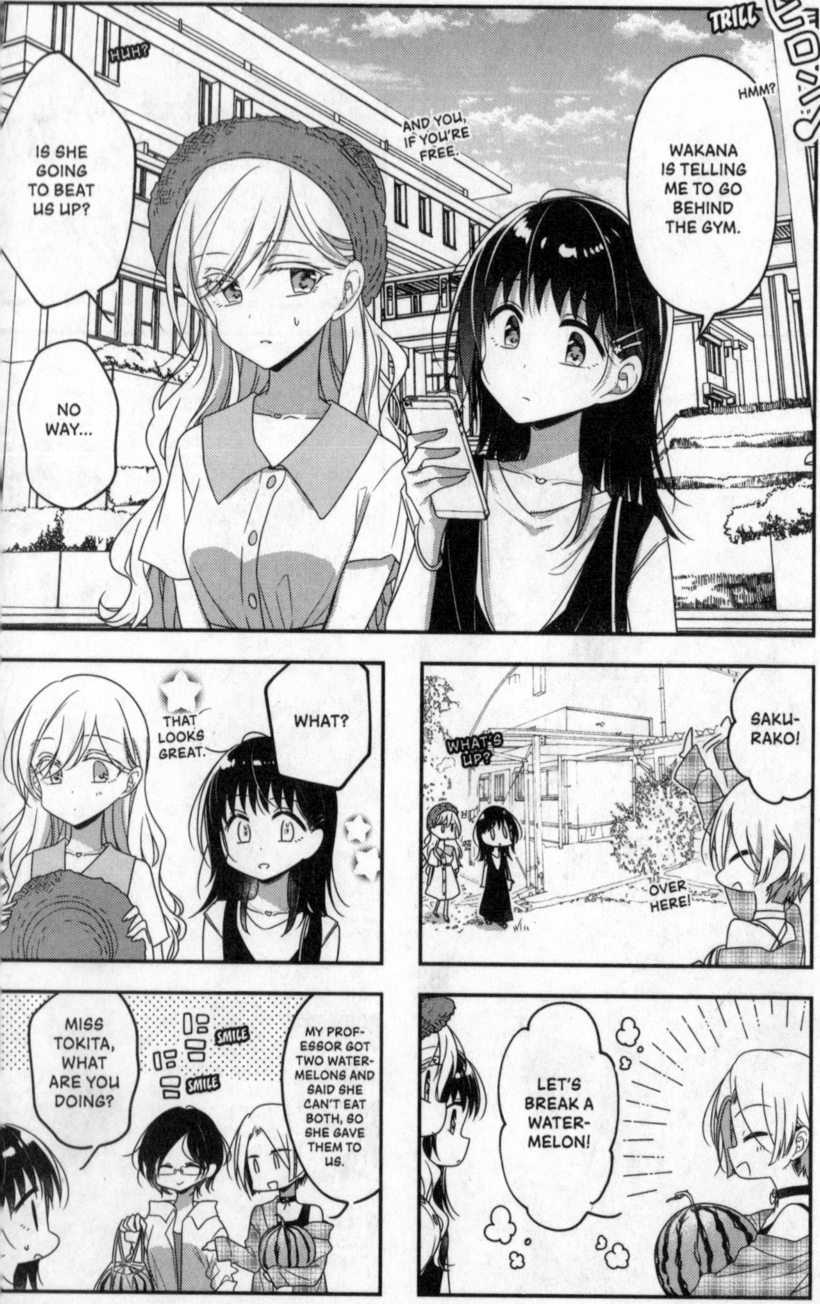
TRILL
HMM?
WAKANA IS TELLING ME TO GO BEHIND THE GYM.
AND YOU, IF YOU'RE FREE.
HUH?
IS SHE GOING TO BEAT US UP?
NO WAY...
SAKU-RAKO!
WHAT'S UP?
OVER HERE!
WHAT?
THAT LOOKS GREAT.
LET'S BREAK A WATER-MELON!
MY PROF-ESSOR GOT TWO WATER-MELONS AND SAID SHE CAN'T EAT BOTH, SO SHE GAVE THEM TO US.
SMILE
SMILE
MISS TOKITA, WHAT ARE YOU DOING?

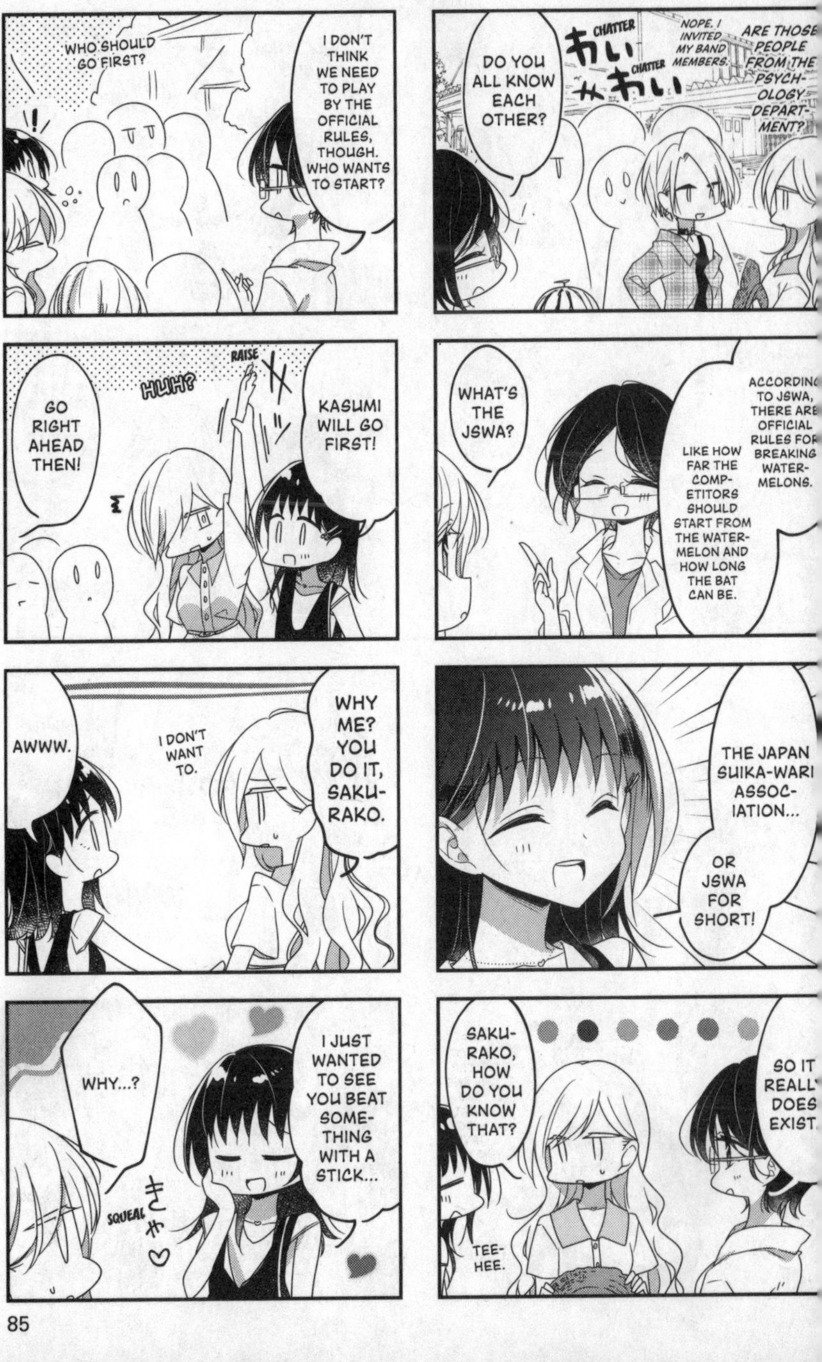

ARE THOSE PEOPLE FROM THE PSYCH-OLOGY DEPART-MENT?
NOPE. I INVITED MY BAND MEMBERS.
CHATTER わい CHATTER わい
DO YOU ALL KNOW EACH OTHER?
ACCORDIN TO JSWA, THERE ARE OFFICIAL RULES FOR BREAKING WATER-MELONS.
LIKE HOW FAR THE COMP-ETITORS SHOULD START FROM THE WATER-MELON AND HOW LONG THE BAT CAN BE.
WHAT'S THE JSWA?
THE JAPAN SUIKA-WARI ASSOC-IATION...
OR JSWA FOR SHORT!
SO IT REALL DOES EXIST.
SAKU-RAKO, HOW DO YOU KNOW THAT?
TEE-HEE.
I DON'T THINK WE NEED TO PLAY BY THE OFFICIAL RULES, THOUGH. WHO WANTS TO START?
WHO SHOULD GO FIRST?
!
KASUMI WILL GO FIRST!
RAISE
HUH?
GO RIGHT AHEAD THEN!
WHY ME? YOU DO IT, SAKU-RAKO.
I DON'T WANT TO.
AWWW.
I JUST WANTED TO SEE YOU BEAT SOME-THING WITH A STICK...
きゃ
SQUEAL
WHY...?

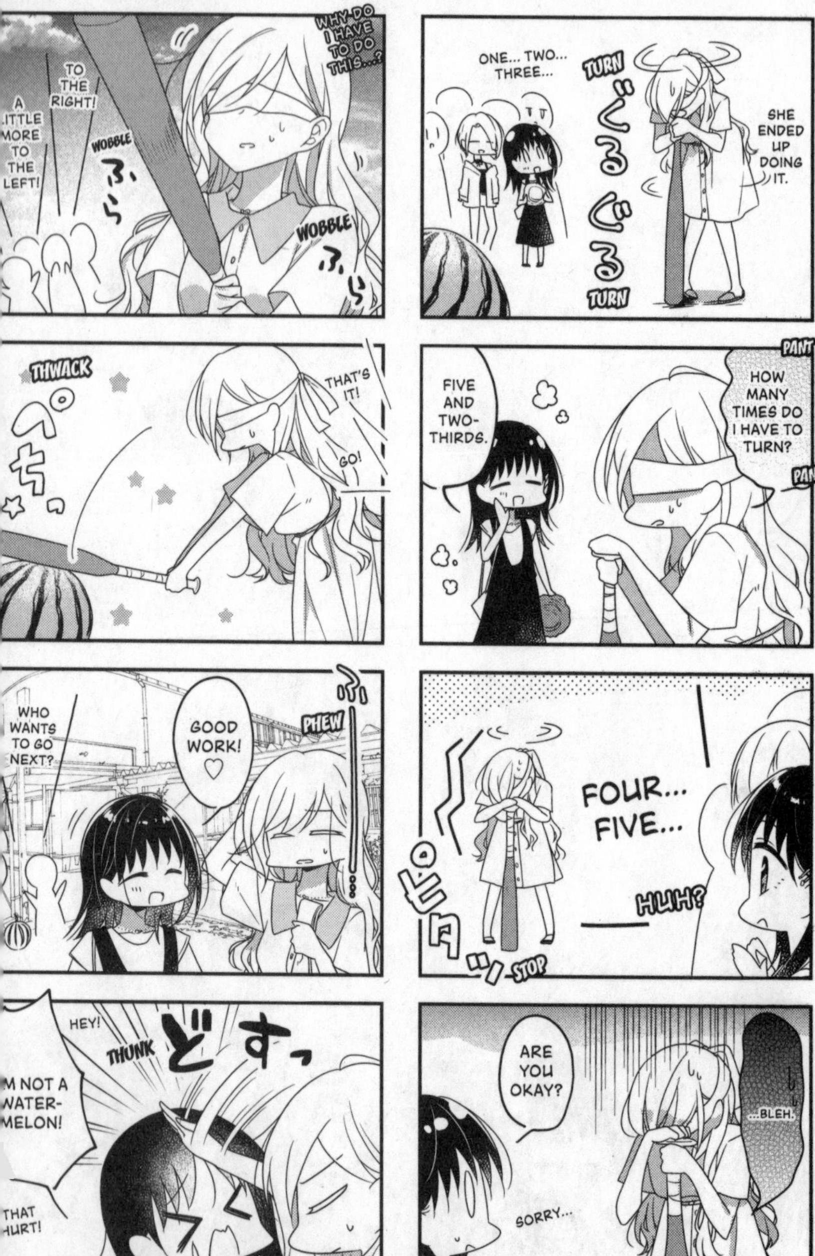
ONE... TWO... THREE...
TURN ぐるぐる TURN
SHE ENDED UP DOING IT.
WHY DO I HAVE TO DO THIS...?
TO THE RIGHT!
A LITTLE MORE TO THE LEFT!
WOBBLE ふら
WOBBLE ふら
PANT はぁっ はぁ…… PANT
HOW MANY TIMES DO I HAVE TO TURN?
FIVE AND TWO-THIRDS.
THAT'S IT!
GO!
THWACK ぺちっ
FOUR... FIVE...
HUH?
STOP ピタッ
PHEW ふぅ…
GOOD WORK! ♡
WHO WANTS TO GO NEXT?
ARE YOU OKAY?
...BLEH.
SORRY...
THUNK どすっ
HEY!
M NOT A WATER-MELON!
THAT HURT!

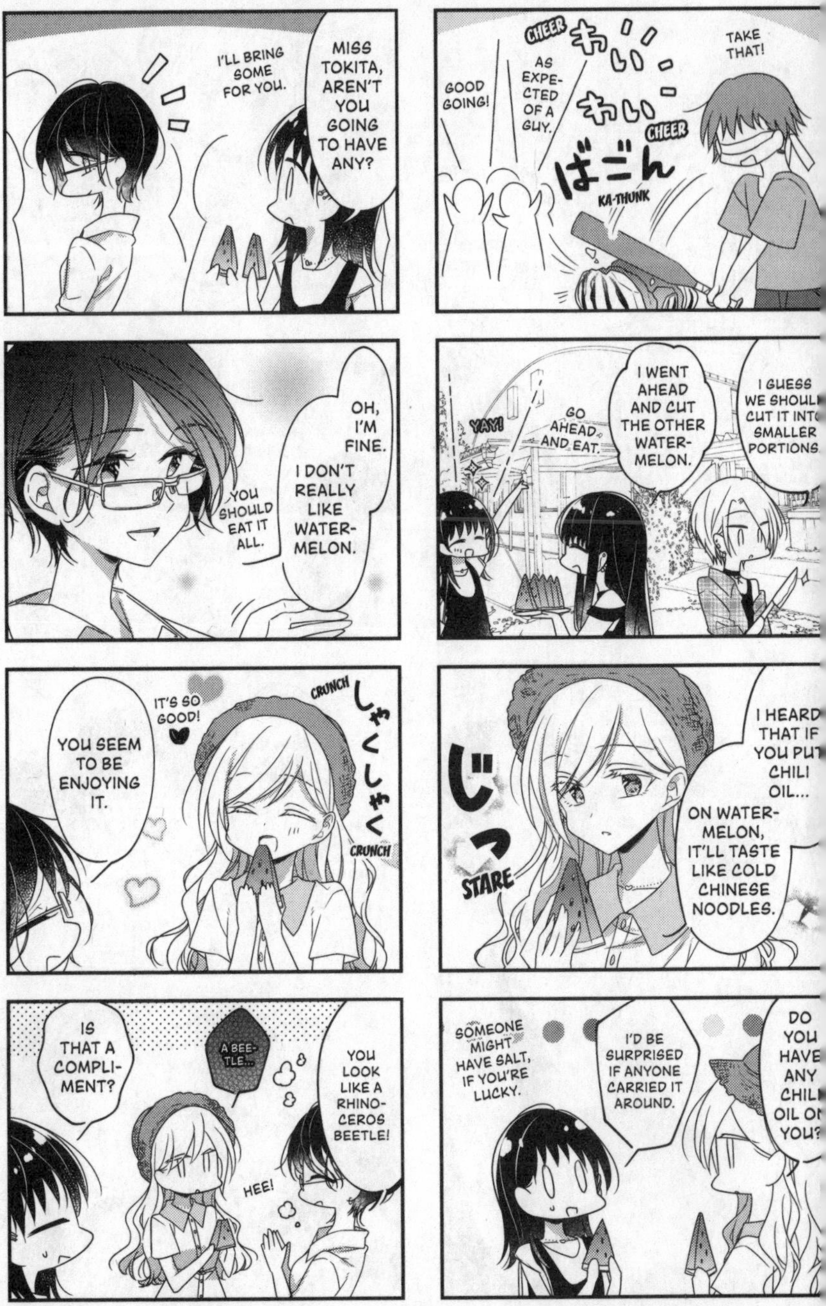

TAKE THAT!
CHEER わいわい CHEER
AS EXPECTED OF A GUY.
GOOD GOING!
ばごん KA-THUNK
I GUESS WE SHOUL CUT IT INTO SMALLER PORTIONS.
I WENT AHEAD AND CUT THE OTHER WATER-MELON.
GO AHEAD AND EAT.
YAY!
I HEARD THAT IF YOU PUT CHILI OIL...
ON WATER-MELON, IT'LL TASTE LIKE COLD CHINESE NOODLES.
じっ STARE
DO YOU HAVE ANY CHILI OIL ON YOU?
I'D BE SURPRISED IF ANYONE CARRIED IT AROUND.
SOMEONE MIGHT HAVE SALT, IF YOU'RE LUCKY.
MISS TOKITA, AREN'T YOU GOING TO HAVE ANY?
I'LL BRING SOME FOR YOU.
OH, I'M FINE.
I DON'T REALLY LIKE WATER-MELON.
YOU SHOULD EAT IT ALL.
しゃくしゃく CRUNCH CRUNCH
IT'S SO GOOD!
YOU SEEM TO BE ENJOYING IT.
YOU LOOK LIKE A RHINO-CEROS BEETLE!
HEE!
A BEE-TLE...
IS THAT A COMPLI-MENT?

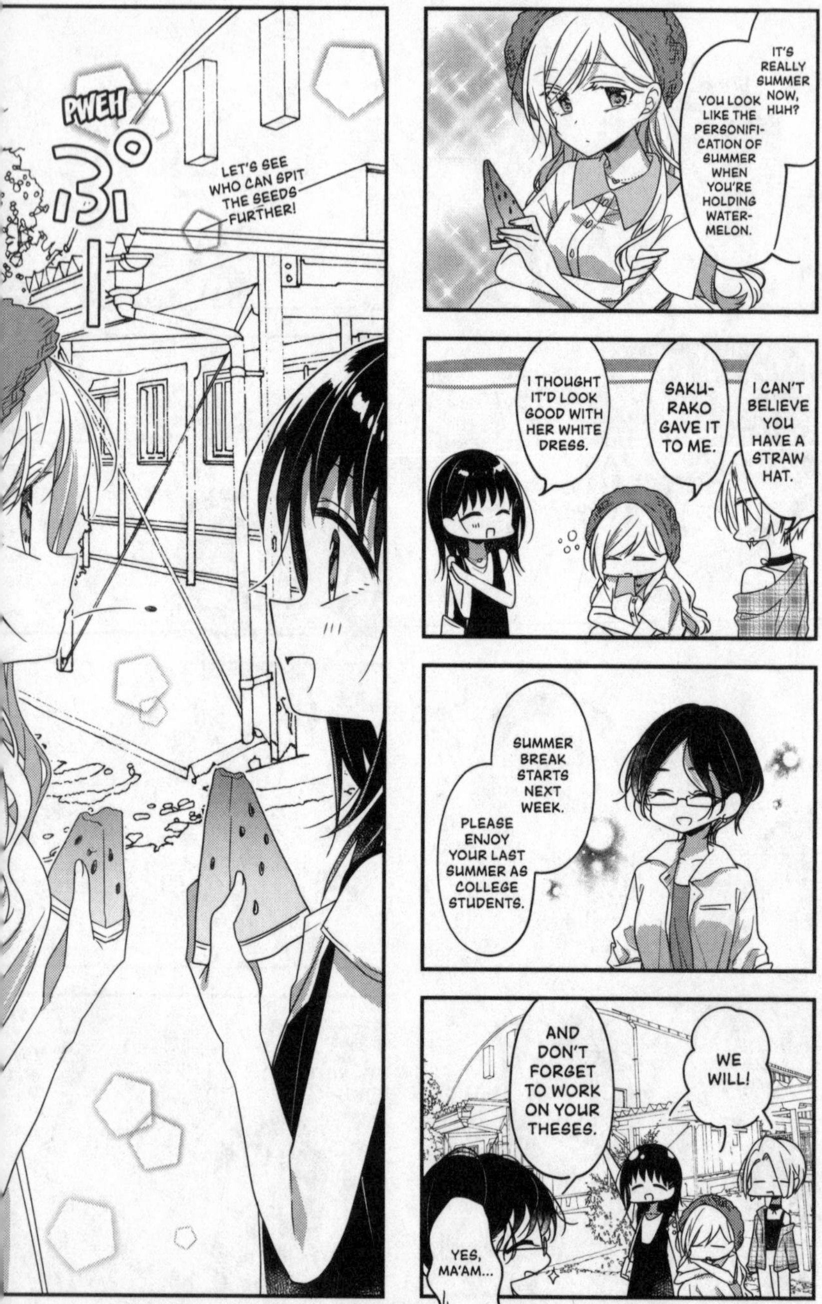
IT'S REALLY SUMMER NOW, HUH?
YOU LOOK LIKE THE PERSONIFICATION OF SUMMER WHEN YOU'RE HOLDING WATERMELON.
I CAN'T BELIEVE YOU HAVE A STRAW HAT.
SAKURAKO GAVE IT TO ME.
I THOUGHT IT'D LOOK GOOD WITH HER WHITE DRESS.
SUMMER BREAK STARTS NEXT WEEK.
PLEASE ENJOY YOUR LAST SUMMER AS COLLEGE STUDENTS.
WE WILL!
AND DON'T FORGET TO WORK ON YOUR THESES.
YES, MA'AM...
LET'S SEE WHO CAN SPIT THE SEEDS FURTHER!
PWEH

Illustration gallery of Yukik

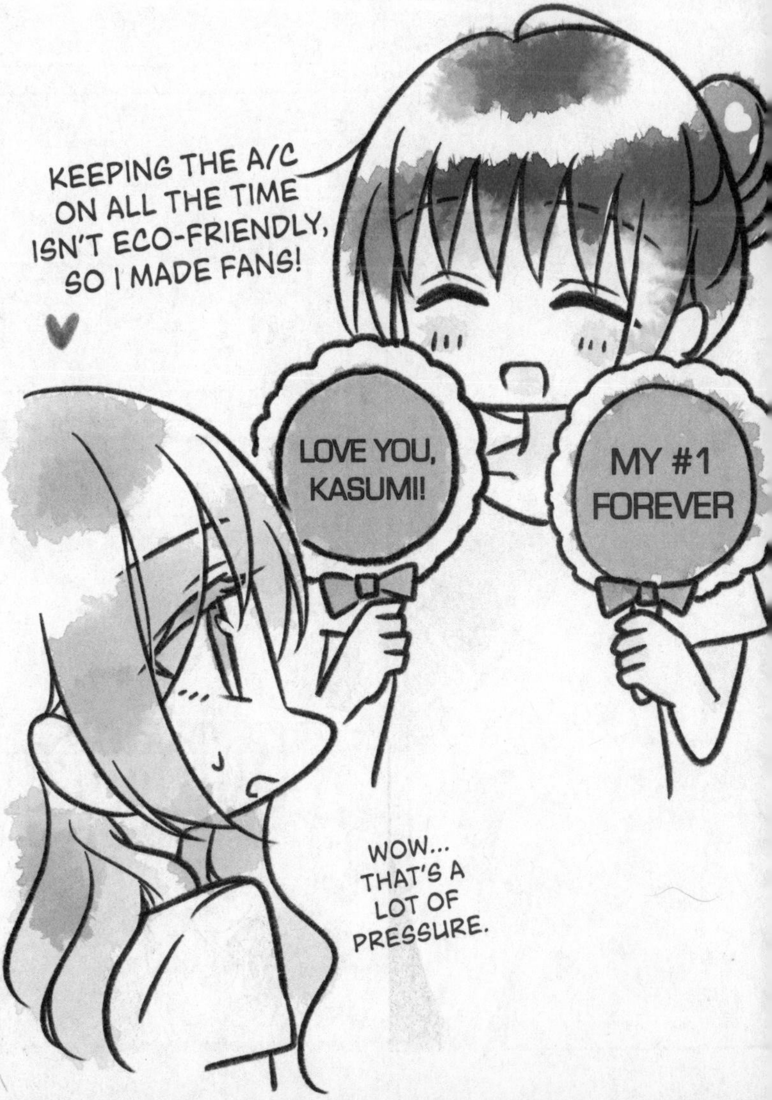
KEEPING THE A/C ON ALL THE TIME ISN'T ECO-FRIENDLY, SO I MADE FANS!
LOVE YOU, KASUMI!
MY #1 FOREVER
WOW... THAT'S A LOT OF PRESSURE.

Futaribeya
A ROOM FOR TWO

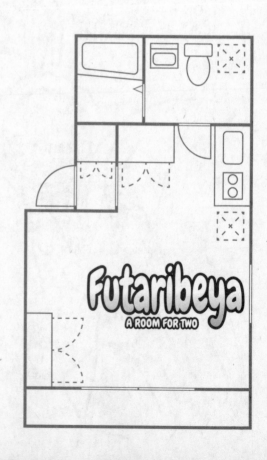

Special Chapter #3 - "Thoughts on an Uneventful Day"

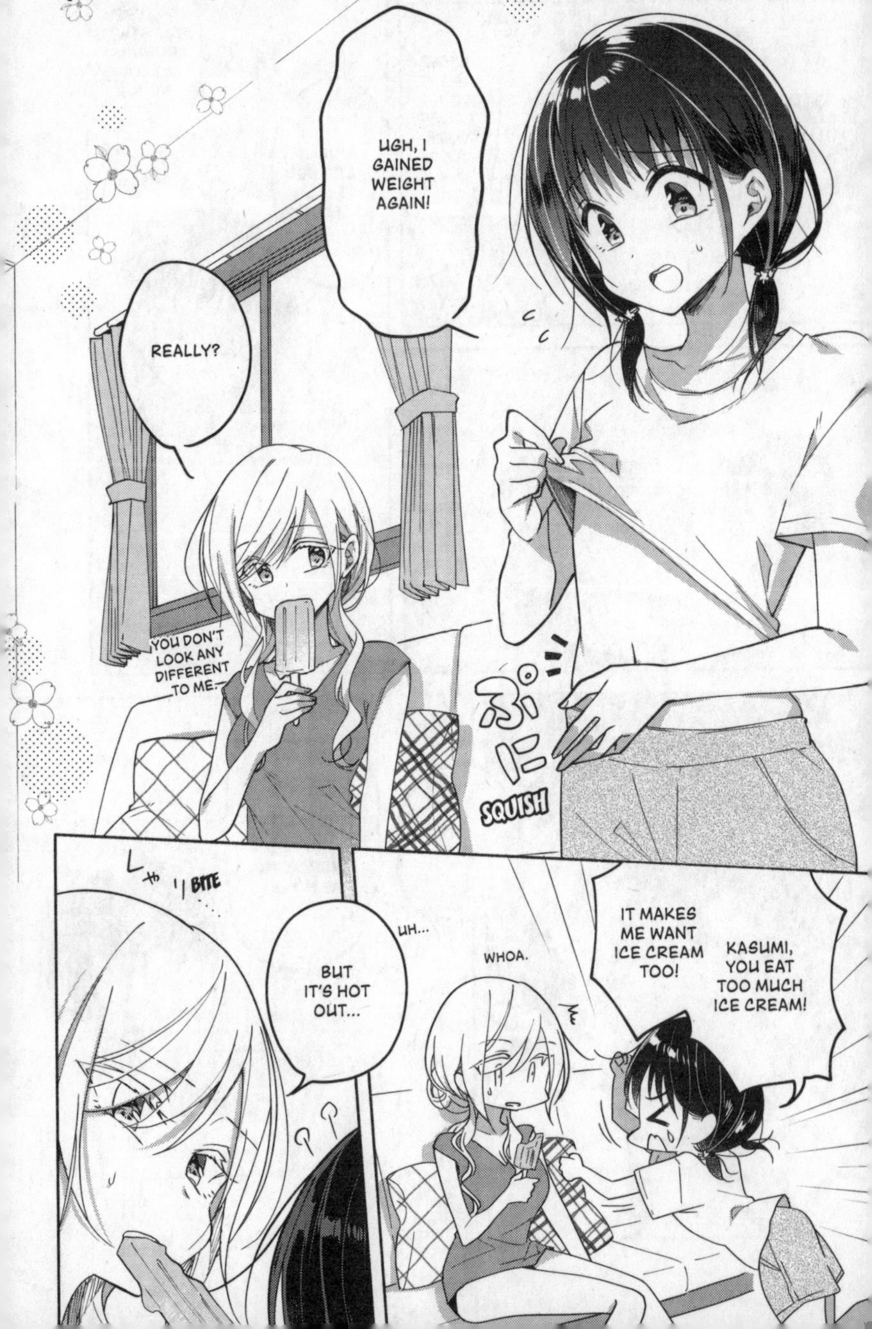
UGH, I GAINED WEIGHT AGAIN!
REALLY?
ぷに
SQUISH
YOU DON'T LOOK ANY DIFFERENT TO ME.
KASUMI, YOU EAT TOO MUCH ICE CREAM!
IT MAKES ME WANT ICE CREAM TOO!
WHOA.
UH...
BITE
BUT IT'S HOT OUT...

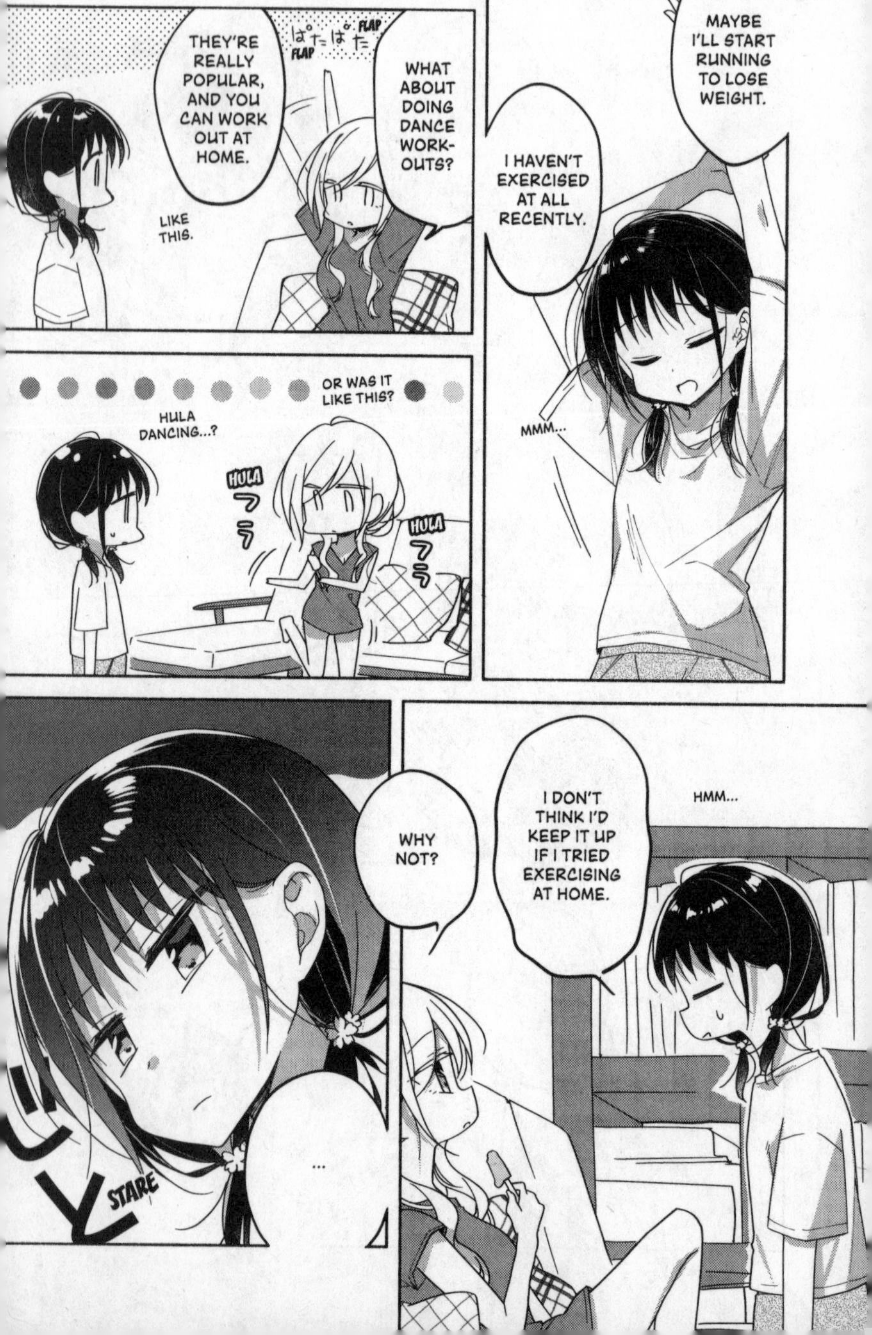
MAYBE I'LL START RUNNING TO LOSE WEIGHT.
I HAVEN'T EXERCISED AT ALL RECENTLY.
MMM...
WHAT ABOUT DOING DANCE WORK-OUTS?
ぱたぱた
FLAP FLAP
THEY'RE REALLY POPULAR, AND YOU CAN WORK OUT AT HOME.
LIKE THIS.
OR WAS IT LIKE THIS?
フラ
HULA
フラ
HULA
HULA DANCING...?
HMM...
I DON'T THINK I'D KEEP IT UP IF I TRIED EXERCISING AT HOME.
WHY NOT?
...
STARE

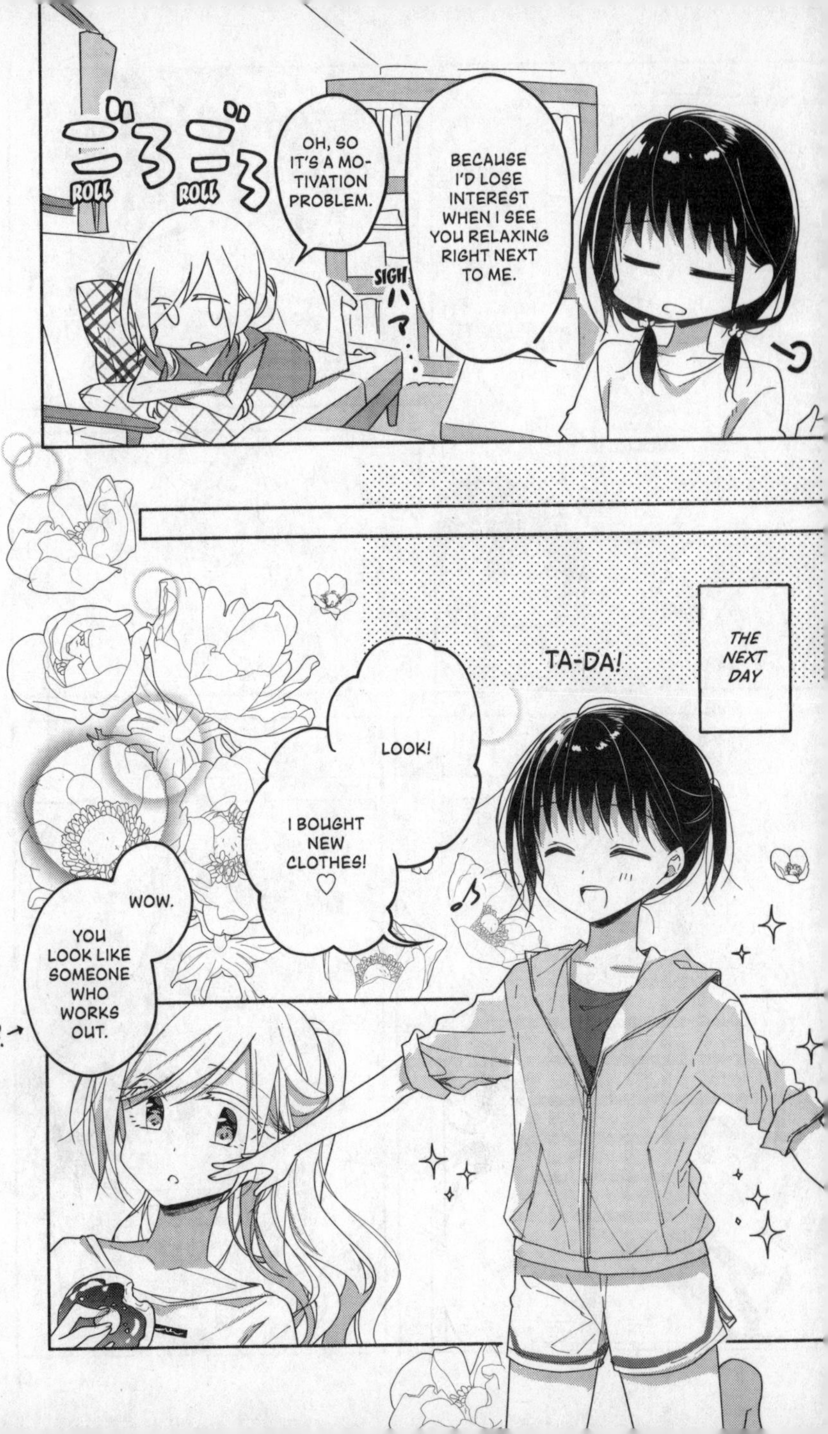
BECAUSE I'D LOSE INTEREST WHEN I SEE YOU RELAXING RIGHT NEXT TO ME.
SIGH
ハァ…
OH, SO IT'S A MO-TIVATION PROBLEM.
ごろごろ
ROLL ROLL
THE NEXT DAY
TA-DA!
LOOK!
I BOUGHT NEW CLOTHES! ♡
WOW.
YOU LOOK LIKE SOMEONE WHO WORKS OUT.
?

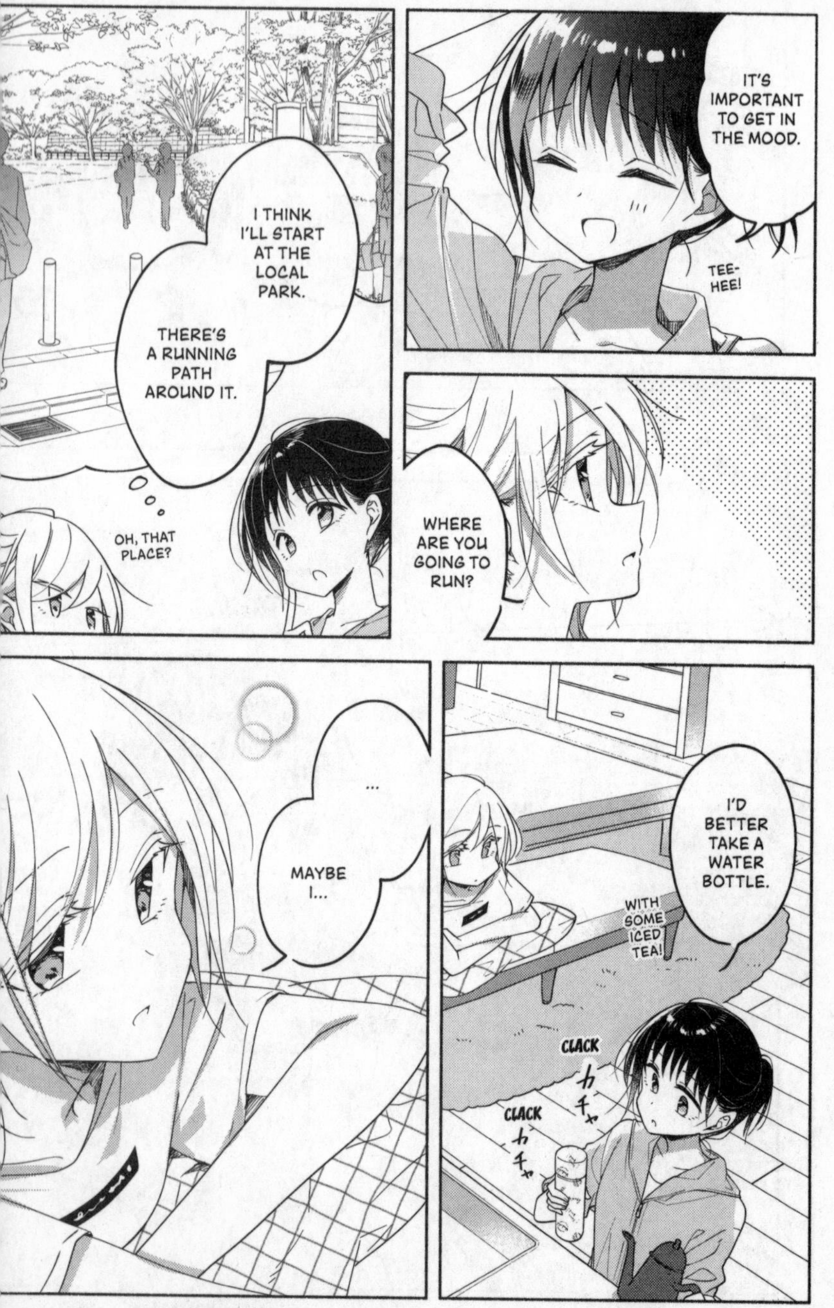
IT'S IMPORTANT TO GET IN THE MOOD.
TEE-HEE!
WHERE ARE YOU GOING TO RUN?
I THINK I'LL START AT THE LOCAL PARK.
THERE'S A RUNNING PATH AROUND IT.
OH, THAT PLACE?
I'D BETTER TAKE A WATER BOTTLE.
WITH SOME ICED TEA!
CLACK
カチャ
CLACK
カチャ
...
MAYBE I...

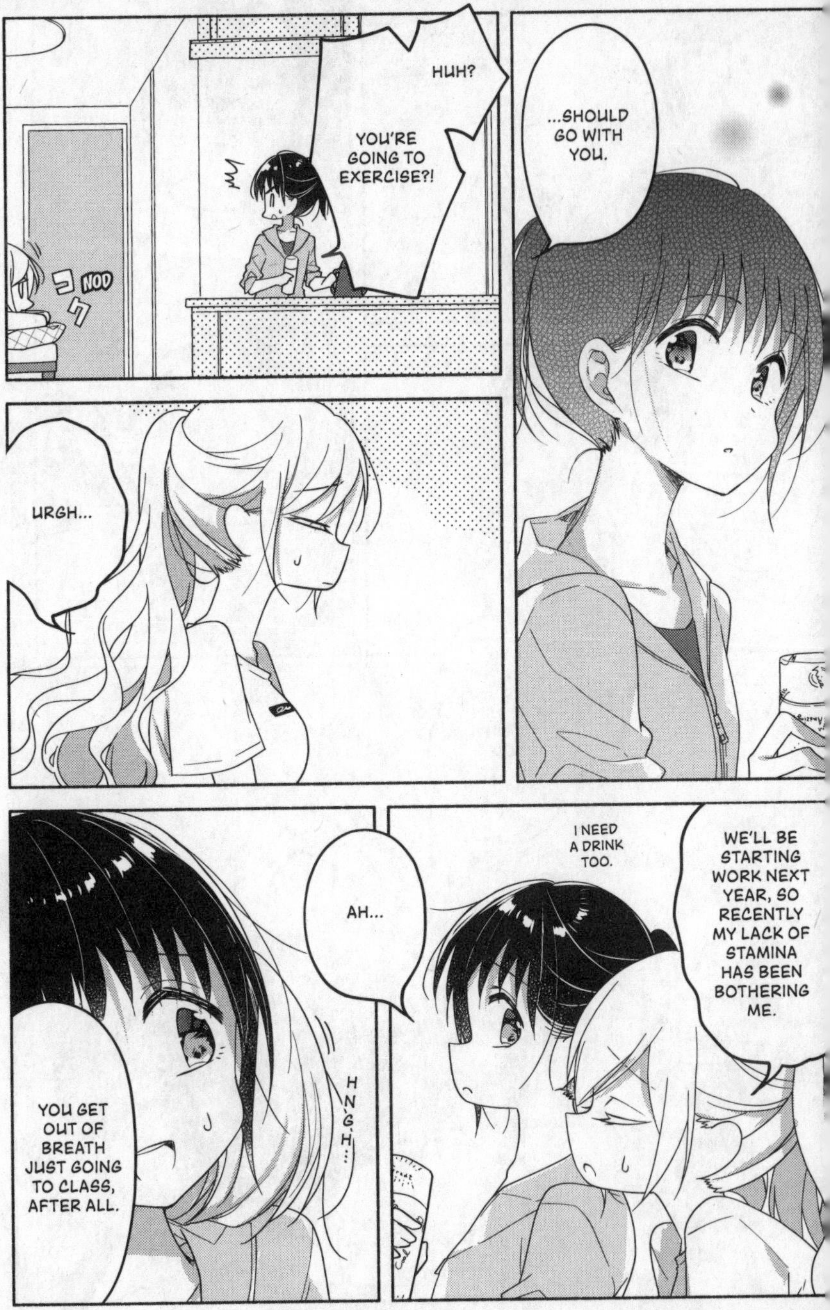
...SHOULD GO WITH YOU.
HUH?
YOU'RE GOING TO EXERCISE?!
NOD
URGH...
WE'LL BE STARTING WORK NEXT YEAR, SO RECENTLY MY LACK OF STAMINA HAS BEEN BOTHERING ME.
I NEED A DRINK TOO.
AH...
HNGH...
YOU GET OUT OF BREATH JUST GOING TO CLASS, AFTER ALL.

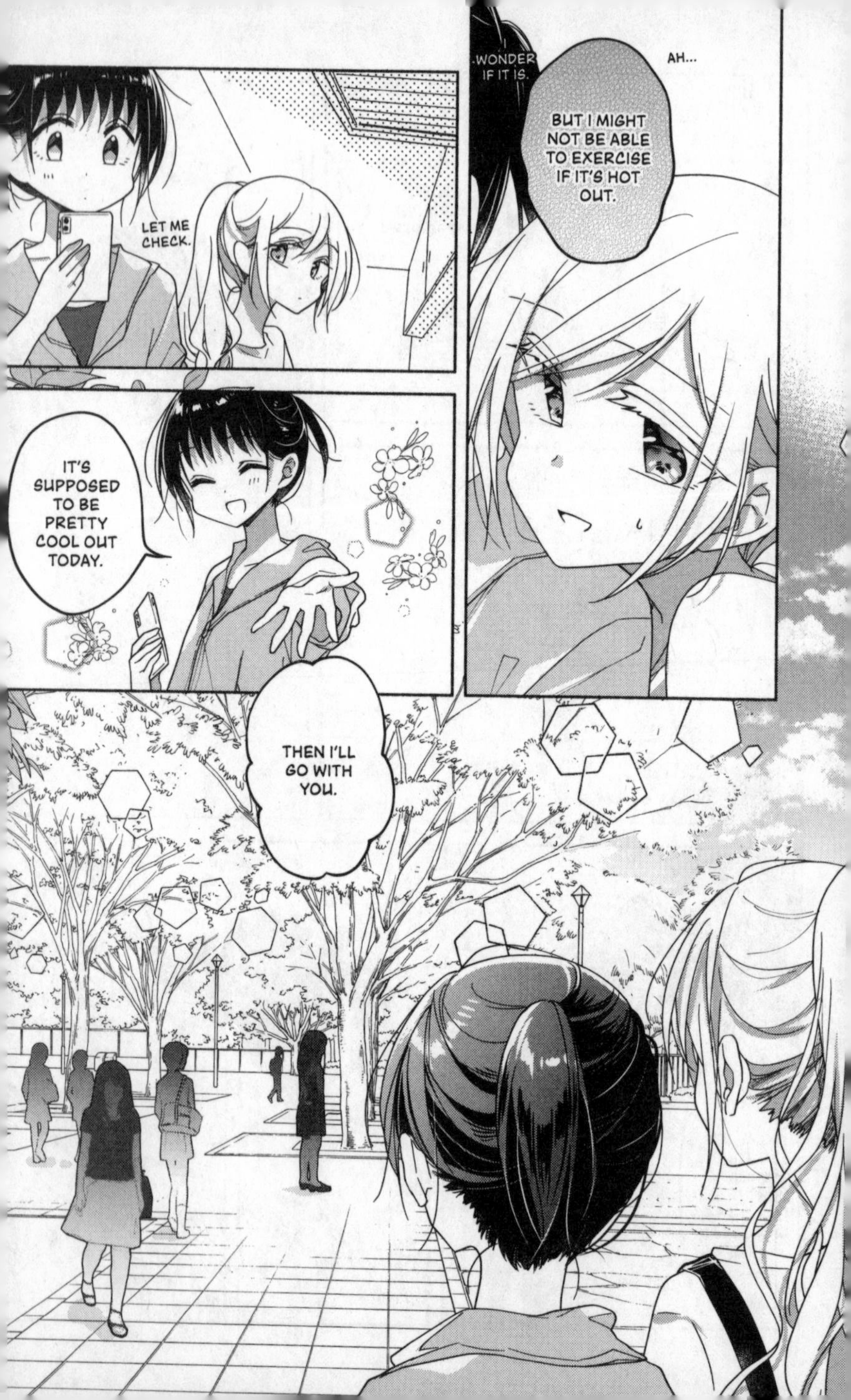
AH...
BUT I MIGHT NOT BE ABLE TO EXERCISE IF IT'S HOT OUT.
I WONDER IF IT IS.
LET ME CHECK.
IT'S SUPPOSED TO BE PRETTY COOL OUT TODAY.
THEN I'LL GO WITH YOU.

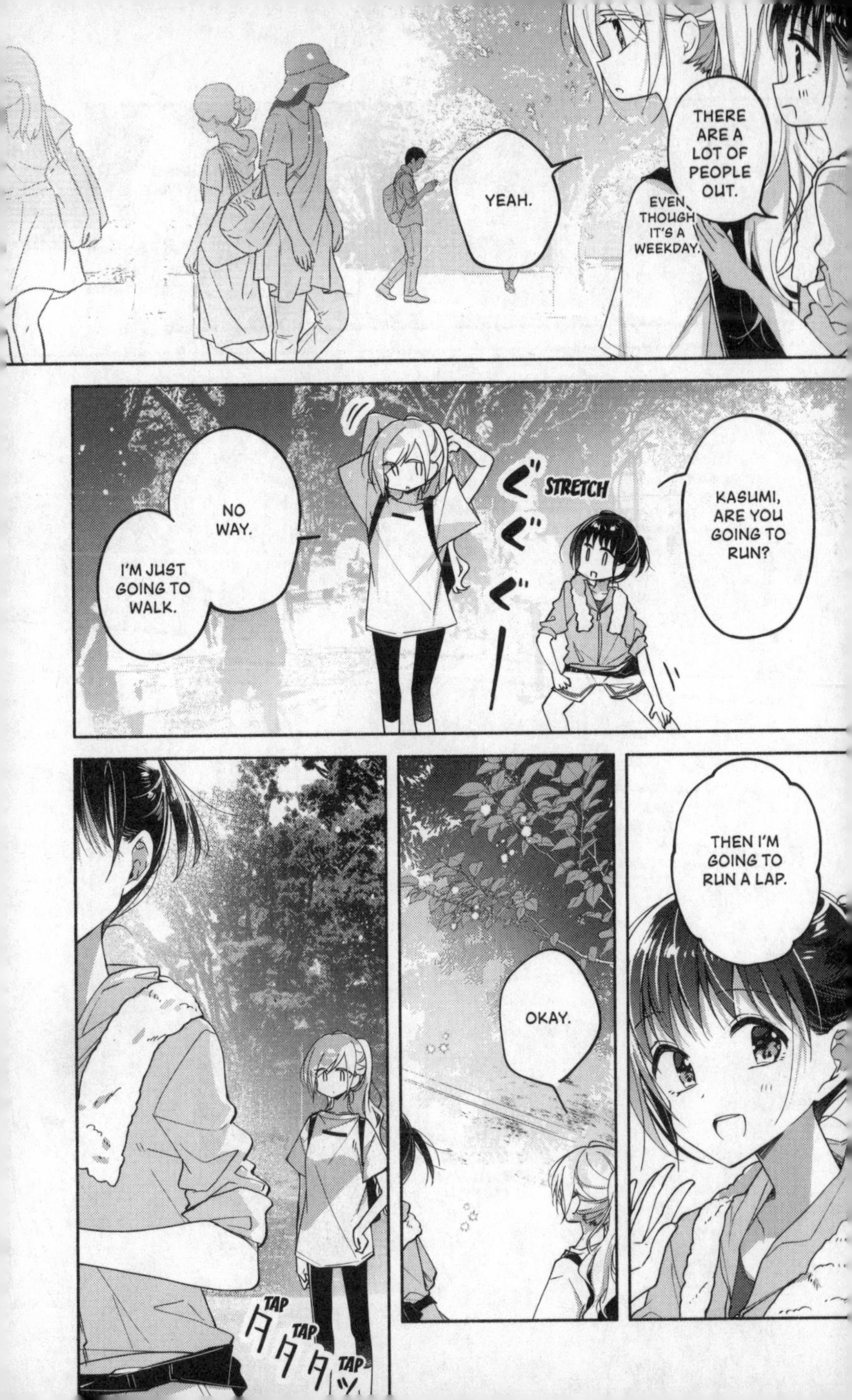
THERE ARE A LOT OF PEOPLE OUT.
EVEN THOUGH IT'S A WEEKDAY.
YEAH.
KASUMI, ARE YOU GOING TO RUN?
STRETCH
NO WAY.
I'M JUST GOING TO WALK.
THEN I'M GOING TO RUN A LAP.
OKAY.
TAP
TAP
TAP

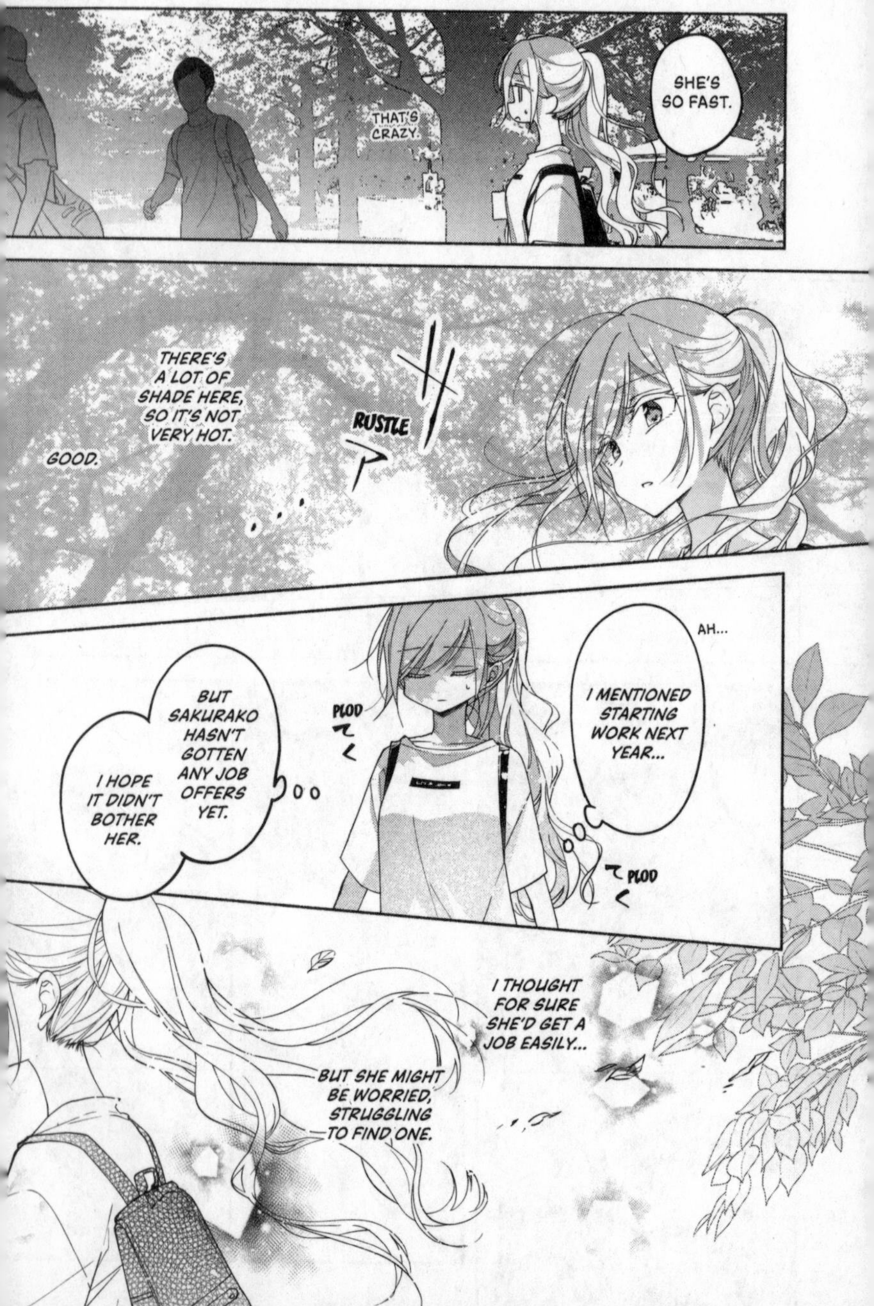
SHE'S SO FAST.
THAT'S CRAZY.
RUSTLE
THERE'S A LOT OF SHADE HERE, SO IT'S NOT VERY HOT.
GOOD.
...
AH...
I MENTIONED STARTING WORK NEXT YEAR...
PLOD
PLOD
BUT SAKURAKO HASN'T GOTTEN ANY JOB OFFERS YET.
I HOPE IT DIDN'T BOTHER HER.
I THOUGHT FOR SURE SHE'D GET A JOB EASILY...
BUT SHE MIGHT BE WORRIED, STRUGGLING TO FIND ONE.

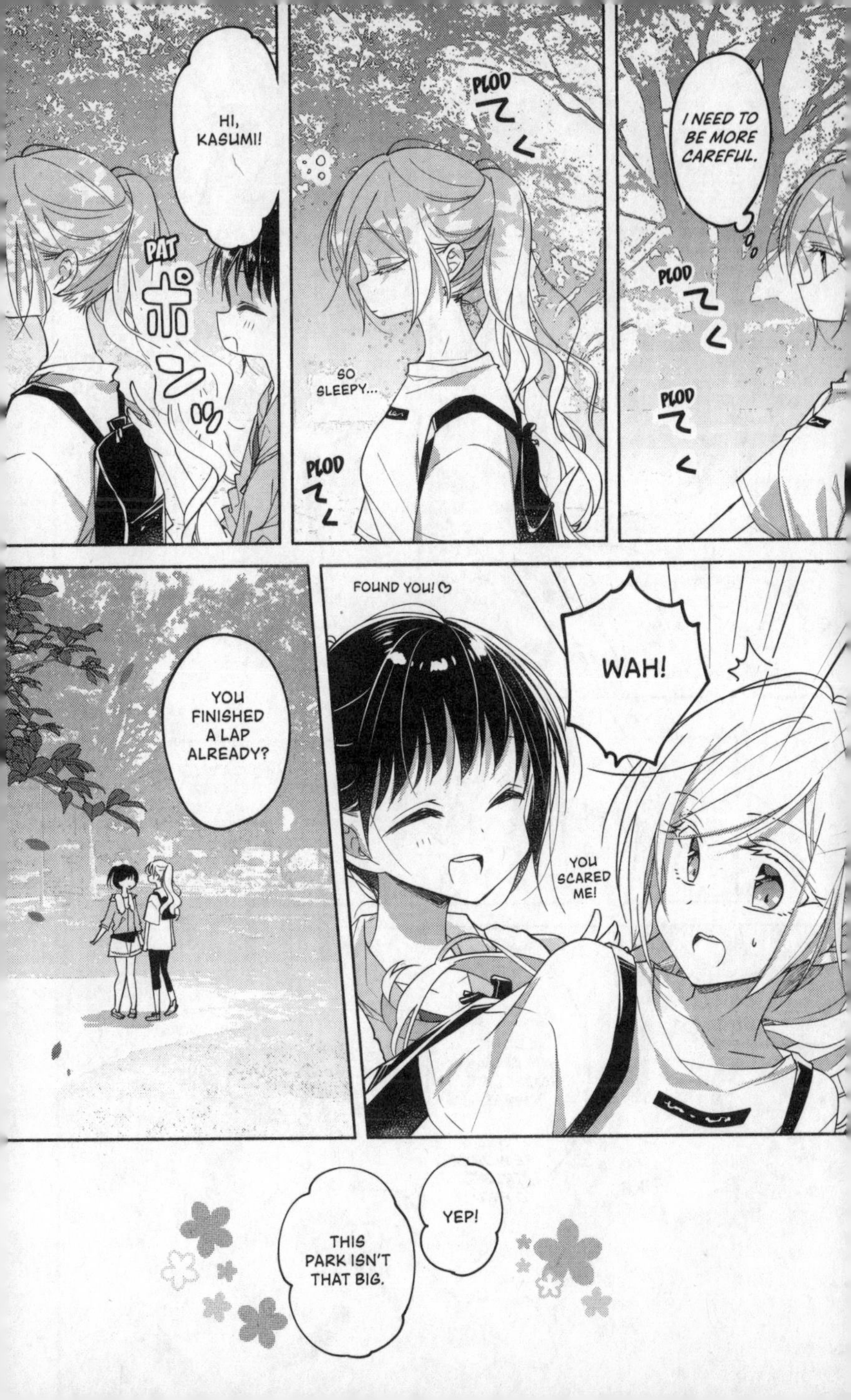

PLOD
I NEED TO BE MORE CAREFUL.
PLOD
PLOD
SO SLEEPY...
PLOD
HI, KASUMI!
PAT
FOUND YOU! ♡
WAH!
YOU SCARED ME!
YOU FINISHED A LAP ALREADY?
YEP!
THIS PARK ISN'T THAT BIG.

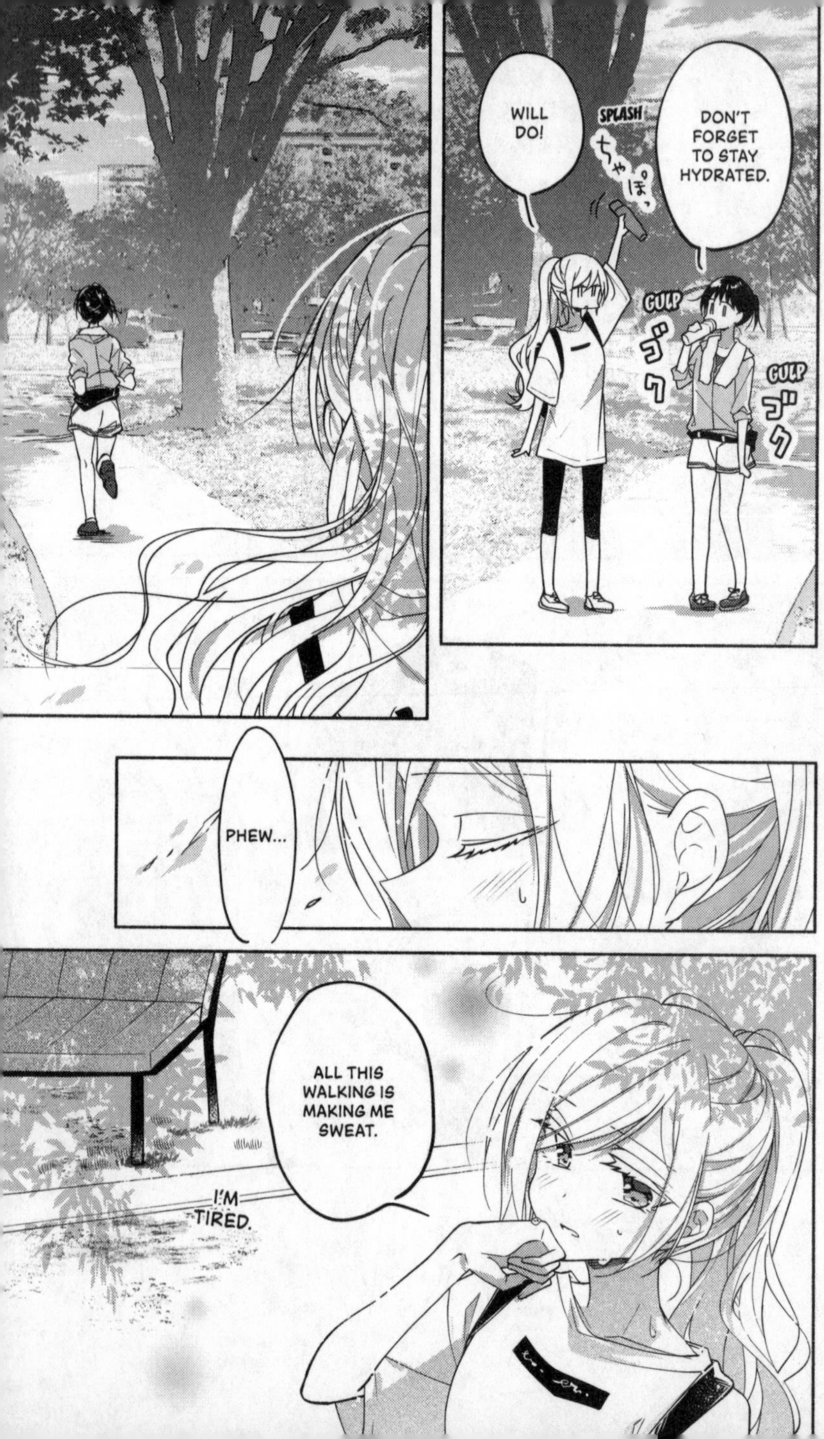
DON'T FORGET TO STAY HYDRATED.
GULP
ゴク
GULP
ゴク
SPLASH
ちゃぽっ
WILL DO!
PHEW...
ALL THIS WALKING IS MAKING ME SWEAT.
I'M TIRED.

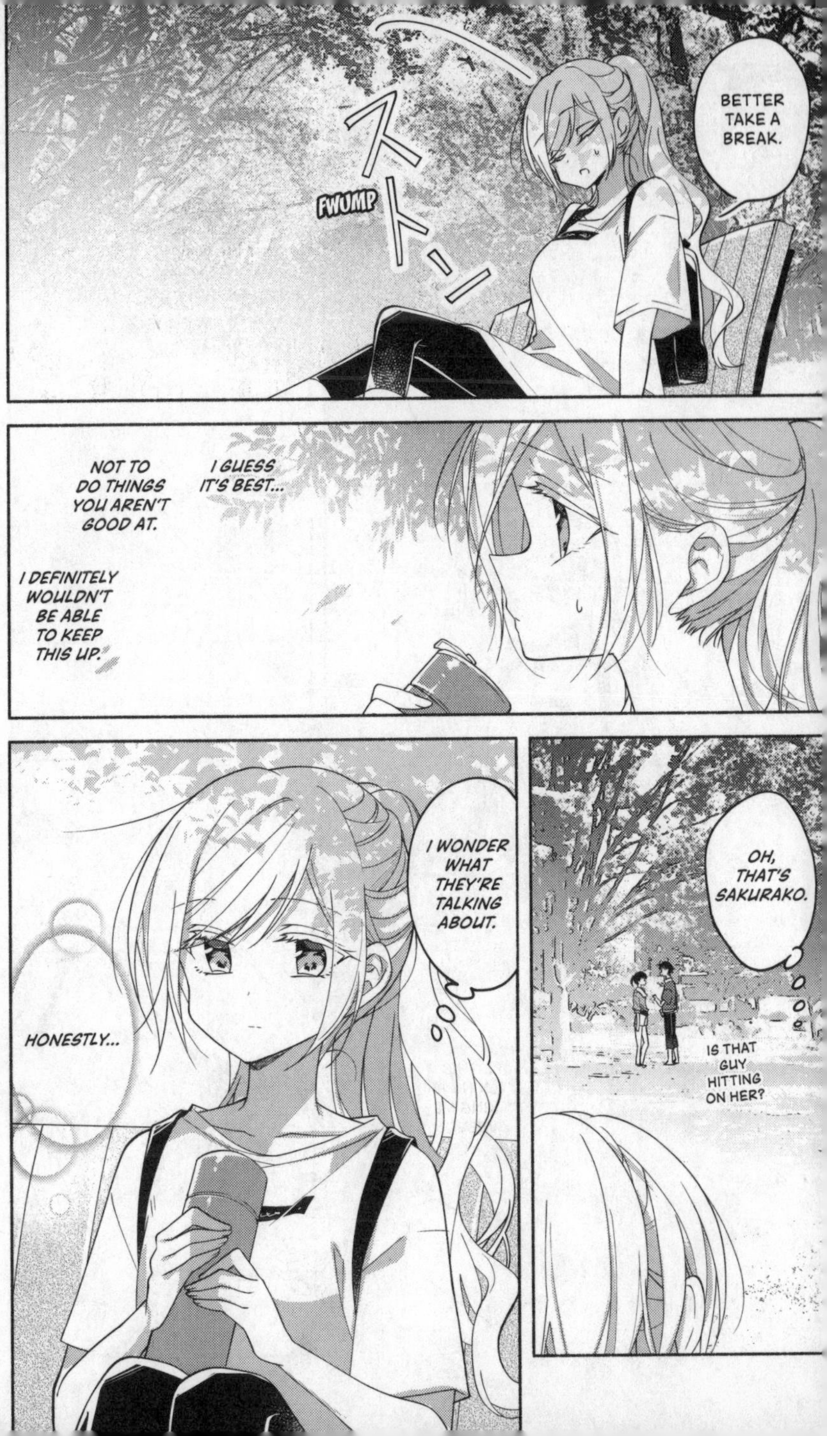
BETTER TAKE A BREAK.
ストーン
FWUMP
I GUESS IT'S BEST...
NOT TO DO THINGS YOU AREN'T GOOD AT.
I DEFINITELY WOULDN'T BE ABLE TO KEEP THIS UP.
OH, THAT'S SAKURAKO.
IS THAT GUY HITTING ON HER?
I WONDER WHAT THEY'RE TALKING ABOUT.
HONESTLY...

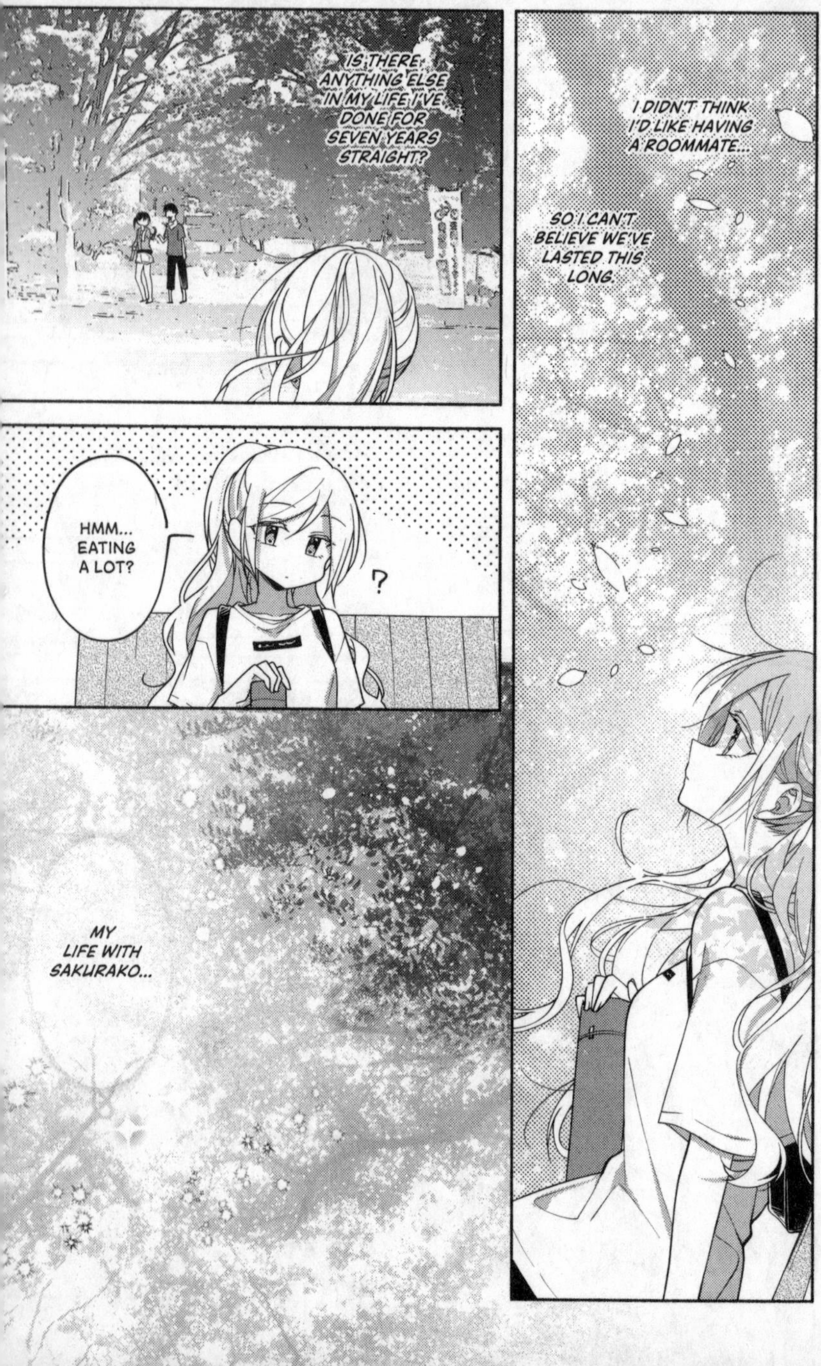
I DIDN'T THINK I'D LIKE HAVING A ROOMMATE...
SO I CAN'T BELIEVE WE'VE LASTED THIS LONG.
IS THERE ANYTHING ELSE IN MY LIFE I'VE DONE FOR SEVEN YEARS STRAIGHT?
HMM... EATING A LOT?
?
MY LIFE WITH SAKURAKO...

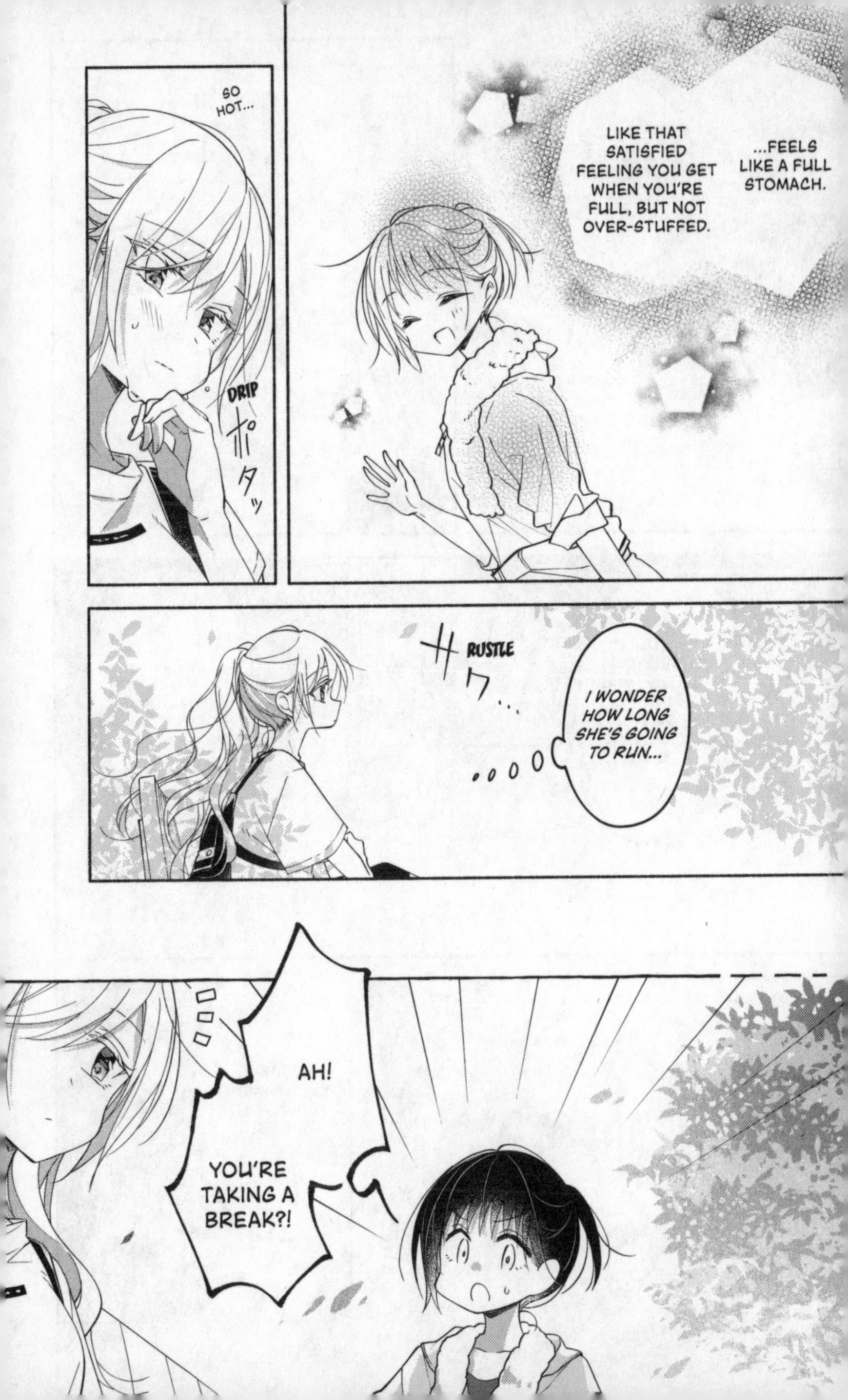
...FEELS LIKE A FULL STOMACH.
LIKE THAT SATISFIED FEELING YOU GET WHEN YOU'RE FULL, BUT NOT OVER-STUFFED.
SO HOT...
DRIP
ポタッ
I WONDER HOW LONG SHE'S GOING TO RUN...
RUSTLE
サク...
AH!
YOU'RE TAKING A BREAK?!

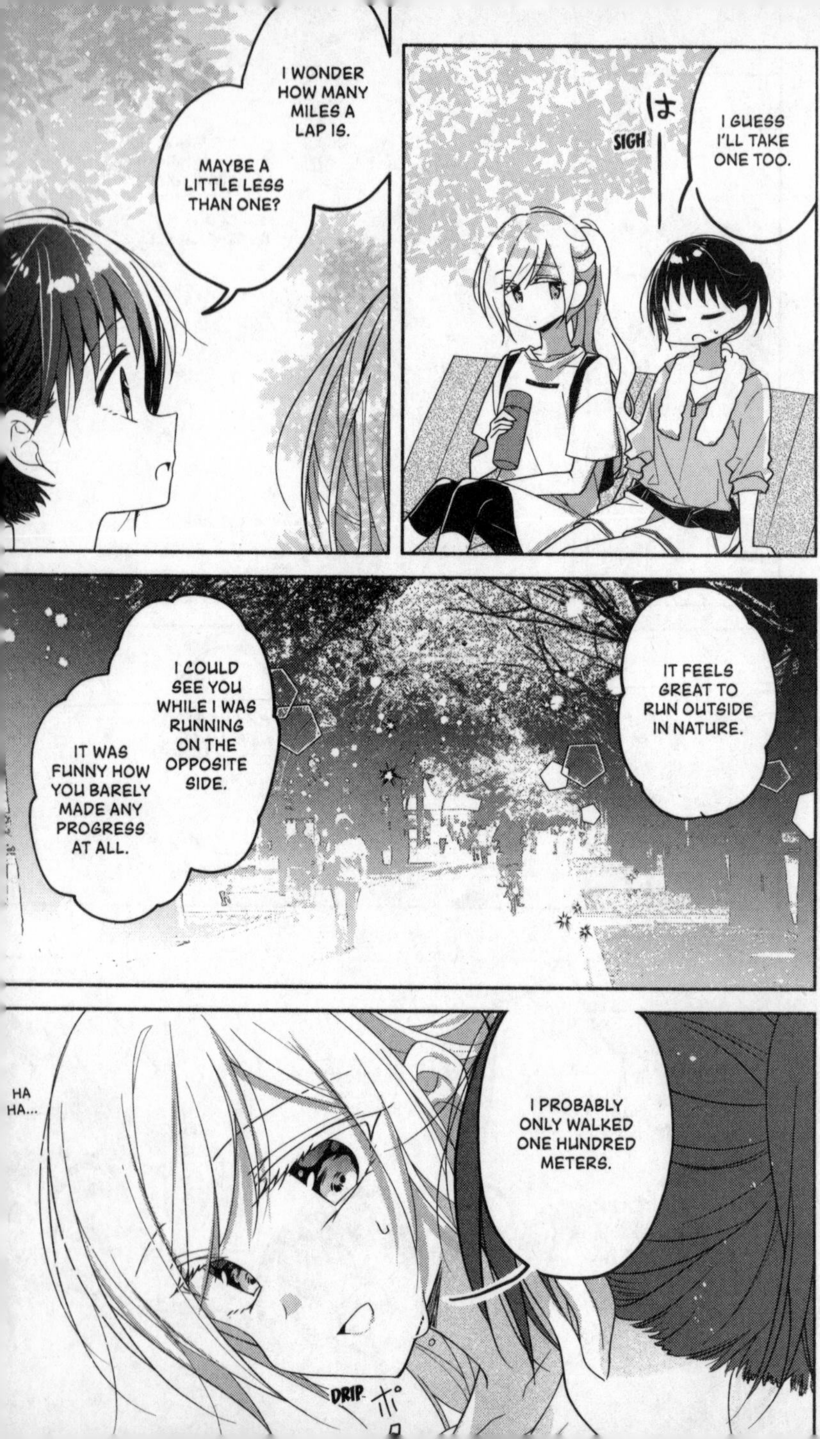
は
SIGH
I GUESS I'LL TAKE ONE TOO.
I WONDER HOW MANY MILES A LAP IS.
MAYBE A LITTLE LESS THAN ONE?
IT FEELS GREAT TO RUN OUTSIDE IN NATURE.
I COULD SEE YOU WHILE I WAS RUNNING ON THE OPPOSITE SIDE.
IT WAS FUNNY HOW YOU BARELY MADE ANY PROGRESS AT ALL.
I PROBABLY ONLY WALKED ONE HUNDRED METERS.
HA HA...
DRIP
ポ

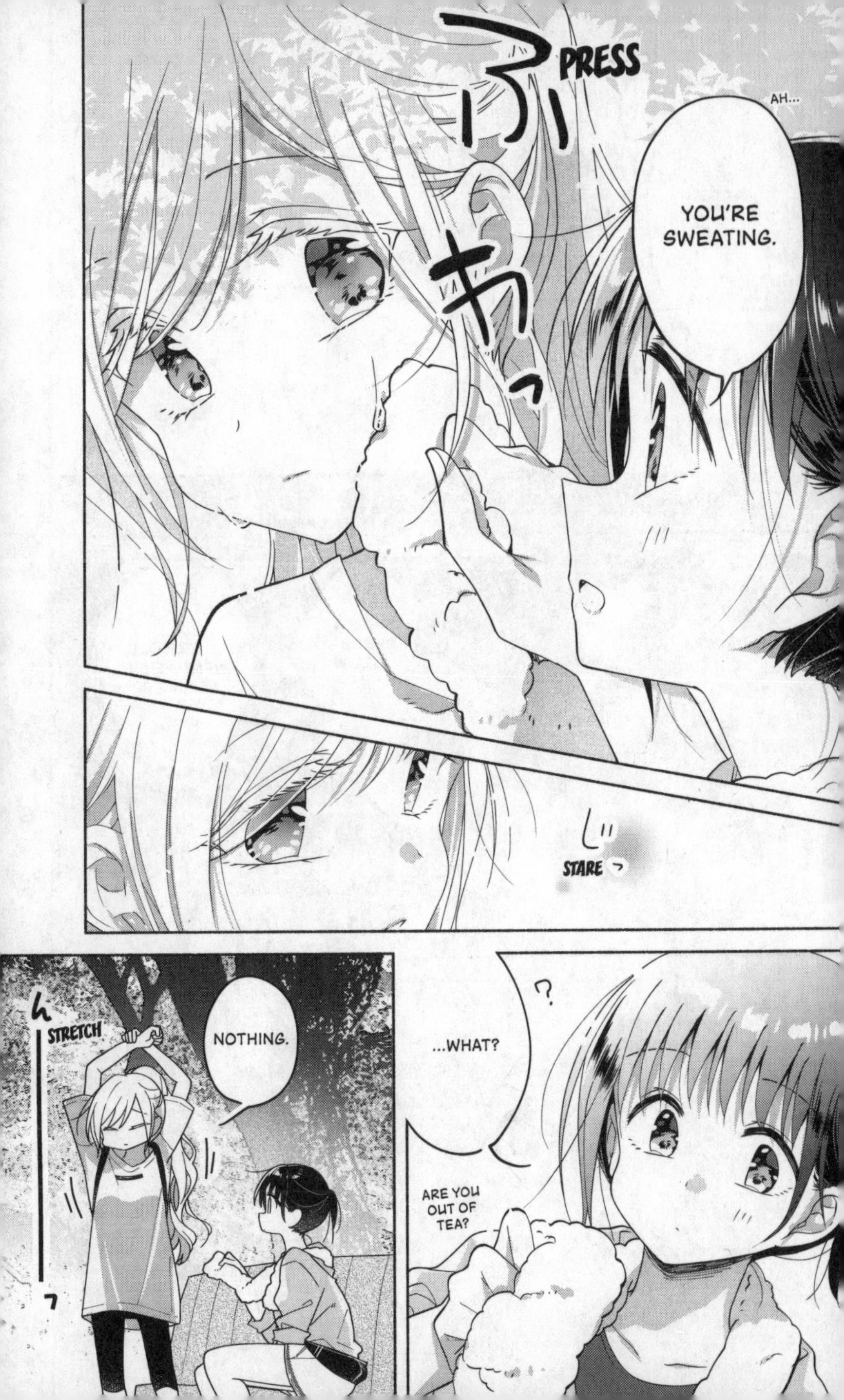
AH...
YOU'RE SWEATING.
PRESS
STARE
...WHAT?
ARE YOU OUT OF TEA?
NOTHING.
STRETCH

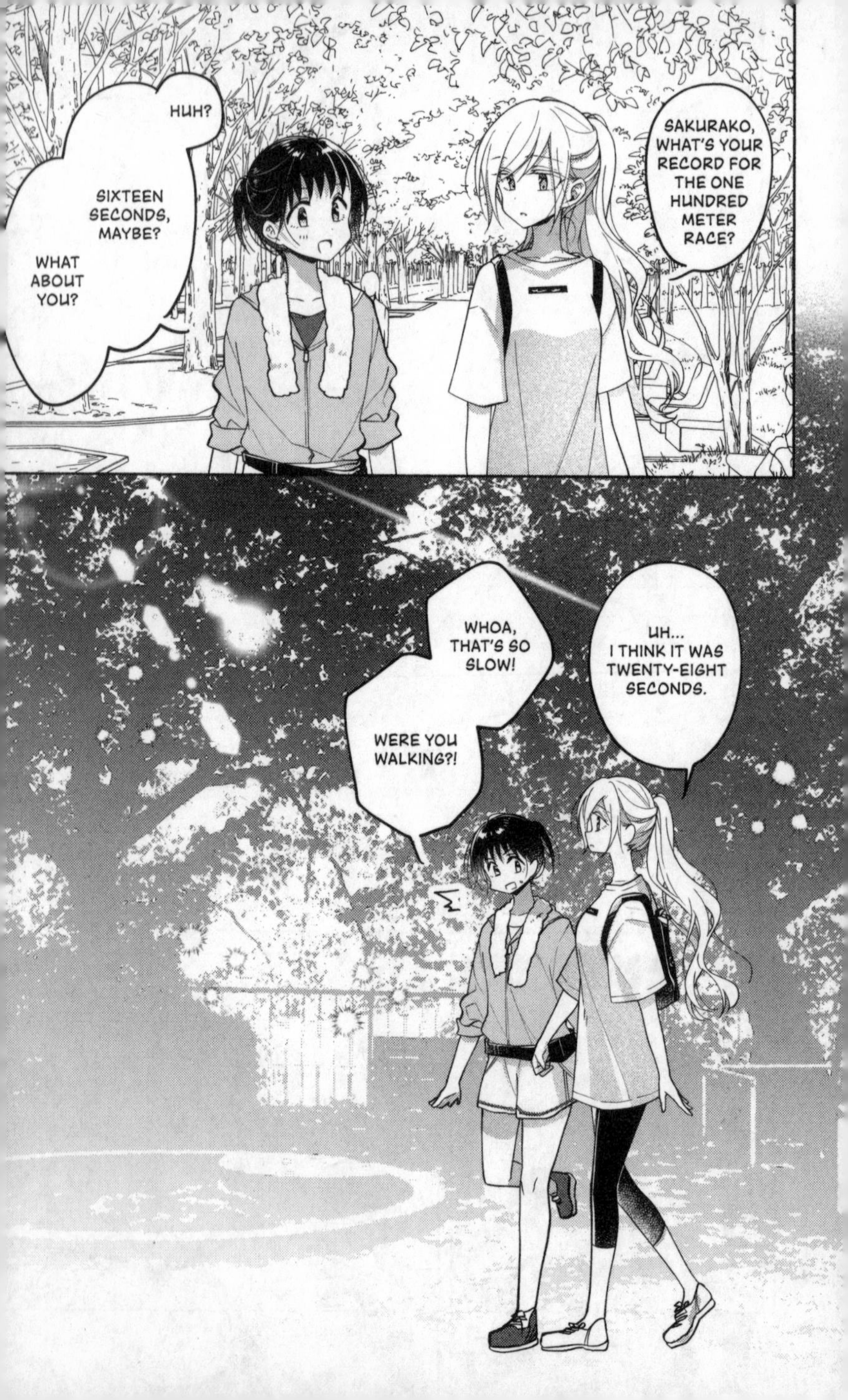
SAKURAKO, WHAT'S YOUR RECORD FOR THE ONE HUNDRED METER RACE?
HUH?
SIXTEEN SECONDS, MAYBE?
WHAT ABOUT YOU?
UH... I THINK IT WAS TWENTY-EIGHT SECONDS.
WHOA, THAT'S SO SLOW!
WERE YOU WALKING?!

Illustration gallery of Yukik

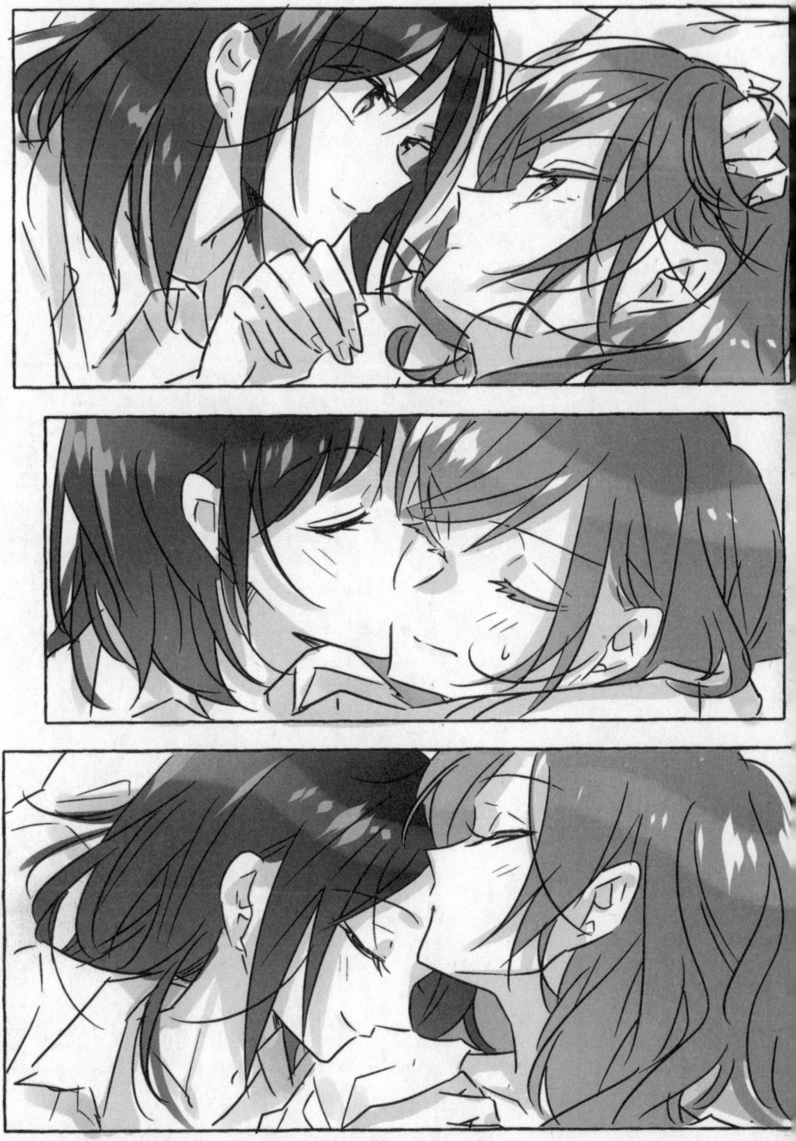

NOT THAT IT MATTERS, BUT MAY 23RD IS KISS DAY.

Futaribeya
A ROOM FOR TWO

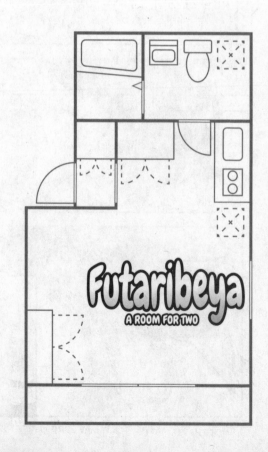

Chapter 66

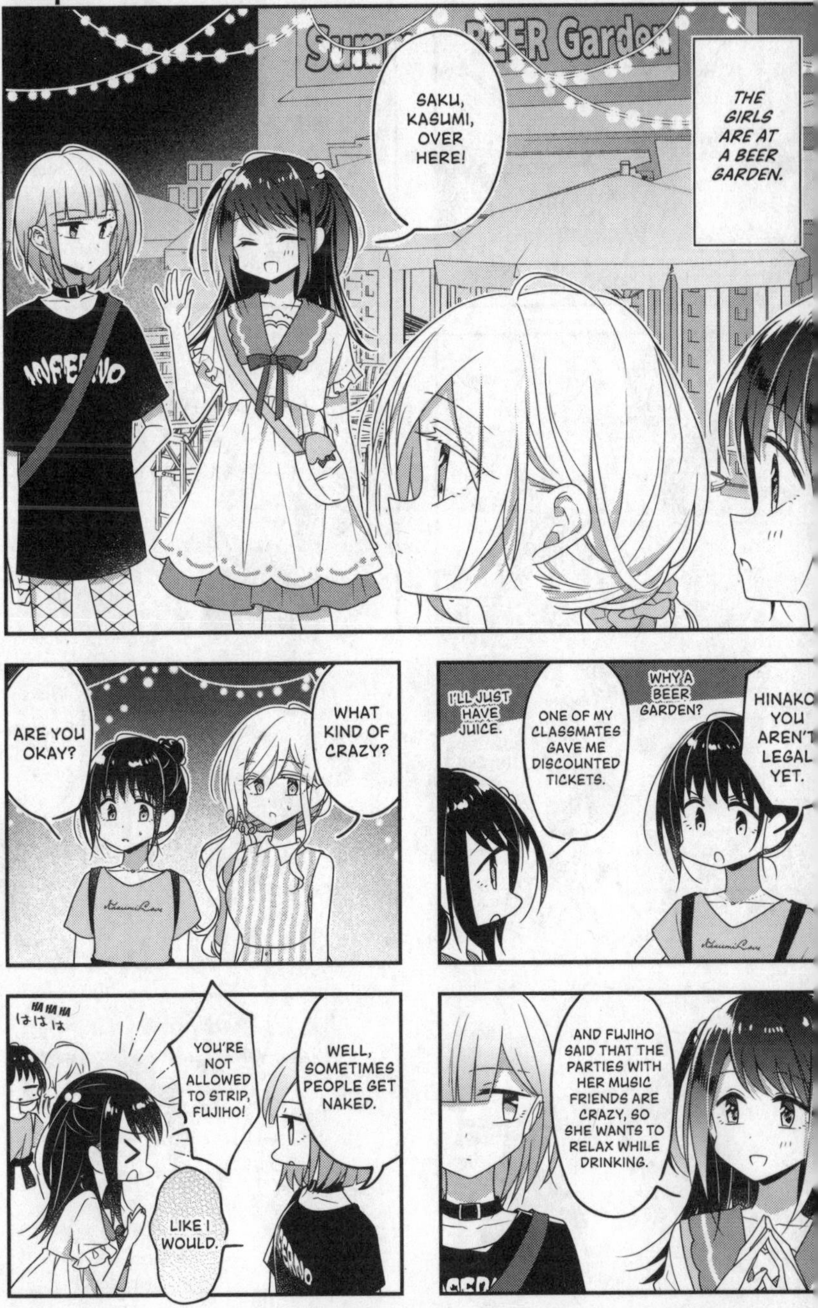
THE GIRLS ARE AT A BEER GARDEN.
SAKU, KASUMI, OVER HERE!
HINAKO YOU AREN'T LEGAL YET.
WHY A BEER GARDEN?
ONE OF MY CLASSMATES GAVE ME DISCOUNTED TICKETS.
I'LL JUST HAVE JUICE.
AND FUJIHO SAID THAT THE PARTIES WITH HER MUSIC FRIENDS ARE CRAZY, SO SHE WANTS TO RELAX WHILE DRINKING.
WHAT KIND OF CRAZY?
ARE YOU OKAY?
WELL, SOMETIMES PEOPLE GET NAKED.
YOU'RE NOT ALLOWED TO STRIP, FUJIHO!
HA HA HA
ははは
LIKE I WOULD.

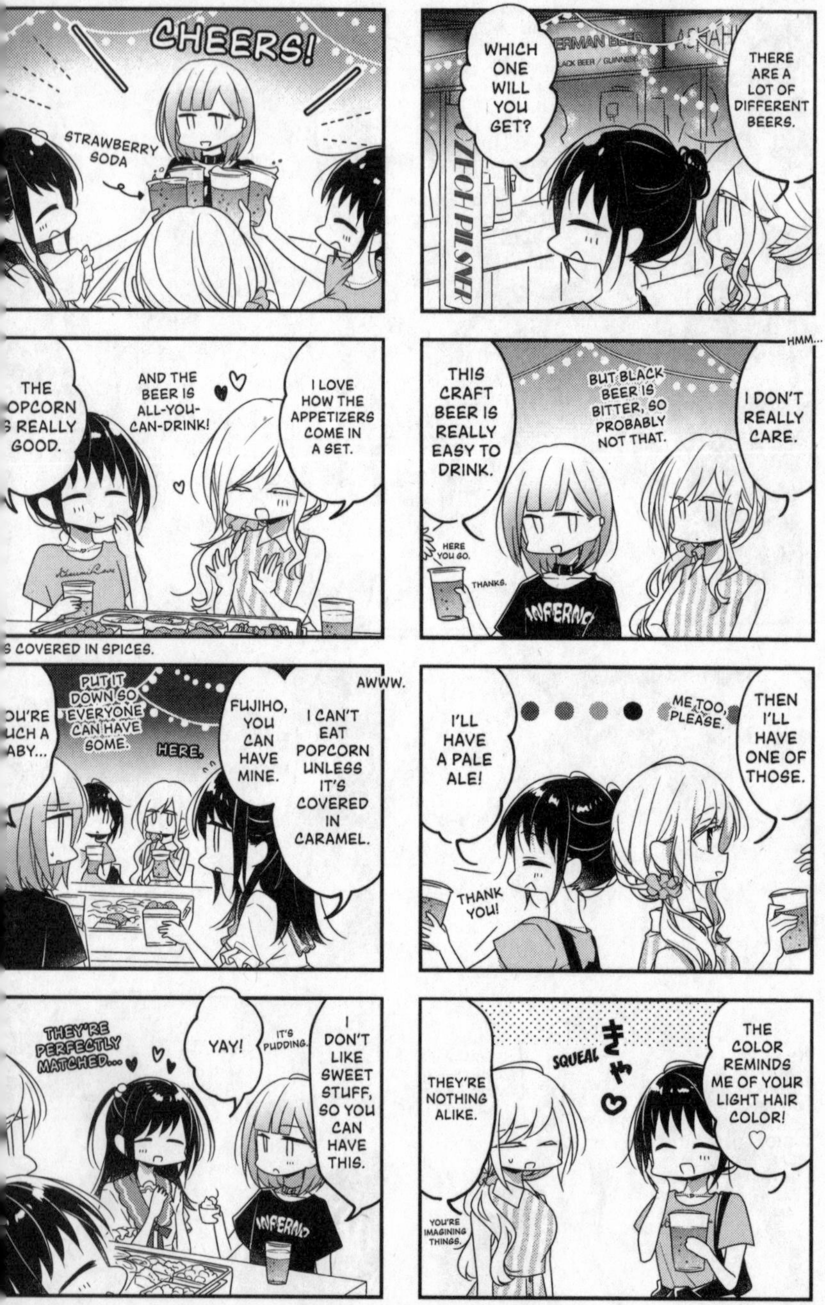
THERE ARE A LOT OF DIFFERENT BEERS.
WHICH ONE WILL YOU GET?
CZECH PILSNER
HMM...
I DON'T REALLY CARE.
BUT BLACK BEER IS BITTER, SO PROBABLY NOT THAT.
THIS CRAFT BEER IS REALLY EASY TO DRINK.
HERE YOU GO.
THANKS.
INFERNO
THEN I'LL HAVE ONE OF THOSE.
ME TOO, PLEASE.
I'LL HAVE A PALE ALE!
THANK YOU!
THE COLOR REMINDS ME OF YOUR LIGHT HAIR COLOR!
SQUEAL
THEY'RE NOTHING ALIKE.
YOU'RE IMAGINING THINGS.
CHEERS!
STRAWBERRY SODA
I LOVE HOW THE APPETIZERS COME IN A SET.
AND THE BEER IS ALL-YOU-CAN-DRINK!
THE POPCORN S REALLY GOOD.
S COVERED IN SPICES.
AWWW.
I CAN'T EAT POPCORN UNLESS IT'S COVERED IN CARAMEL.
FUJIHO, YOU CAN HAVE MINE.
HERE.
PUT IT DOWN SO EVERYONE CAN HAVE SOME.
OU'RE UCH A ABY...
I DON'T LIKE SWEET STUFF, SO YOU CAN HAVE THIS.
IT'S PUDDING.
YAY!
INFERNO
THEY'RE PERFECTLY MATCHED...

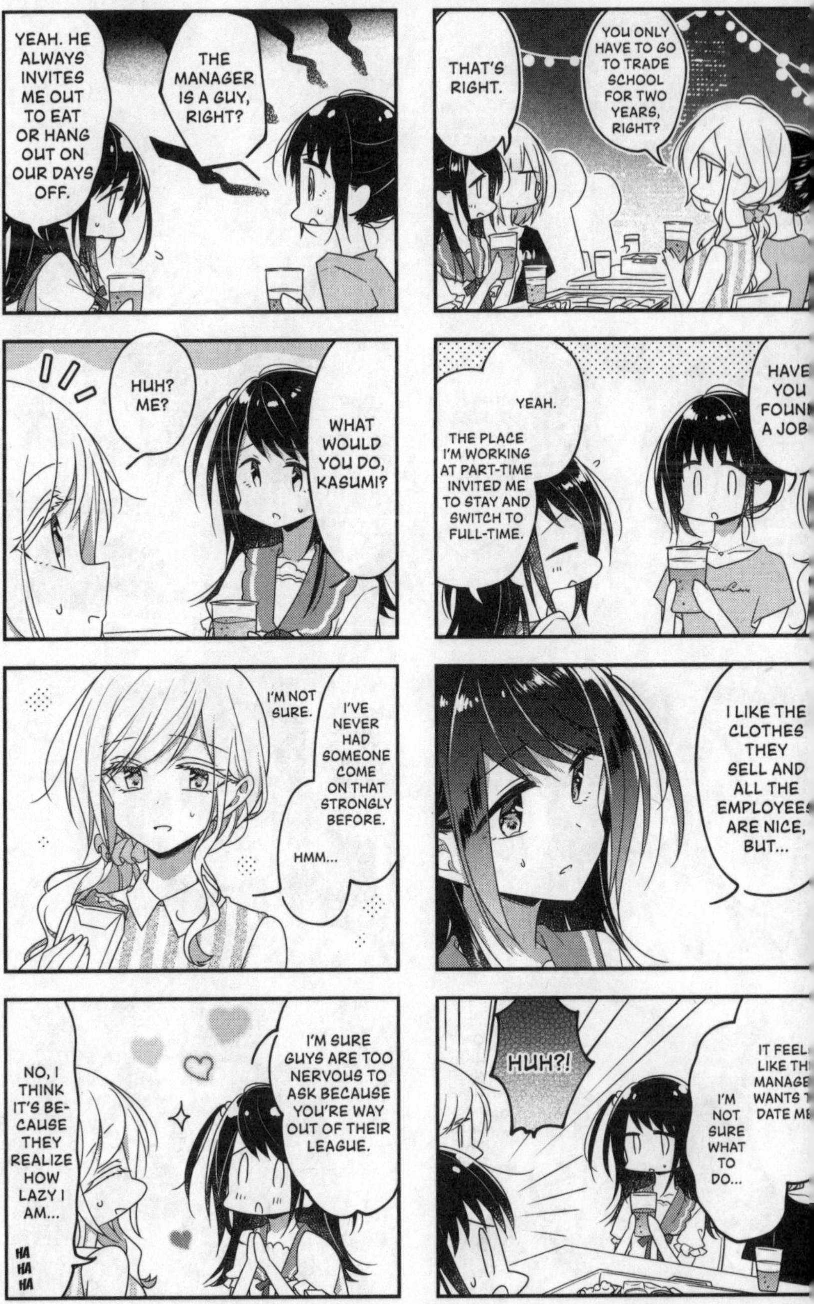
YOU ONLY HAVE TO GO TO TRADE SCHOOL FOR TWO YEARS, RIGHT?
THAT'S RIGHT.
HAVE YOU FOUN A JOB
YEAH.
THE PLACE I'M WORKING AT PART-TIME INVITED ME TO STAY AND SWITCH TO FULL-TIME.
I LIKE THE CLOTHES THEY SELL AND ALL THE EMPLOYEE ARE NICE, BUT...
IT FEEL LIKE TH MANAGE WANTS T DATE ME
I'M NOT SURE WHAT TO DO...
HUH?!
THE MANAGER IS A GUY, RIGHT?
YEAH. HE ALWAYS INVITES ME OUT TO EAT OR HANG OUT ON OUR DAYS OFF.
WHAT WOULD YOU DO, KASUMI?
HUH? ME?
I'M NOT SURE.
I'VE NEVER HAD SOMEONE COME ON THAT STRONGLY BEFORE.
HMM...
I'M SURE GUYS ARE TOO NERVOUS TO ASK BECAUSE YOU'RE WAY OUT OF THEIR LEAGUE.
NO, I THINK IT'S BE-CAUSE THEY REALIZE HOW LAZY I AM...
HA HA HA

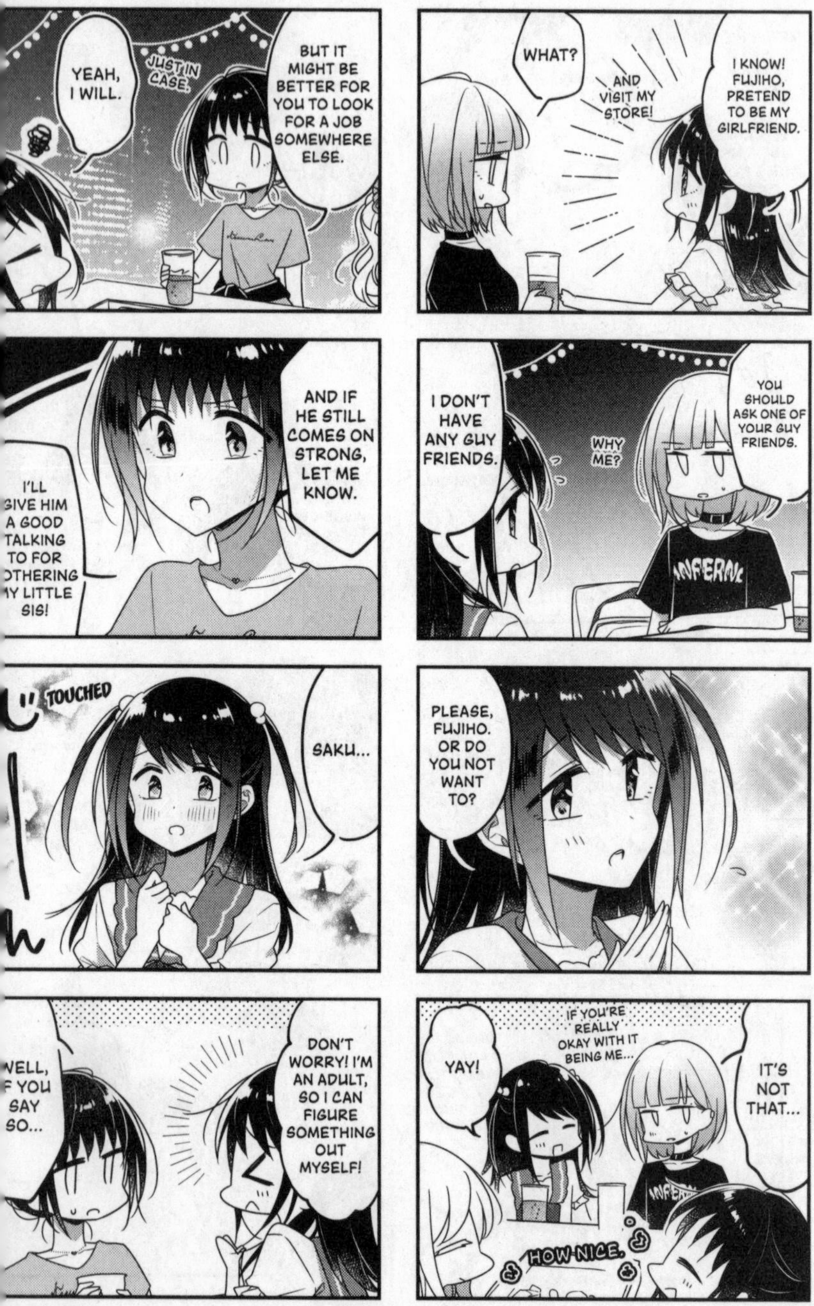

I KNOW! FUJIHO, PRETEND TO BE MY GIRLFRIEND.
AND VISIT MY STORE!
WHAT?
BUT IT MIGHT BE BETTER FOR YOU TO LOOK FOR A JOB SOMEWHERE ELSE.
JUST IN CASE.
YEAH, I WILL.
YOU SHOULD ASK ONE OF YOUR GUY FRIENDS.
WHY ME?
I DON'T HAVE ANY GUY FRIENDS.
AND IF HE STILL COMES ON STRONG, LET ME KNOW.
I'LL GIVE HIM A GOOD TALKING TO FOR BOTHERING MY LITTLE SIS!
PLEASE, FUJIHO. OR DO YOU NOT WANT TO?
SAKU...
TOUCHED
IT'S NOT THAT...
IF YOU'RE REALLY OKAY WITH IT BEING ME...
YAY!
HOW NICE.
DON'T WORRY! I'M AN ADULT, SO I CAN FIGURE SOMETHING OUT MYSELF!
WELL, IF YOU SAY SO...

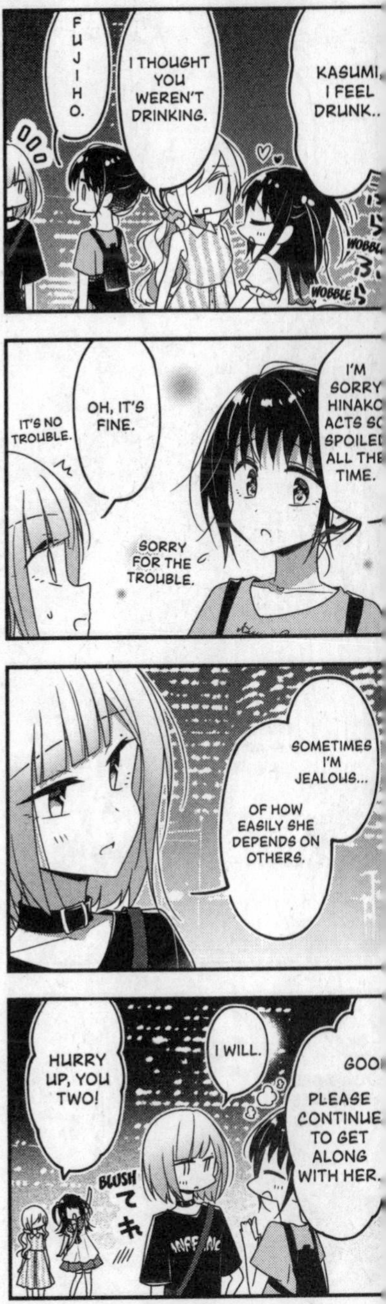
KASUMI, I FEEL DRUNK..
WOBBLE
WOBBLE
I THOUGHT YOU WEREN'T DRINKING.
FUJIHO.
I'M SORRY HINAKO ACTS SO SPOILED ALL THE TIME.
OH, IT'S FINE.
IT'S NO TROUBLE.
SORRY FOR THE TROUBLE.
SOMETIMES I'M JEALOUS...
OF HOW EASILY SHE DEPENDS ON OTHERS.
GOO
PLEASE CONTINUE TO GET ALONG WITH HER.
I WILL.
HURRY UP, YOU TWO!
BLUSH
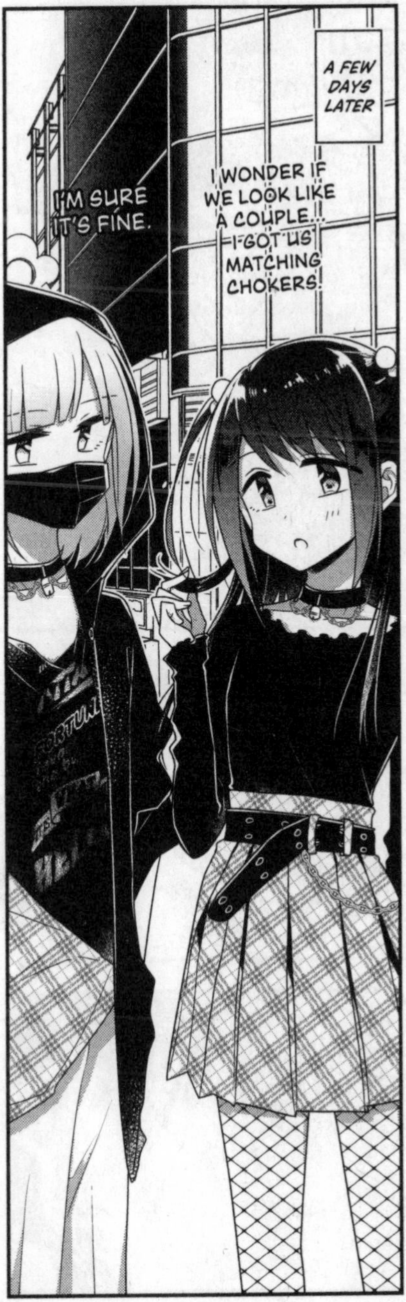
A FEW DAYS LATER
I WONDER IF WE LOOK LIKE A COUPLE... I GOT US MATCHING CHOKERS!
I'M SURE IT'S FINE.

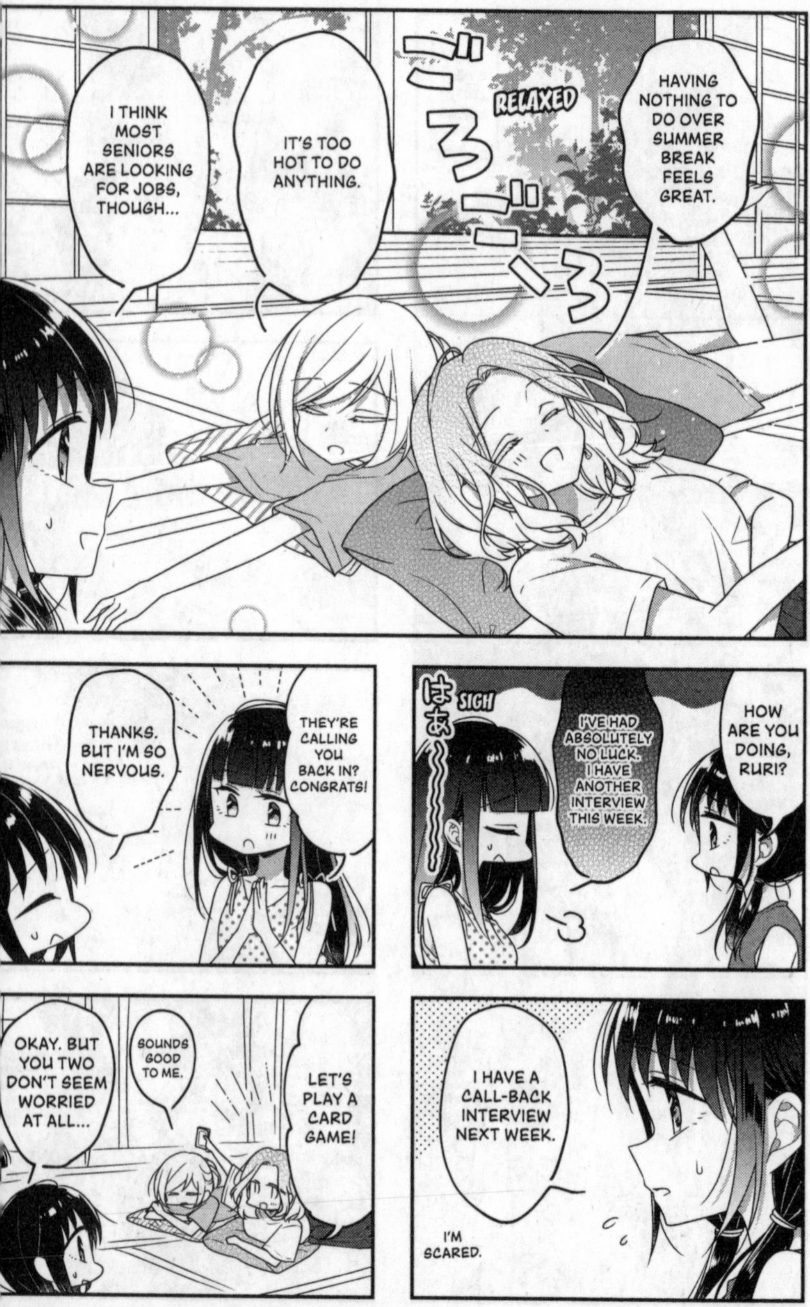
HAVING NOTHING TO DO OVER SUMMER BREAK FEELS GREAT.
ごろごろ
RELAXED
IT'S TOO HOT TO DO ANYTHING.
I THINK MOST SENIORS ARE LOOKING FOR JOBS, THOUGH...
HOW ARE YOU DOING, RURI?
I'VE HAD ABSOLUTELY NO LUCK. I HAVE ANOTHER INTERVIEW THIS WEEK.
はぁ～
SIGH
THEY'RE CALLING YOU BACK IN? CONGRATS!
THANKS. BUT I'M SO NERVOUS.
I HAVE A CALL-BACK INTERVIEW NEXT WEEK.
I'M SCARED.
LET'S PLAY A CARD GAME!
SOUNDS GOOD TO ME.
OKAY. BUT YOU TWO DON'T SEEM WORRIED AT ALL...

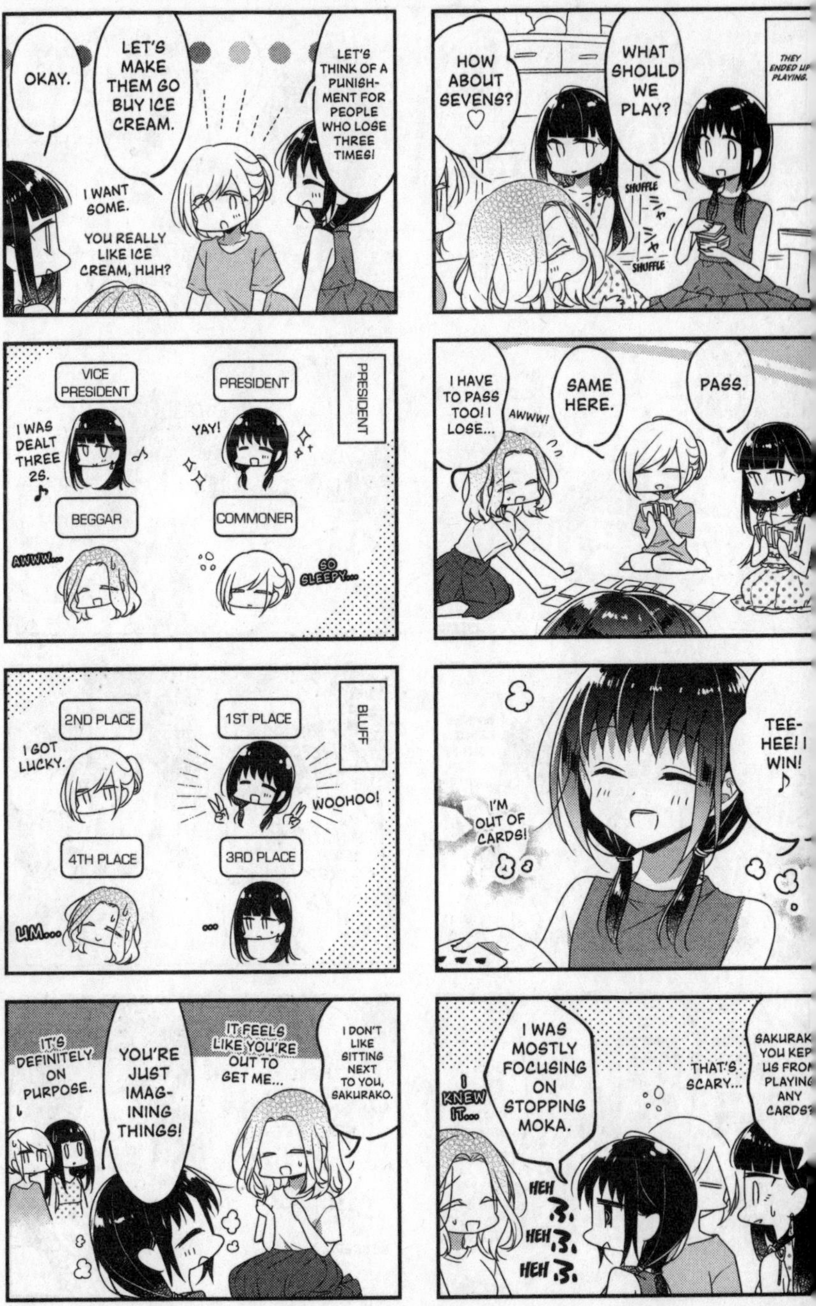
THEY ENDED UP PLAYING.
WHAT SHOULD WE PLAY?
HOW ABOUT SEVENS? ♡
SHUFFLE
SHUFFLE
PASS.
SAME HERE.
I HAVE TO PASS TOO! I LOSE...
AWWW!
TEE-HEE! I WIN! ♪
I'M OUT OF CARDS!
SAKURAK YOU KEP US FRO PLAYING ANY CARDS?
THAT'S SCARY...
I WAS MOSTLY FOCUSING ON STOPPING MOKA.
I KNEW IT...
HEH
HEH
HEH
LET'S THINK OF A PUNISH-MENT FOR PEOPLE WHO LOSE THREE TIMES!
LET'S MAKE THEM GO BUY ICE CREAM.
OKAY.
I WANT SOME.
YOU REALLY LIKE ICE CREAM, HUH?
PRESIDENT
PRESIDENT
YAY!
VICE PRESIDENT
I WAS DEALT THREE 2S. ♪
COMMONER
SO SLEEPY...
BEGGAR
AWWW...
BLUFF
1ST PLACE
WOOHOO!
2ND PLACE
I GOT LUCKY.
3RD PLACE
...
4TH PLACE
UM...
I DON'T LIKE SITTING NEXT TO YOU, SAKURAKO.
IT FEELS LIKE YOU'RE OUT TO GET ME...
YOU'RE JUST IMAG-INING THINGS!
IT'S DEFINITELY ON PURPOSE.

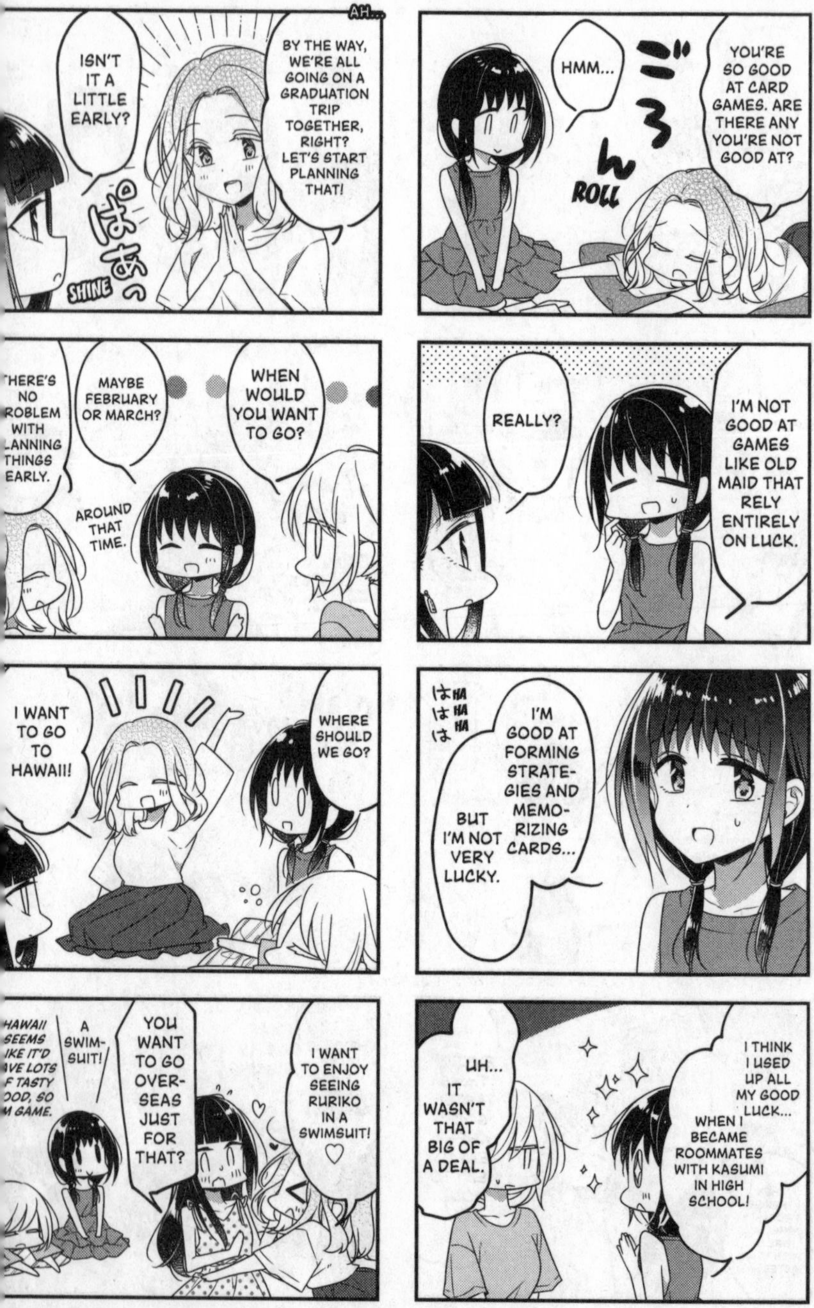
YOU'RE SO GOOD AT CARD GAMES. ARE THERE ANY YOU'RE NOT GOOD AT?
ごろん
ROLL
HMM...
I'M NOT GOOD AT GAMES LIKE OLD MAID THAT RELY ENTIRELY ON LUCK.
REALLY?
ははは
HA HA HA
I'M GOOD AT FORMING STRATEGIES AND MEMORIZING CARDS...
BUT I'M NOT VERY LUCKY.
I THINK I USED UP ALL MY GOOD LUCK...
WHEN I BECAME ROOMMATES WITH KASUMI IN HIGH SCHOOL!
UH...
IT WASN'T THAT BIG OF A DEAL.
AH...
BY THE WAY, WE'RE ALL GOING ON A GRADUATION TRIP TOGETHER, RIGHT? LET'S START PLANNING THAT!
ぱあっ
SHINE
ISN'T IT A LITTLE EARLY?
WHEN WOULD YOU WANT TO GO?
MAYBE FEBRUARY OR MARCH?
AROUND THAT TIME.
HERE'S NO ROBLEM WITH LANNING THINGS EARLY.
WHERE SHOULD WE GO?
I WANT TO GO TO HAWAII!
I WANT TO ENJOY SEEING RURIKO IN A SWIMSUIT! ♡
YOU WANT TO GO OVERSEAS JUST FOR THAT?
A SWIMSUIT!
HAWAII SEEMS IKE IT'D AVE LOTS F TASTY OOD, SO M GAME.

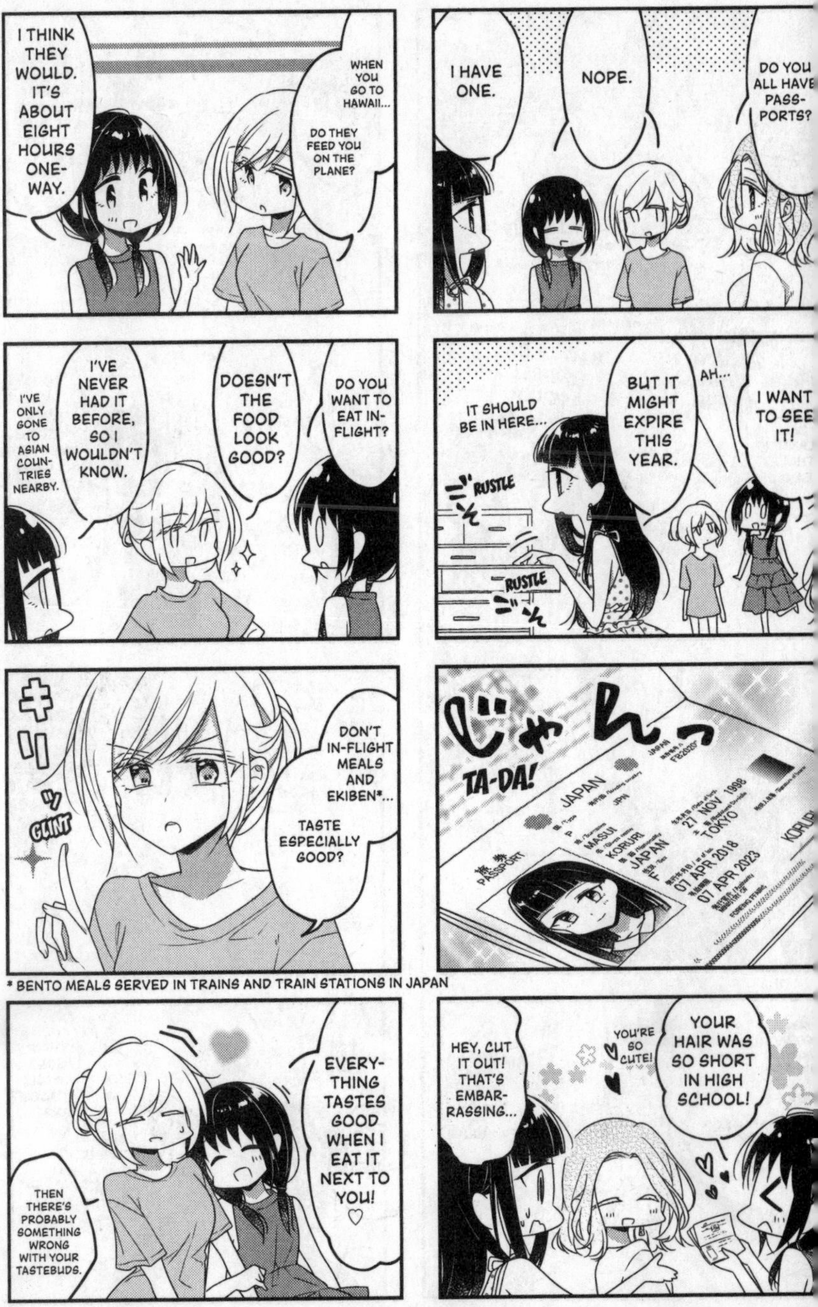
DO YOU ALL HAVE PASS-PORTS?
NOPE.
I HAVE ONE.
WHEN YOU GO TO HAWAII...
DO THEY FEED YOU ON THE PLANE?
I THINK THEY WOULD. IT'S ABOUT EIGHT HOURS ONE-WAY.
I WANT TO SEE IT!
AH...
BUT IT MIGHT EXPIRE THIS YEAR.
IT SHOULD BE IN HERE...
RUSTLE
RUSTLE
DO YOU WANT TO EAT IN-FLIGHT?
DOESN'T THE FOOD LOOK GOOD?
I'VE NEVER HAD IT BEFORE, SO I WOULDN'T KNOW.
I'VE ONLY GONE TO ASIAN COUNTRIES NEARBY.
じゃんっ
TA-DA!
PASSPORT
JAPAN
MASUI
KORURI
27 NOV 1998
TOKYO
07 APR 2018
07 APR 2023
キリッ
GLINT
DON'T IN-FLIGHT MEALS AND EKIBEN*...
TASTE ESPECIALLY GOOD?
YOUR HAIR WAS SO SHORT IN HIGH SCHOOL!
YOU'RE SO CUTE!
HEY, CUT IT OUT! THAT'S EMBARRASSING...
EVERYTHING TASTES GOOD WHEN I EAT IT NEXT TO YOU! ♡
THEN THERE'S PROBABLY SOMETHING WRONG WITH YOUR TASTEBUDS.

* BENTO MEALS SERVED IN TRAINS AND TRAIN STATIONS IN JAPAN

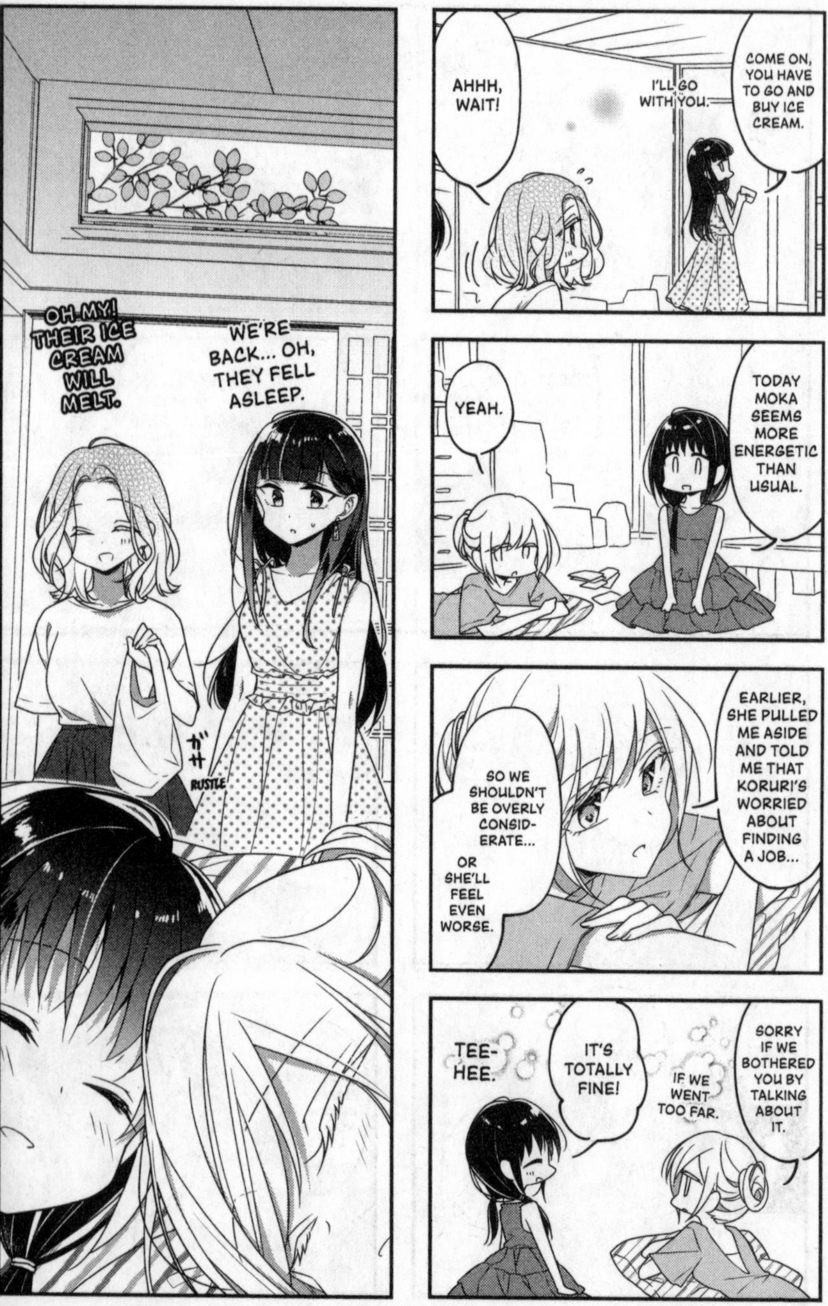
COME ON, YOU HAVE TO GO AND BUY ICE CREAM.
I'LL GO WITH YOU.
AHHH, WAIT!
TODAY MOKA SEEMS MORE ENERGETIC THAN USUAL.
YEAH.
EARLIER, SHE PULLED ME ASIDE AND TOLD ME THAT KORURI'S WORRIED ABOUT FINDING A JOB...
SO WE SHOULDN'T BE OVERLY CONSIDERATE...
OR SHE'LL FEEL EVEN WORSE.
SORRY IF WE BOTHERED YOU BY TALKING ABOUT IT.
IF WE WENT TOO FAR.
IT'S TOTALLY FINE!
TEE-HEE.
WE'RE BACK... OH, THEY FELL ASLEEP.
ガサ
RUSTLE
OH MY! THEIR ICE CREAM WILL MELT.

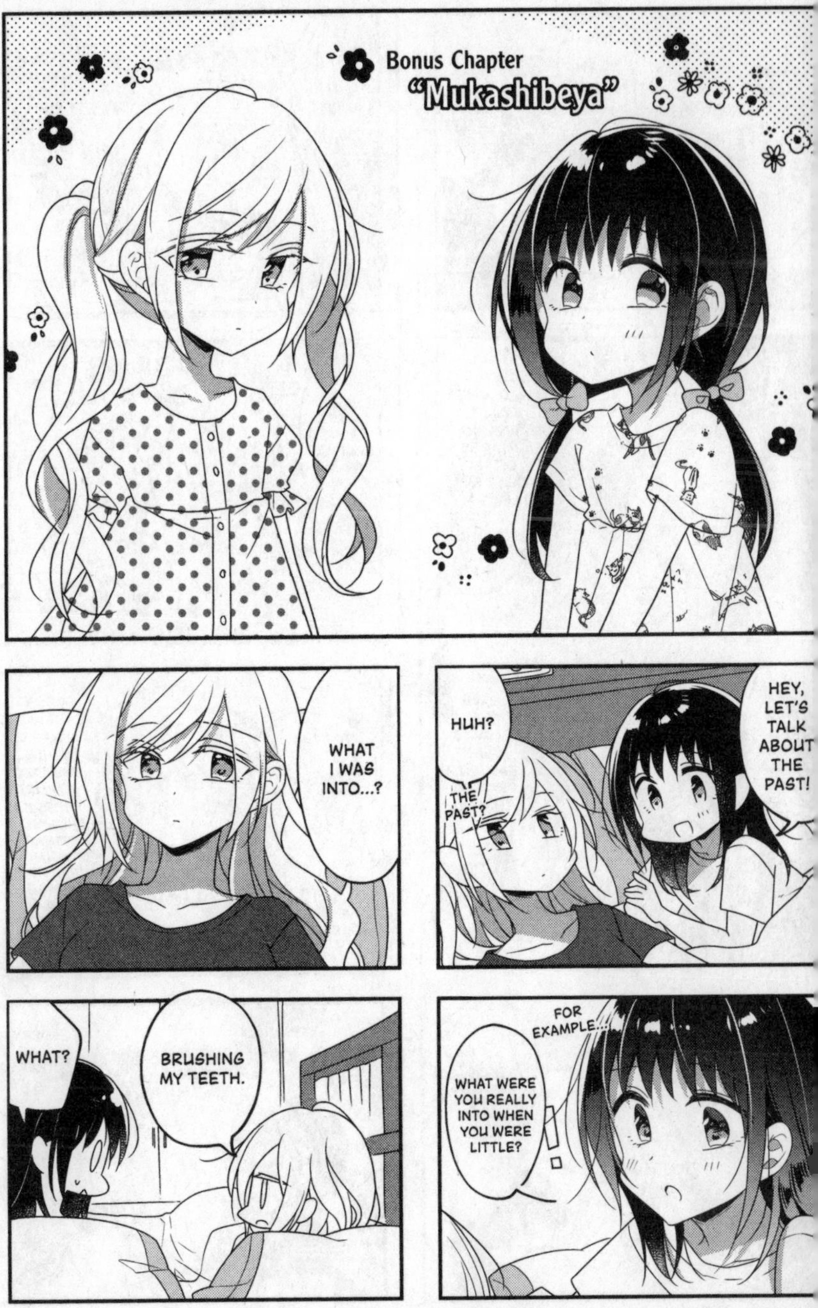
Bonus Chapter
"Mukashibeya"
HEY, LET'S TALK ABOUT THE PAST!
HUH?
THE PAST?
WHAT I WAS INTO...?
FOR EXAMPLE...
WHAT WERE YOU REALLY INTO WHEN YOU WERE LITTLE?
BRUSHING MY TEETH.
WHAT?

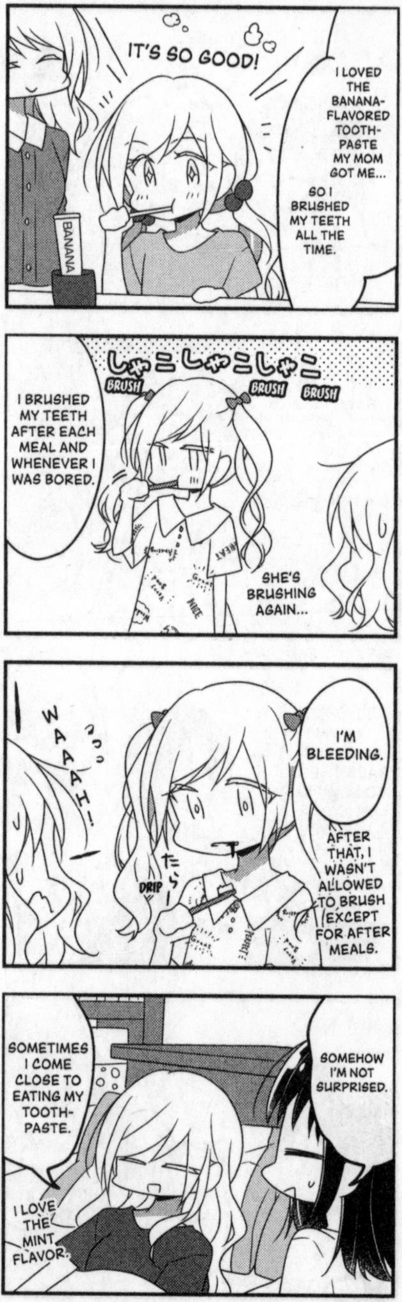
I LOVED THE BANANA-FLAVORED TOOTHPASTE MY MOM GOT ME...
SO I BRUSHED MY TEETH ALL THE TIME.
IT'S SO GOOD!
BANANA
しゃこしゃこしゃこ
BRUSH
BRUSH
BRUSH
I BRUSHED MY TEETH AFTER EACH MEAL AND WHENEVER I WAS BORED.
SHE'S BRUSHING AGAIN...
I'M BLEEDING.
AFTER THAT, I WASN'T ALLOWED TO BRUSH EXCEPT FOR AFTER MEALS.
WAAAAH!
DRIP
SOMEHOW I'M NOT SURPRISED.
SOMETIMES I COME CLOSE TO EATING MY TOOTHPASTE.
I LOVE THE MINT FLAVOR.

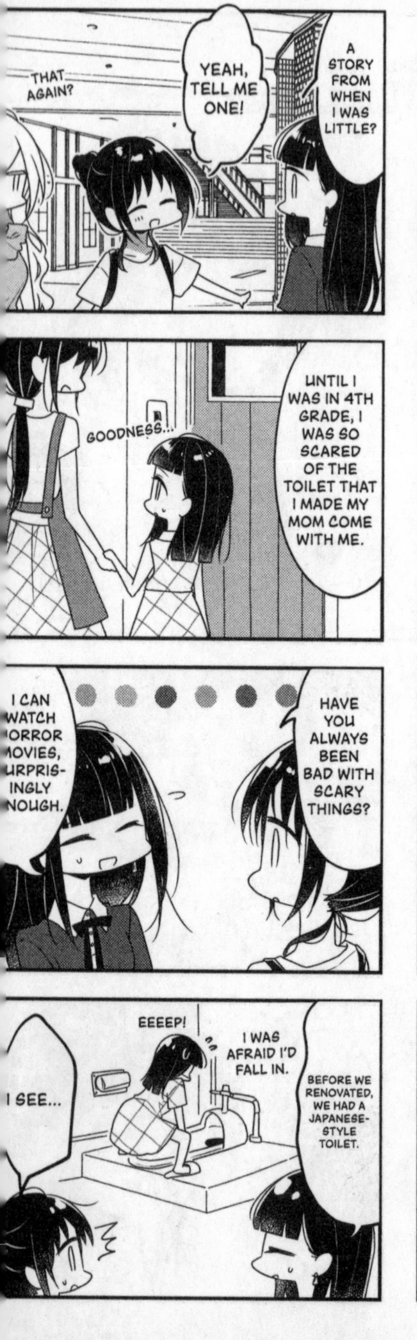
A STORY FROM WHEN I WAS LITTLE?
YEAH, TELL ME ONE!
THAT AGAIN?
UNTIL I WAS IN 4TH GRADE, I WAS SO SCARED OF THE TOILET THAT I MADE MY MOM COME WITH ME.
GOODNESS...
HAVE YOU ALWAYS BEEN BAD WITH SCARY THINGS?
I CAN WATCH ORROR OVIES, URPRIS-INGLY NOUGH.
BEFORE WE RENOVATED, WE HAD A JAPANESE-STYLE TOILET.
I WAS AFRAID I'D FALL IN.
EEEEP!
I SEE...

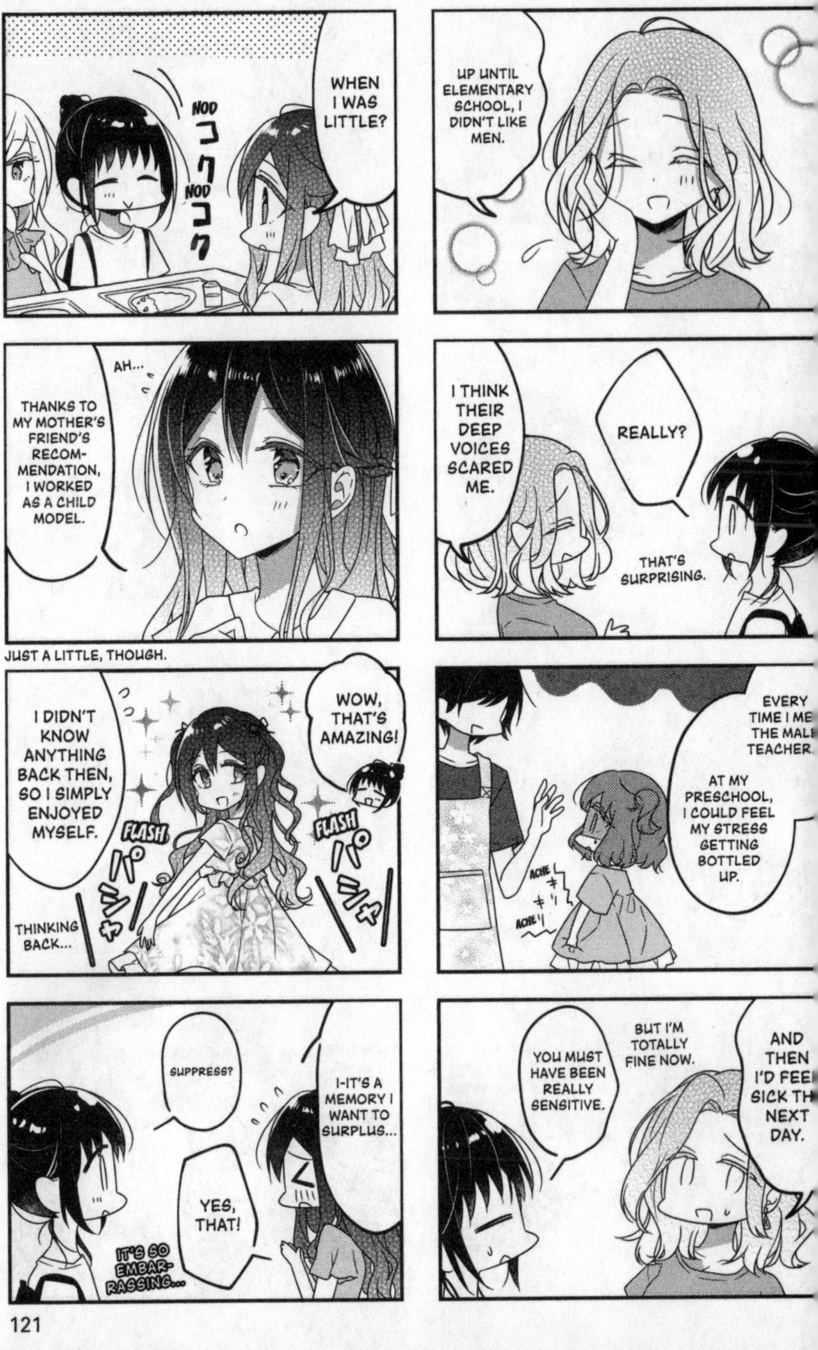

UP UNTIL ELEMENTARY SCHOOL, I DIDN'T LIKE MEN.
I THINK THEIR DEEP VOICES SCARED ME.
REALLY?
THAT'S SURPRISING.
EVERY TIME I ME THE MALE TEACHER
AT MY PRESCHOOL, I COULD FEEL MY STRESS GETTING BOTTLED UP.
ACHE
ACHE
AND THEN I'D FEE SICK TH NEXT DAY.
BUT I'M TOTALLY FINE NOW.
YOU MUST HAVE BEEN REALLY SENSITIVE.
WHEN I WAS LITTLE?
NOD コク
NOD コク
THANKS TO MY MOTHER'S FRIEND'S RECOM-MENDATION, I WORKED AS A CHILD MODEL.
AH...
JUST A LITTLE, THOUGH.
WOW, THAT'S AMAZING!
I DIDN'T KNOW ANYTHING BACK THEN, SO I SIMPLY ENJOYED MYSELF.
FLASH パシャ
FLASH パシャ
THINKING BACK...
I-IT'S A MEMORY I WANT TO SURPLUS...
SUPPRESS?
YES, THAT!
IT'S SO EMBARRASSING...

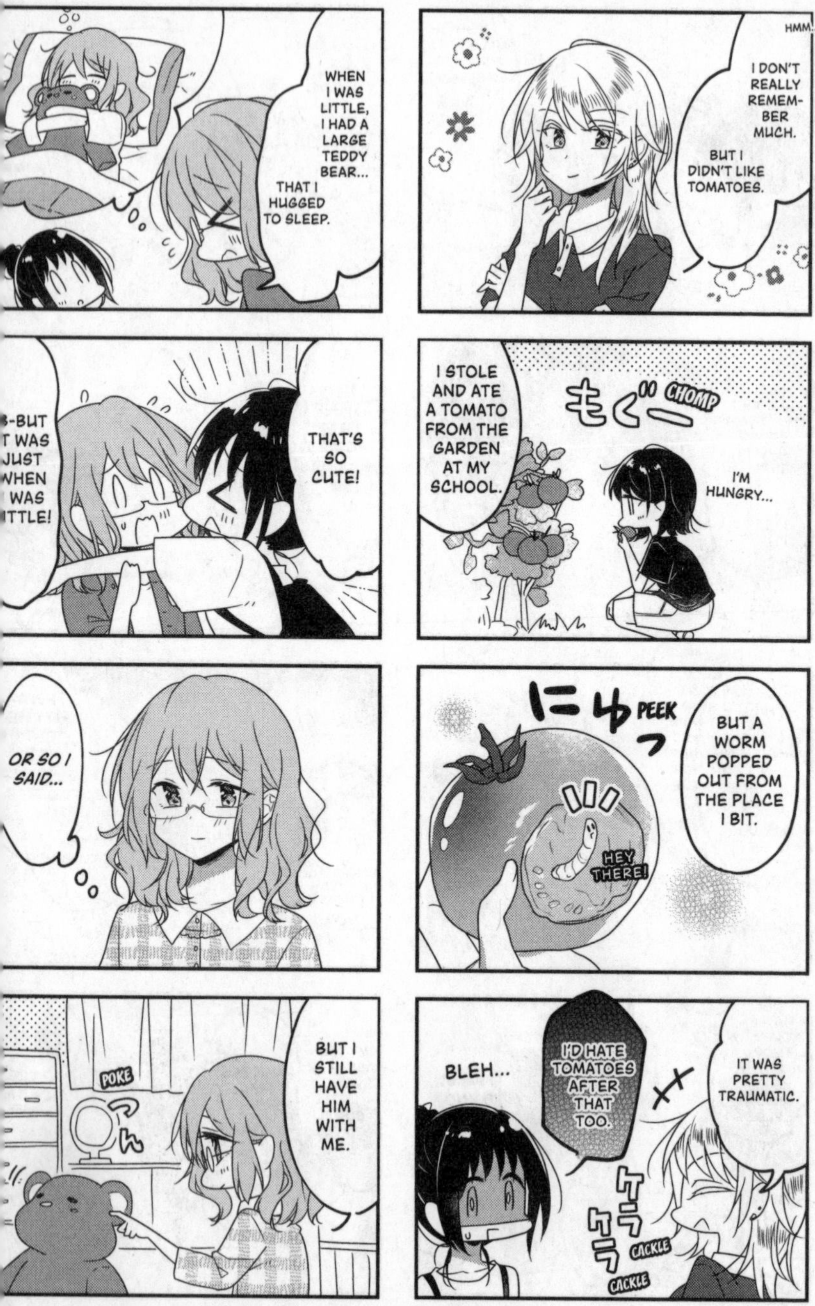
HMM...
I DON'T REALLY REMEMBER MUCH.
BUT I DIDN'T LIKE TOMATOES.
I STOLE AND ATE A TOMATO FROM THE GARDEN AT MY SCHOOL.
もぐー CHOMP
I'M HUNGRY...
にゅっ PEEK
BUT A WORM POPPED OUT FROM THE PLACE I BIT.
HEY THERE!
IT WAS PRETTY TRAUMATIC.
I'D HATE TOMATOES AFTER THAT TOO.
BLEH...
ケラケラ CACKLE CACKLE
WHEN I WAS LITTLE, I HAD A LARGE TEDDY BEAR...
THAT I HUGGED TO SLEEP.
THAT'S SO CUTE!
OR SO I SAID...
BUT I STILL HAVE HIM WITH ME.
つん POKE

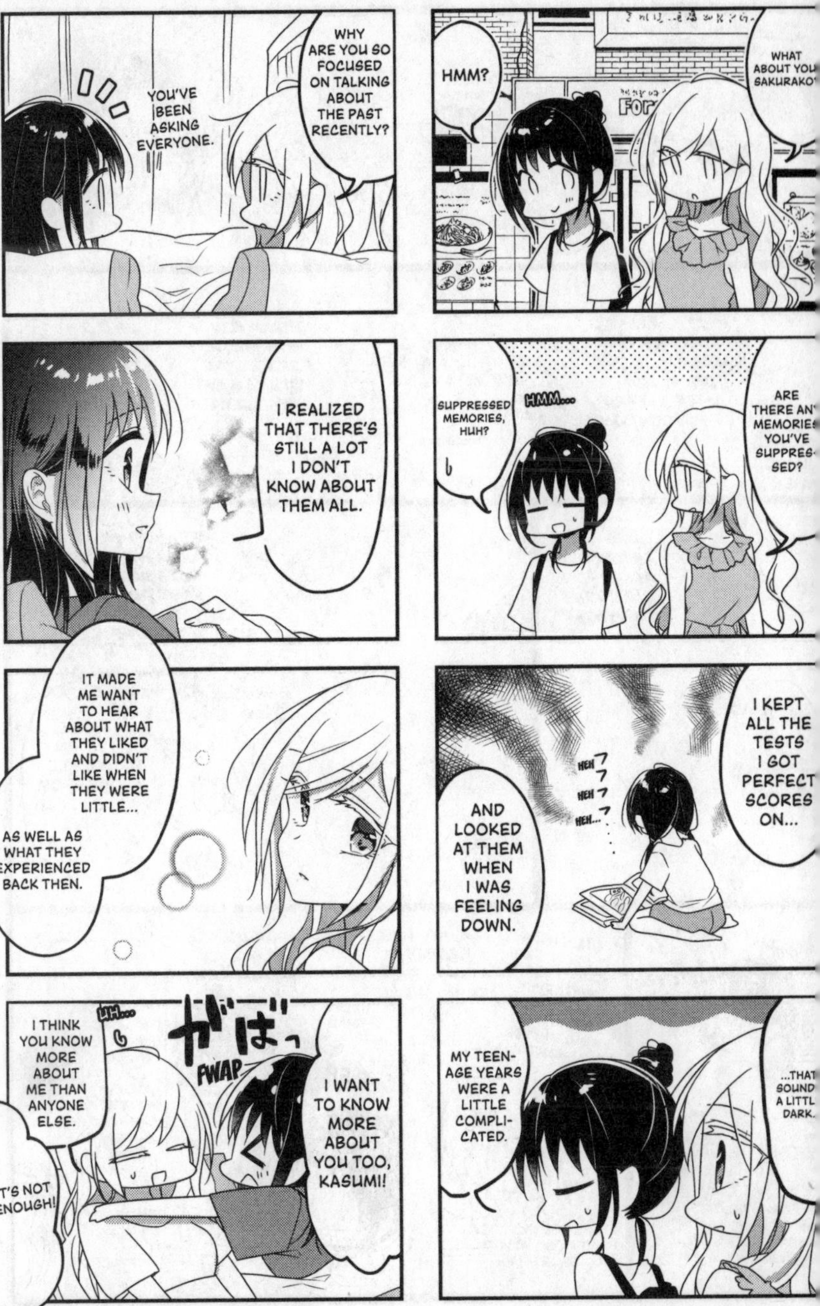
WHAT ABOUT YOU SAKURAKO
HMM?
ARE THERE AN MEMORIE YOU'VE SUPPRES-SED?
HMM...
SUPPRESSED MEMORIES, HUH?
I KEPT ALL THE TESTS I GOT PERFECT SCORES ON...
HEH HEH HEH...
AND LOOKED AT THEM WHEN I WAS FEELING DOWN.
...THAT SOUND A LITTL DARK.
MY TEEN-AGE YEARS WERE A LITTLE COMPLI-CATED.
WHY ARE YOU SO FOCUSED ON TALKING ABOUT THE PAST RECENTLY?
YOU'VE BEEN ASKING EVERYONE.
I REALIZED THAT THERE'S STILL A LOT I DON'T KNOW ABOUT THEM ALL.
IT MADE ME WANT TO HEAR ABOUT WHAT THEY LIKED AND DIDN'T LIKE WHEN THEY WERE LITTLE...
AS WELL AS WHAT THEY EXPERIENCED BACK THEN.
I WANT TO KNOW MORE ABOUT YOU TOO, KASUMI!
がばっ
FWAP
UH...
I THINK YOU KNOW MORE ABOUT ME THAN ANYONE ELSE.
IT'S NOT ENOUGH!

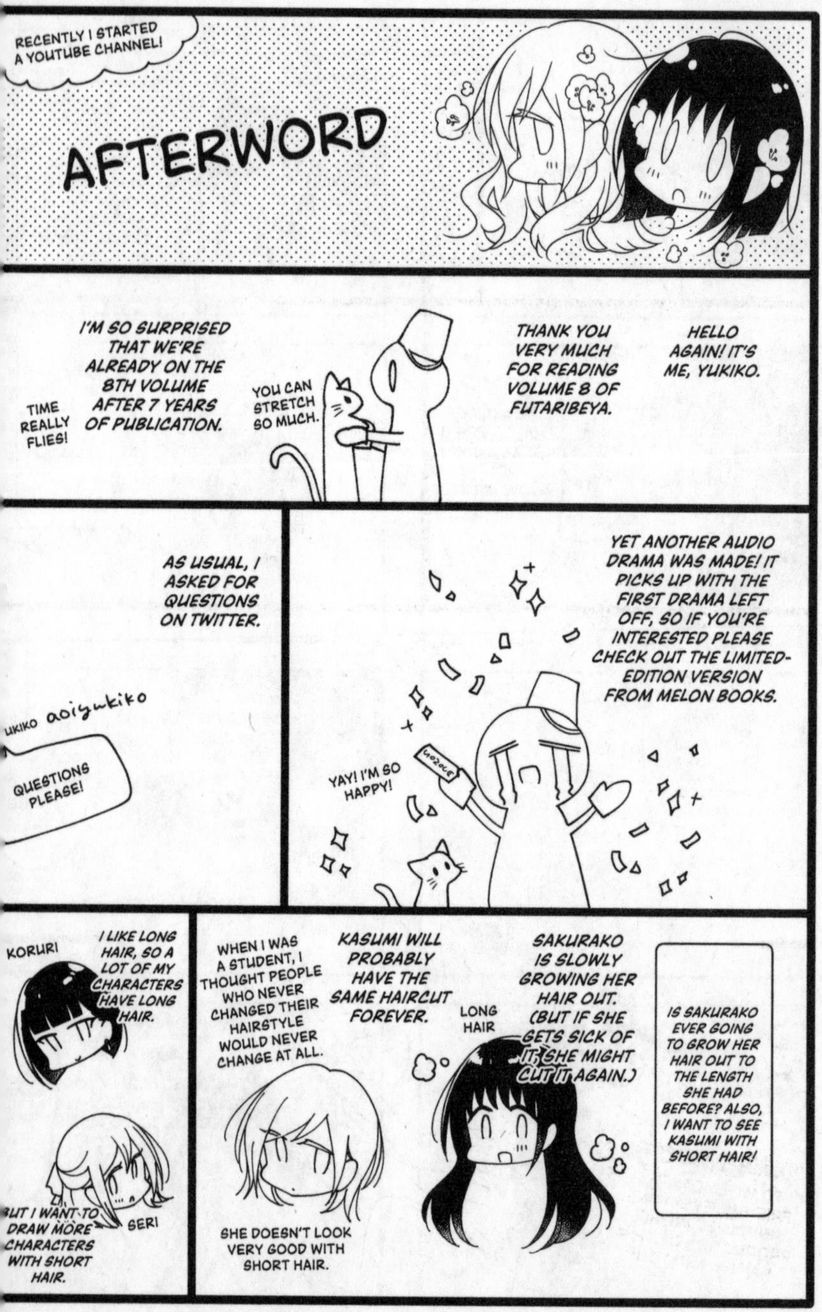
AFTERWORD
RECENTLY I STARTED A YOUTUBE CHANNEL!
HELLO AGAIN! IT'S ME, YUKIKO.
THANK YOU VERY MUCH FOR READING VOLUME 8 OF FUTARIBEYA.
YOU CAN STRETCH SO MUCH.
I'M SO SURPRISED THAT WE'RE ALREADY ON THE 8TH VOLUME AFTER 7 YEARS OF PUBLICATION.
TIME REALLY FLIES!
YET ANOTHER AUDIO DRAMA WAS MADE! IT PICKS UP WITH THE FIRST DRAMA LEFT OFF, SO IF YOU'RE INTERESTED PLEASE CHECK OUT THE LIMITED-EDITION VERSION FROM MELON BOOKS.
YAY! I'M SO HAPPY!
AS USUAL, I ASKED FOR QUESTIONS ON TWITTER.
UKIKO aoiyukiko
QUESTIONS PLEASE!
IS SAKURAKO EVER GOING TO GROW HER HAIR OUT TO THE LENGTH SHE HAD BEFORE? ALSO, I WANT TO SEE KASUMI WITH SHORT HAIR!
SAKURAKO IS SLOWLY GROWING HER HAIR OUT. (BUT IF SHE GETS SICK OF IT, SHE MIGHT CUT IT AGAIN.)
LONG HAIR
KASUMI WILL PROBABLY HAVE THE SAME HAIRCUT FOREVER.
WHEN I WAS A STUDENT, I THOUGHT PEOPLE WHO NEVER CHANGED THEIR HAIRSTYLE WOULD NEVER CHANGE AT ALL.
SHE DOESN'T LOOK VERY GOOD WITH SHORT HAIR.
I LIKE LONG HAIR, SO A LOT OF MY CHARACTERS HAVE LONG HAIR.
KORURI
SERI
UT I WANT TO DRAW MORE CHARACTERS WITH SHORT HAIR.

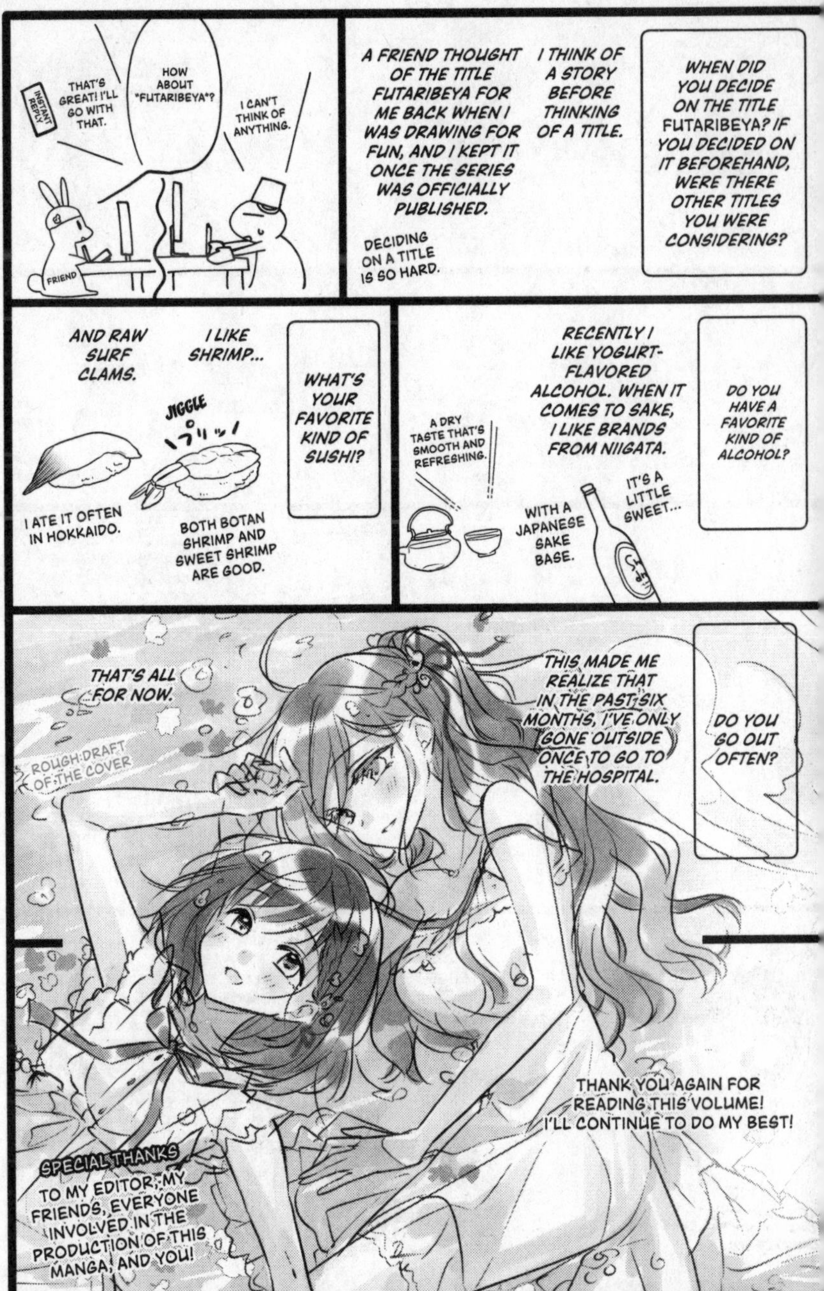
WHEN DID YOU DECIDE ON THE TITLE FUTARIBEYA? IF YOU DECIDED ON IT BEFOREHAND, WERE THERE OTHER TITLES YOU WERE CONSIDERING?
I THINK OF A STORY BEFORE THINKING OF A TITLE.
A FRIEND THOUGHT OF THE TITLE FUTARIBEYA FOR ME BACK WHEN I WAS DRAWING FOR FUN, AND I KEPT IT ONCE THE SERIES WAS OFFICIALLY PUBLISHED.
DECIDING ON A TITLE IS SO HARD.
I CAN'T THINK OF ANYTHING.
HOW ABOUT "FUTARIBEYA"?
THAT'S GREAT! I'LL GO WITH THAT.
INSTANT REPLY
FRIEND
DO YOU HAVE A FAVORITE KIND OF ALCOHOL?
RECENTLY I LIKE YOGURT-FLAVORED ALCOHOL. WHEN IT COMES TO SAKE, I LIKE BRANDS FROM NIIGATA.
IT'S A LITTLE SWEET...
WITH A JAPANESE SAKE BASE.
A DRY TASTE THAT'S SMOOTH AND REFRESHING.
WHAT'S YOUR FAVORITE KIND OF SUSHI?
I LIKE SHRIMP...
AND RAW SURF CLAMS.
JIGGLE
BOTH BOTAN SHRIMP AND SWEET SHRIMP ARE GOOD.
I ATE IT OFTEN IN HOKKAIDO.
DO YOU GO OUT OFTEN?
THIS MADE ME REALIZE THAT IN THE PAST SIX MONTHS, I'VE ONLY GONE OUTSIDE ONCE TO GO TO THE HOSPITAL.
THAT'S ALL FOR NOW.
ROUGH DRAFT OF THE COVER
THANK YOU AGAIN FOR READING THIS VOLUME! I'LL CONTINUE TO DO MY BEST!
SPECIAL THANKS
TO MY EDITOR, MY FRIENDS, EVERYONE INVOLVED IN THE PRODUCTION OF THIS MANGA, AND YOU!

Futaribeya
A ROOM FOR TWO

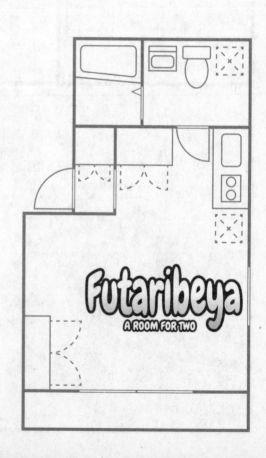

Sakuya Amano

KONOHANA KITAN, VOL. 1

FANTASY

Yuzu is a brand new employee at Konohanatei, the hot-springs inn that sits on the crossroads between worlds.
A simple, clumsy but charmingly earnest girl, Yuzu must now figure out her new life working alongside all the other fox-spirits who run the inn under one cardinal rule - at Konohanatei, every guest is a god!

KONOHANA KITAN, VOL 2
Sakuya Amano

FANTASY

At Konohanatei, every guest is considered a god — but when an actual deity, the Great Spirit of Bubbles, comes to the inn for a bath, Yuzu and her fox friends get (many) more of her than they bargained for!

Other guests stopping by the inn this time include a beautiful girl who weaves with the rain, a cursed Japanese doll, and... a mermaid?! Even Hiiragi, Satsuki's gorgeous older sister, drops in for a visit despite their rocky relationship. Perhaps the peaceful, otherworldly Konohanatei is just the right place to mend strained sibling bonds.

STILL SICK, VOLUME 1

Akashi

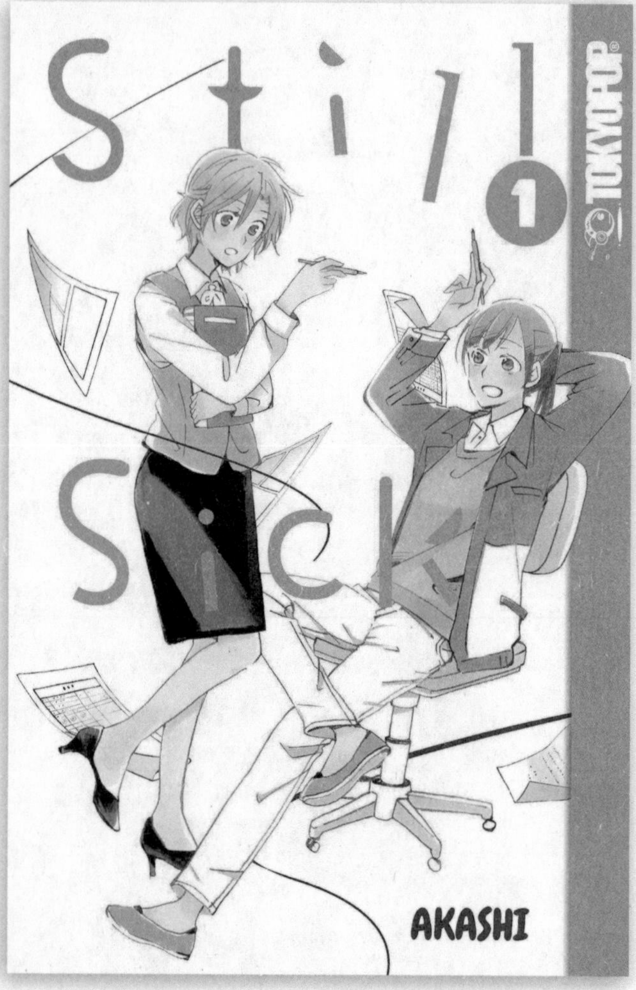

Still Sick
1
TOKYOPOP
AKASHI

♀LOVE x LOVE♀

Makoto Shimizu is just an ordinary office worker, blending in seamlessly with her colleagues on the job... That is, until her coworker Akane Maekawa discovers her well-hidden secret: in her spare time, she draws and sells girls' love comics! Akane is the last person Makoto would think of as a nerd, but as the two grow closer, it starts to seem like Akane may have a secret of her own...

TOKYOPOP

STILL SICK, VOLUME 2

Akashi

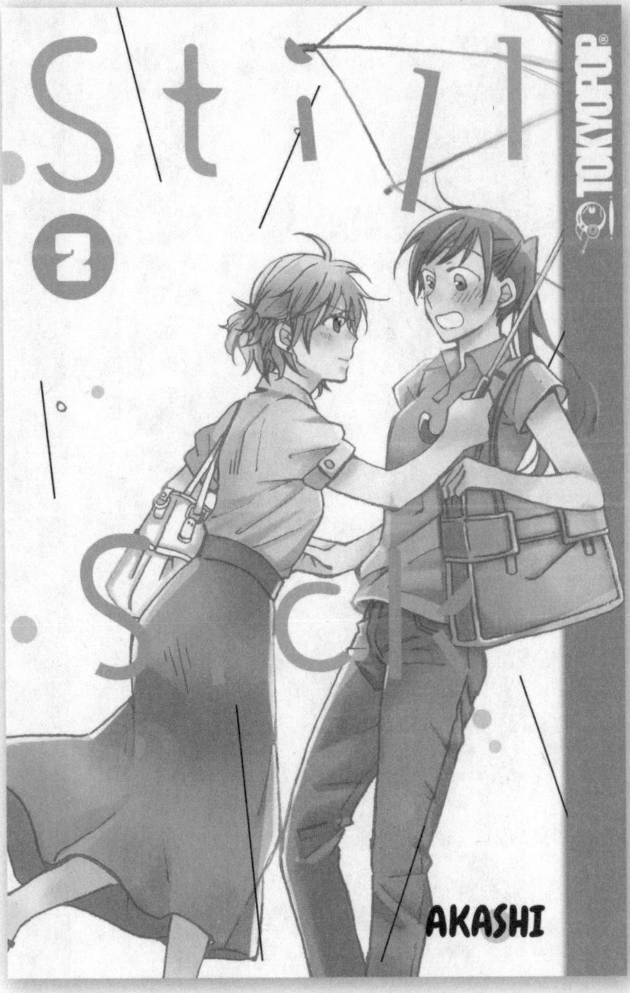
Still Sick
2
TOKYOPOP
AKASHI

LOVE-x-LOVE

After finding out that her coworker Akane used to be a manga creator, Makoto encourages her new friend to recapture that dream. As an amateur comic artist herself, Makoto looks up to Akane and tries to help her overcome the difficulties that made her give up that profession in the past. Although Akane is often her own worst critic, Makoto inspires her to try reshaping her attitude toward her art. But matters become more complicated when Makoto realizes that, somewhere along the way, what started out as a professional friendship over a common interest has developed into... a serious crush!

TOKYOPOP

THE FOX & LITTLE TANUKI, VOLUME 1

Mi Tagawa

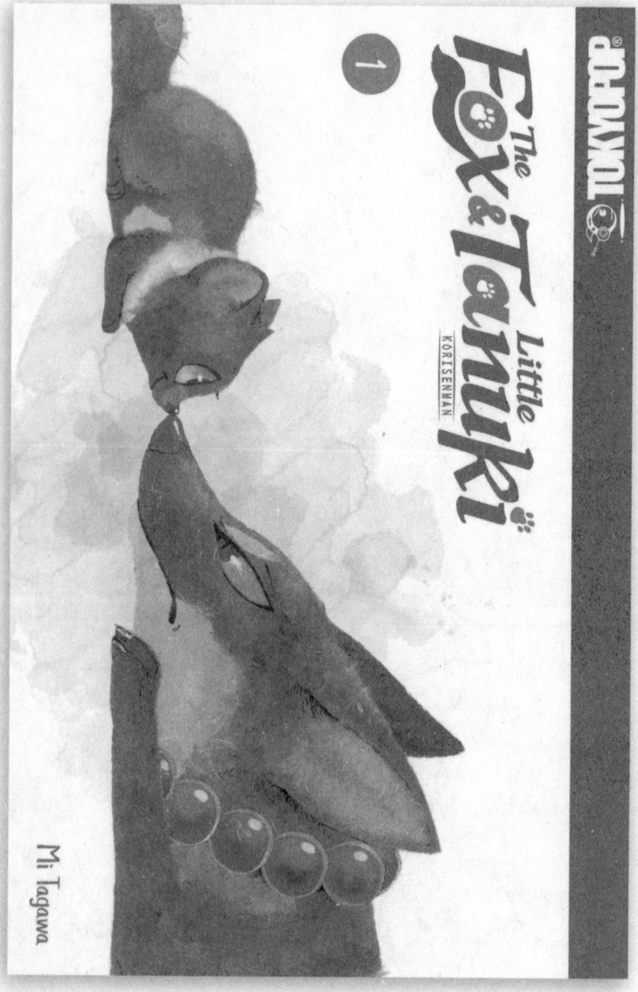
TOKYOPOP
The Fox & Little Tanuki
KORISENNAN
1
Mi Tagawa

FANTASY

It is said that there are some special animals occasionally born with great powers. Senzou the black fox is one of those... but instead of using his powers for good, he abused his strength until the Sun Goddess imprisoned him for his bad behavior. Three hundred years later, he's finally been released, but only on one condition — he can't have any of his abilities back until he successfully helps a tanuki cub named Manpachi become an assistant to the gods. Unfortunately for Senzou, there's no cheating when it comes to completing his task! The magic beads around his neck make sure he can't wander too far from his charge or ignore his duties, and so... Senzou the once-great Fox Spirit must figure out how to be an actually-great babysitter to a innocent little tanuki or risk being stuck without his powers forever!

TOKYOPOP

LAUGHING UNDER THE CLOUDS, VOLUME 1

KarakaraKemuri

FANTASY

Under the curse of Orochi, the great demon serpent reborn every 300 years, Japan has been shrouded in clouds for as long as anyone can remember... The era of the samurai is at an end, and carrying swords has been outlawed. To combat the rising crime rates, an inescapable prison was built in the middle of Lake Biwa. When brothers Tenka, Soramaru and Chutaro Kumo are hired to capture and transport offenders to their final lodgings in this prison, they unexpectedly find themselves faced with a greater destiny than any of them could have imagined.

No Vampire, No Happy Ending
1
TOKYOPOP
SHINYA SHINYA

NO VAMPIRE, NO HAPPY ENDING, VOLUME 1

Shinya Shinya

LOVE-x-LOVE

Arika is what you could charitably call a vampire "enthusiast." When she stumbles across the beautiful and mysterious vampire Divo however, her excitement quickly turns to disappointment as she discovers he's not exactly like the seductive, manipulative villains in her stories. His looks win first place, but his head's a space case. Armed with her extensive knowledge of vampire lore, Arika downgrades Divo to a beta vampire and begins their long, long... long journey to educate him in the ways of the undead.

TOKYOPOP

NO VAMPIRE, NO HAPPY ENDING, VOLUME 2

Shinya Shinya

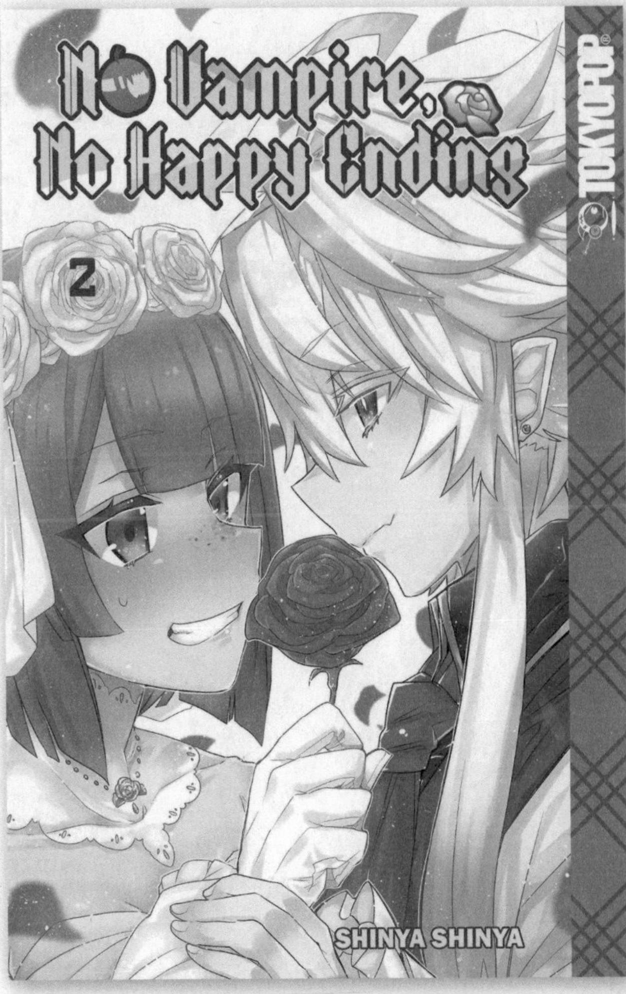
No Vampire, No Happy Ending
2
SHINYA SHINYA
TOKYOPOP

LOVE-x-LOVE

When die-hard vampire enthusiast Arika comes across a mysterious young man named Divo, it seems she struck the jackpot-- she's found a drop-dead gorgeous vampire of her own! Unfortunately, she quickly finds out the disappointing truth: Divo is all beauty, no brains, and no vampire instincts whatsoever. What's a vampire-loving girl to do? Teach him, of course! The grand finale of the laugh-out-loud supernatural love comedy featuring a vampire in beta and the vampire fangirl determined to make him worth her time!

TOKYOPOP

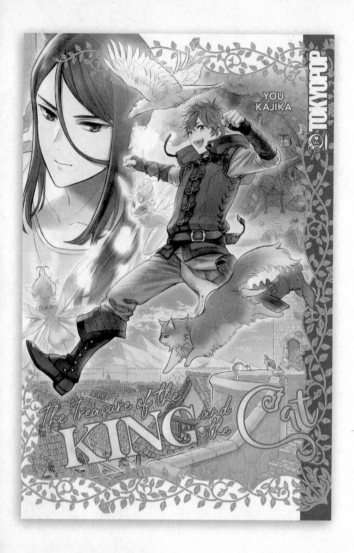

THE TREASURE OF THE KING AND THE CAT

You Kajika

⸎LOVE-x-LOVE⸎

One day, a large number of people suddenly disappeared in the royal capital. When young King Castio goes out to investigate this occurrence, he comes across the culprit... but the criminal puts a spell on him! To help him out, the king calls the wizard O'Feuille to his castle, along with Prince Volks and his loyal retainer Nios. Together, they're determined to solve this strange, fluffy mystery full of cats, swords and magic!

THE CAT PROPOSED

Dento Hayane

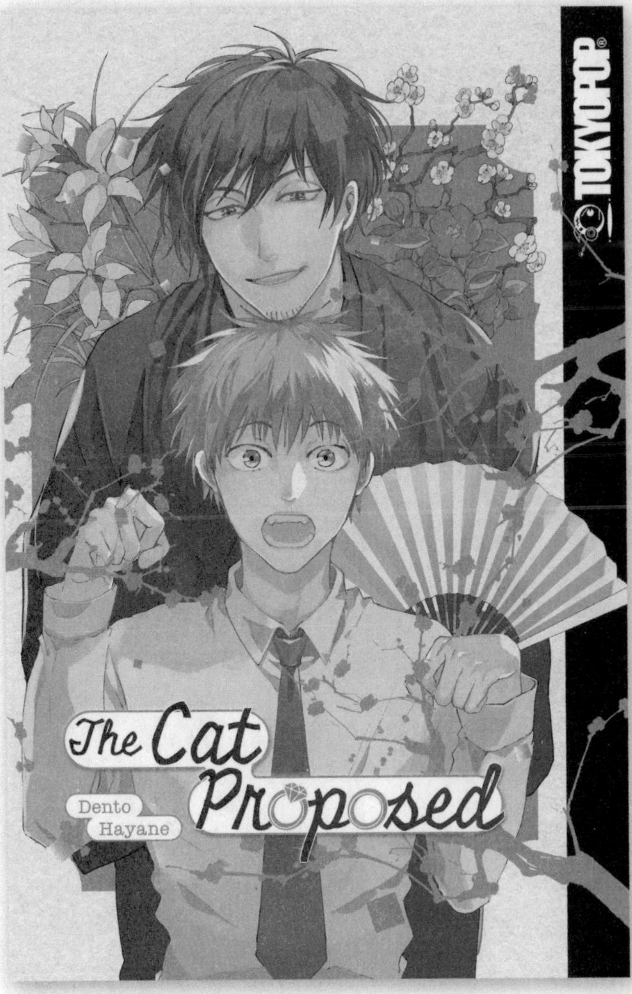
TOKYOPOP
The Cat Proposed
Dento Hayane

LOVE-x-LOVE

TOKYOPOP

Matoi Souta is an overworked office worker tired of his life. Then, on his way home from a long day of work one day, he decides to watch a traditional Japanese play. But something strange happens. He could have sworn he saw one of the actors has cat ears. It turns out that the man is actually a bakeneko — a shapeshifting cat from Japanese folklore. And then, the cat speaks: "From now on, you will be my mate."

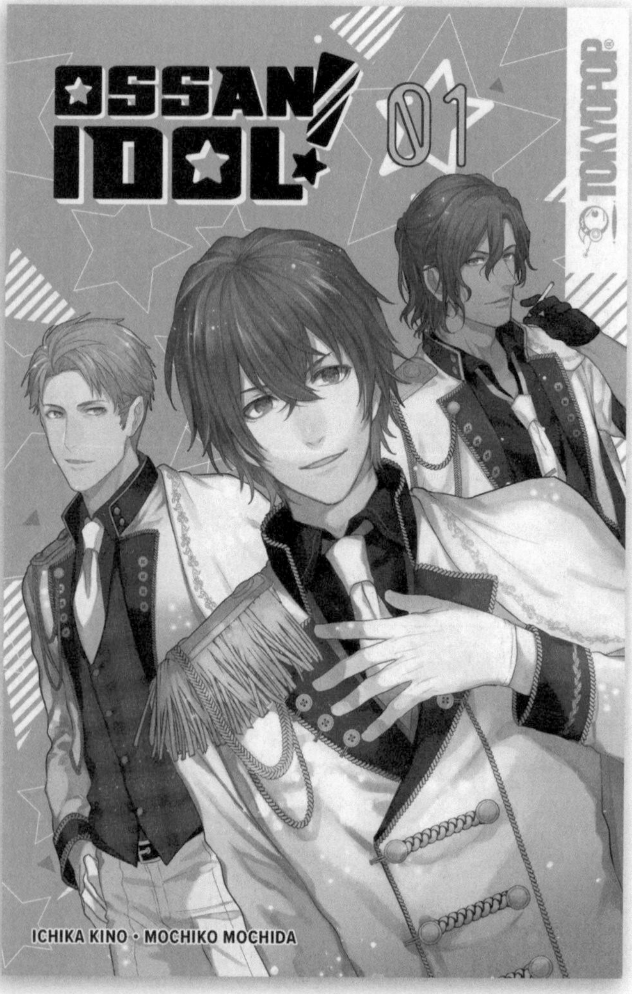
OSSAN IDOL!
01
TOKYOPOP
ICHIKA KINO • MOCHIKO MOCHIDA

OSSAN IDOL! VOLUME 1

Ichika Kino & Mochiko Mochida

IDOL

Miroku Osaki is 36 years old, unemployed, and unhappy. Having been bullied in his childhood and even into his adult life, he became a shut-in after being unfairly laid off. For a long time, the only thing that brought him joy was online gaming. Then, he tried the popular idol game called "Let's Try Dancing!" It was addicting... and transformative! Inspired by the game, Miroku decides to turn his life around. He begins singing karaoke and going to the gym, where he meets Yoichi, the director of an entertainment company who encourages Miroku to pursue his dreams. Miroku only wanted to be good at the game he loves, but when he accidentally uploads a clip of himself singing and dancing, it goes viral! Can he really become an idol, even at his age? Suddenly, it doesn't seem so impossible!

OSSAN IDOL! VOLUME 2

Ichika Kino & Mochiko Mochida

ICHIKA KINO · MOCHIKO MOCHIDA

IDOL

With the help of producer extraordinaire Kamo Lavender, three (almost) middle-aged men are about to take Japan by storm as a group of Ossan Idols!

When Miroku (age 36) accidentally uploaded a video of himself singing and dancing, it quickly went viral. Inspired by his talent and immediate popularity, his friends Yoichi (age 40) and Shiju (age 40) teamed up with him to perform in a competition, where they were discovered by the famous producer himself. Now, the three suddenly have their own radio show, song lyrics, devoted fans, and a debut live performance in a prominent shopping district. Things are really starting to heat up for the unlikely idol group!

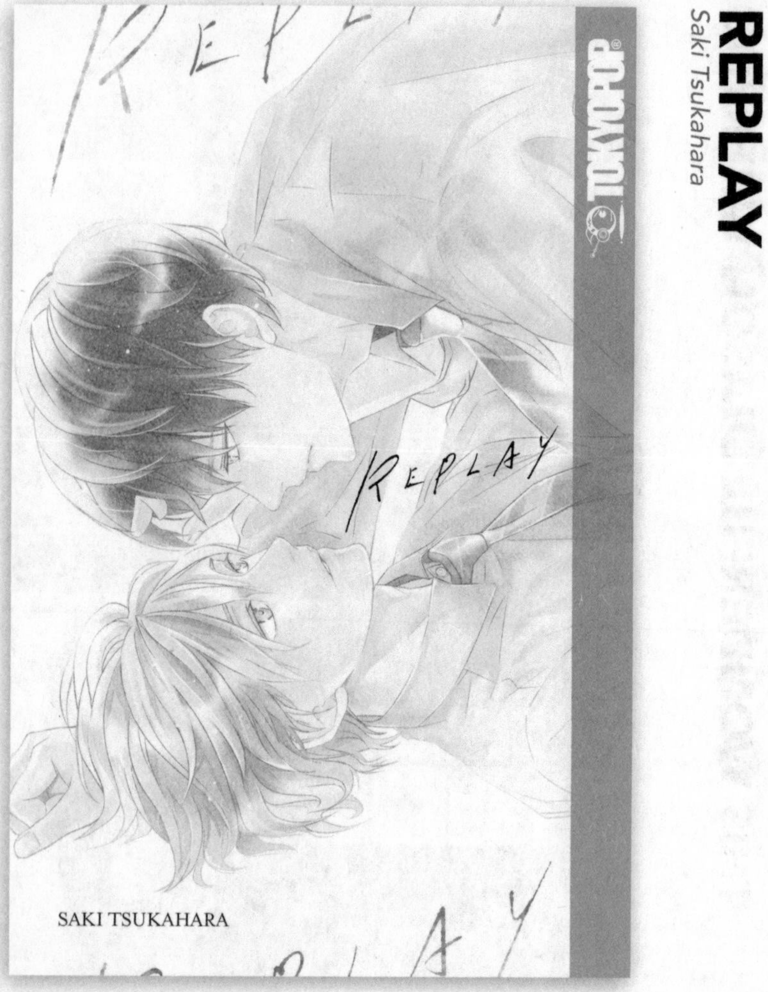
REPLAY
Saki Tsukahara
TOKYOPOP
REPLAY
SAKI TSUKAHARA

LOVE-x-LOVE

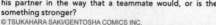

Yuta and Ritsu have been playing baseball together since they were children, but after being defeated in a local tournament over the summer, they must retire from the high school team to study for university entrance exams. Still, Yuta finds himself unable to give up his lingering attachment to baseball. The one person who can truly understand him is Ritsu, who has been acting worryingly distant since they quit the team.

But there's something Yuta himself doesn't understand... Does he think of Ritsu as his partner in the way that a teammate would, or is the affection between them something stronger?

TOKYOPOP

THIS WONDERFUL SEASON WITH YOU

Atsuko Yusen

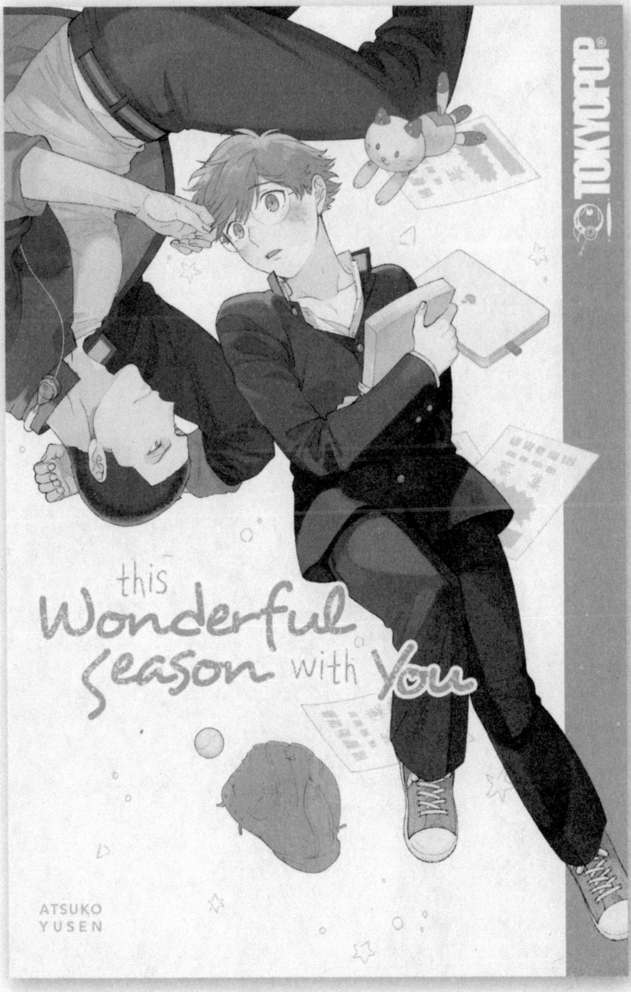
TOKYOPOP
this Wonderful season with You
ATSUKO YUSEN

LOVE-x-LOVE

Enoki is practically the poster-boy for what a typical nerd looks like: short and slight, complete with big round glasses and social awkwardness. His main hobby is making video games, and he's used to not having many friends at school. Then, he meets Shirataki, a former member of the baseball club and his exact opposite; tall, muscular and sporty. Despite their many differences, the spark of friendship between the two boys begins to grow into something more...

TOKYOPOP

THERE ARE THINGS I CAN'T TELL YOU

Edako Mofumofu

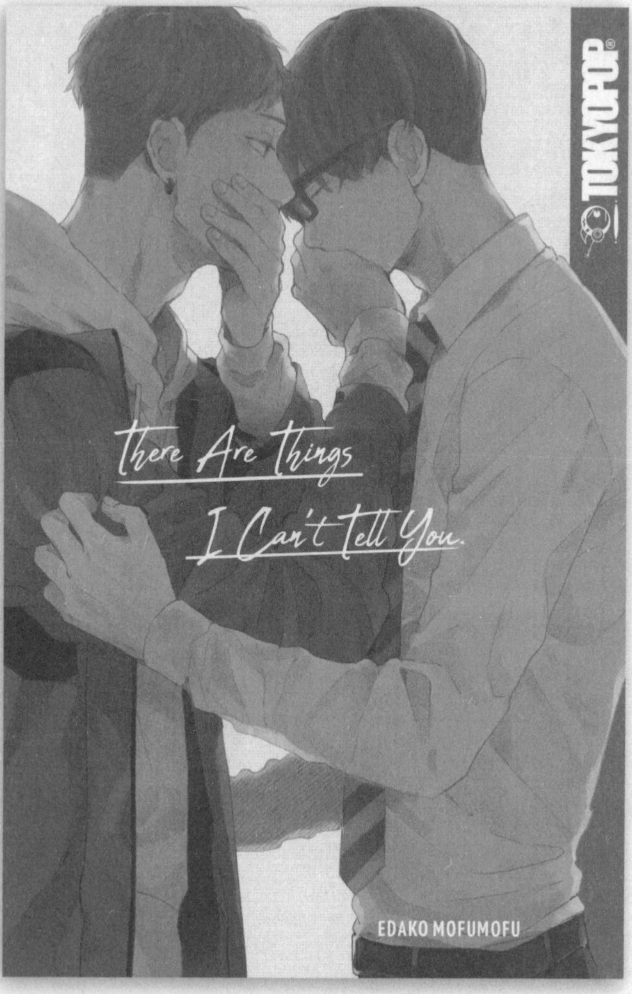
TOKYOPOP
There Are Things
I Can't Tell You.
EDAKO MOFUMOFU

LOVE-x-LOVE | MATURE 18+

Kasumi and Kyousuke are polar opposites when it comes to personality. Kasumi is reserved, soft-spoken and shy; Kyousuke is energetic and has always been popular among their peers. As the saying goes though, opposites have a tendency to attract, and these two have been fast friends since elementary school. To Kasumi, Kyousuke has always been a hero to look up to, someone who supports him and saves him from the bullies. But now, school is over; their relationship suddenly becomes a lot less simple to describe. Facing the world — and one another — as adults, both men find there are things they struggle to say out loud, even to each other.

TOKYOPOP

LIKE TWO PEAS IN A POD

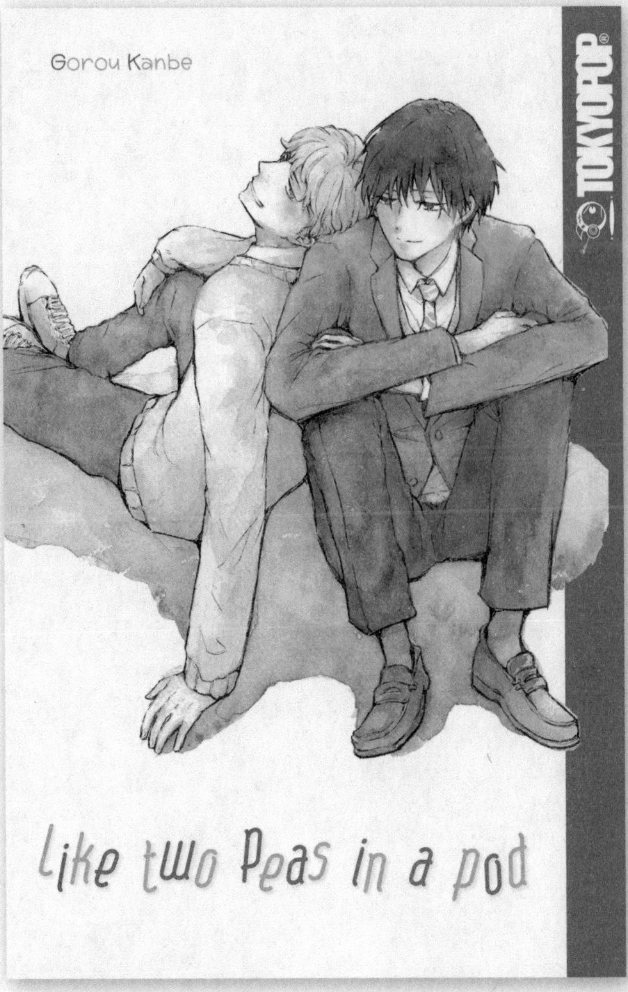

Gorou Kanbe
TOKYOPOP
like two Peas in a pod

LOVE x LOVE

It began with a mistake. When Tanaka and Nakata accidentally mix up their administrative paperwork at the beginning of the school year, they come to an annoying realization... They have almost identical names. And test results. And heights. And taste in fashion. And phone cases. Friction develops in their friendship when it looks like they might even like the same girl!
But as the school year continues, the two discover they have less in common than they first thought...

TOKYOPOP

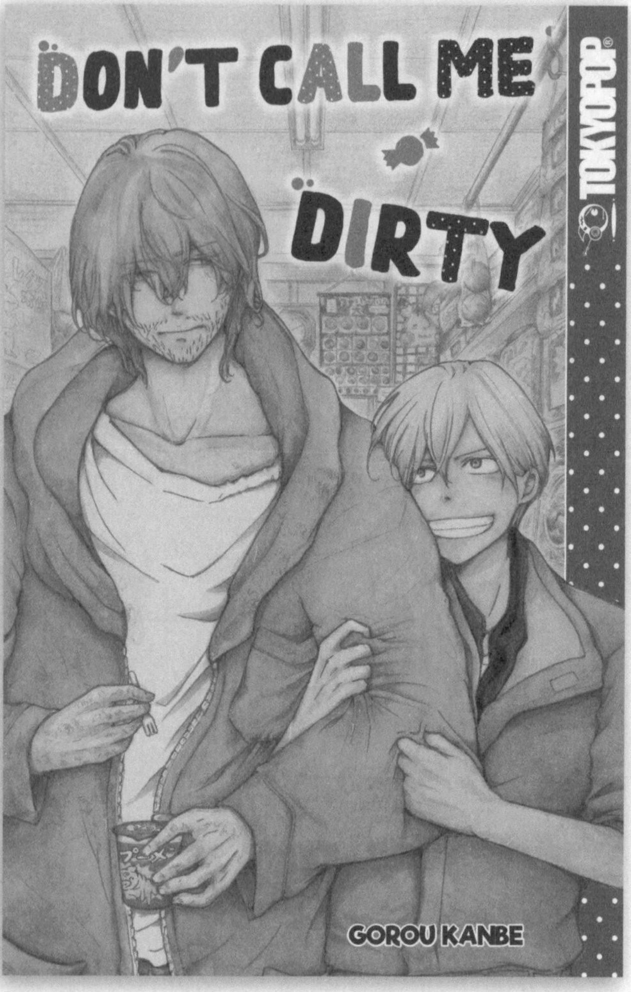
DON'T CALL ME DIRTY
TOKYOPOP
GOROU KANBE

DON'T CALL ME DIRTY

Gorou Kanbe

LOVE x LOVE

After some time attempting a long-distance relationship, Shouji is crestfallen when he finds out his crush isn't gay. Having struggled with his sexuality for years, he tries to distract himself from the rejection, in part by helping out at the neighboring sweets shop. There, Shouji meets a young homeless man called Hama.
Attempting to make their way in a society that labels each of them as 'dirty,' the two men grow closer. Together, they begin to find they have more in common than either of them could have anticipated.

TOKYOPOP

DON'T CALL ME DADDY

Gorou Kanbe

Don't Call Me Daddy

GOROU KANBE

TOKYOPOP®

§LOVE-x-LOVE§

Long before the events of *Don't Call Me Dirty*, Hanao Kaji and Ryuuji Mita were close friends... When Ryuuji is left to raise his son Shouji as a single father, Hanao steps up to help him out. At first, their family life is happy and content, but Hanao's true feelings for Ryuuji become more and more difficult for him to ignore. The pressure of staying closeted eventually becomes too much to bear; Hanao leaves, choosing to run from his feelings and his fears of somehow "messing up" Shouji's life when he starts getting teased at school for having two dads. Years later, when he comes home to care for his aging father and ends up advising Shouji on his blossoming relationship with Hama, Hanao realizes it's time to face his own past... and his future.

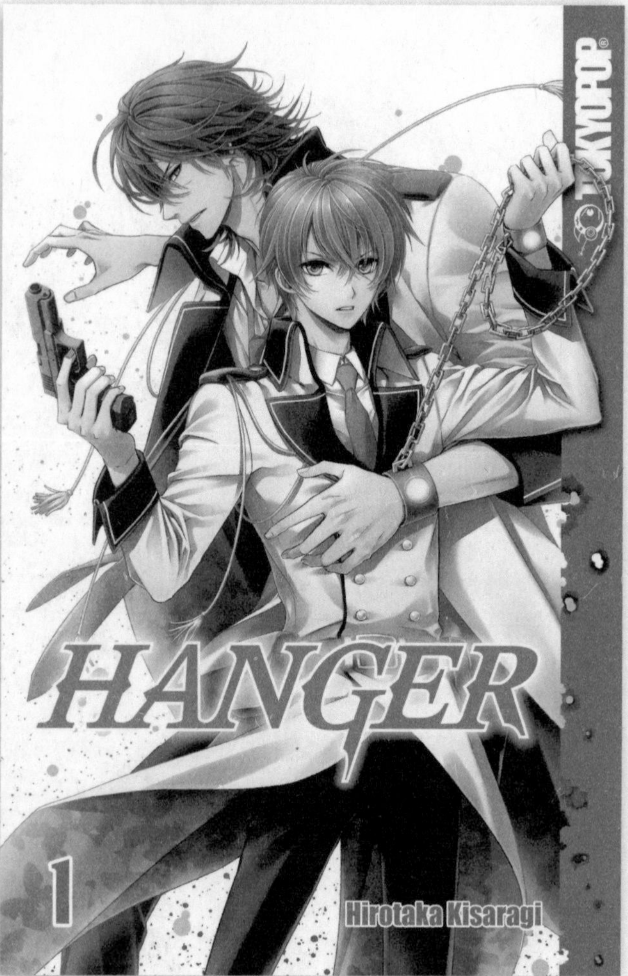
TOKYOPOP
HANGER
1
Hirotaka Kisaragi

HANGER, VOL 1

Hirotaka Kisaragi

LOVE-x-LOVE

In a futuristic Neo-Tokyo, crime is rising rapidly in the wake of a new generation of super-drugs capable of enhancing the user's physical and mental abilities. Hajime Tsukumo is a new recruit on a federal task force trained to go after these powered-up criminals. Now he must team up with Zeroichi, a so-called Hanger looking to reduce his own jail sentence in exchange for helping to take down these chemically-boosted bad guys.

TOKYOPOP

SERVANT & LORD

Lo & Lorinell Yu

Servant & Lord

LO & LORINELL YU

♪LOVE-x-LOVE♪

Christian has always admired handsome, talented composer Daniel. Their shared appreciation for music marked the beginning of a friendship between a willful boy and a sophisticated young man... But when tragedy strikes and circumstances twist around to put Daniel in the service of Christian's wealthy family, their bond is tried in unexpected ways. Years ago, the universal language of music drew them toward one another. Now, Christian has to hope it's still enough to bridge the gap between their vastly different lives.

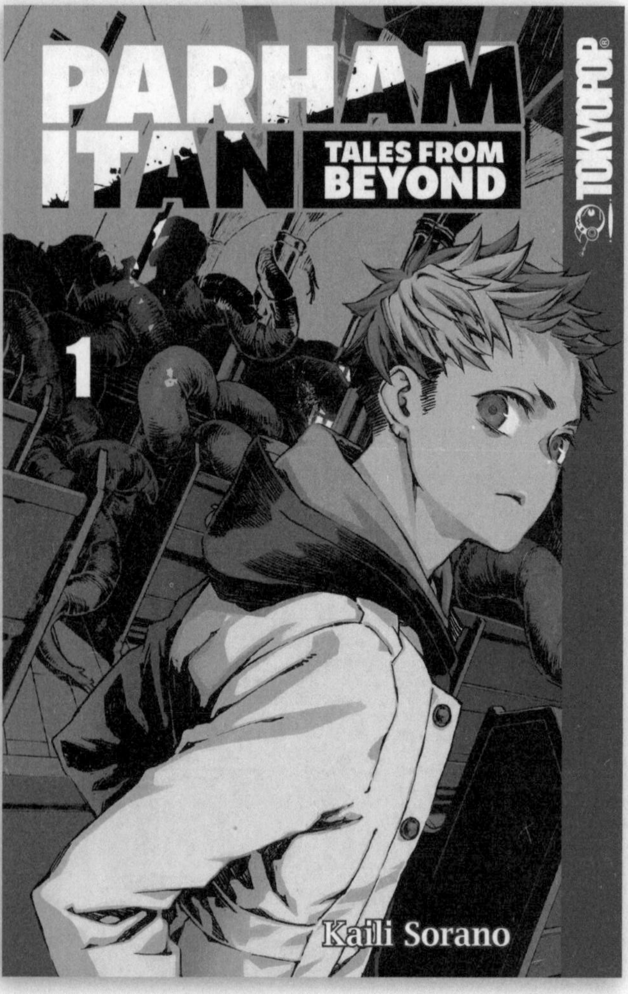
PARHAM ITAN
TALES FROM BEYOND
TOKYOPOP
1
Kaili Sorano

PARHAM ITAN: TALES FROM BEYOND, VOLUME 1

Kaili Sorano

SUPERNATURAL

Yamagishi and Sendo are schoolmates, but that's about as far as their similarities go: one is a short, no-nonsense boxer, while the other is a tall, bookish conspiracy nut. But when they find themselves embroiled in a paranormal phenomenon at school involving plant-faced monster people assimilating innocent victims, it seems they'll have to set aside their differences and work together as best as they can. Of course, it doesn't help that the only one with any answers to this bizarre situation is a mysterious "paranormal investigator" named Akisato, who insists they must find some sort of "key" to stop it all — before giant insects and other preternatural perils from the world "beyond" get to them first. Inspired by Lovecraftian horror and the Call of Cthulhu, this is a brand-new manga series from the creator of Monochrome Factor!

TOKYOPOP

PARHAM ITAN: TALES FROM BEYOND, VOLUME 2
Kaili Sorano

Kaili Sorano

After barely escaping from the Beyond, an alternate dimension swarming with bloodthirsty monsters, high-schoolers Yamagishi and Sendo realize their lives aren't going back to normal anytime soon. Determined to delve deeper into the secrets of the Beyond, they team up with the mysterious paranormal investigator Akisato, under whose grudging guidance they begin to uncover a world of occult sects and black magic. When Yamagishi stumbles across an unknown sigil that he somehow recognizes, it quickly becomes clear his involvement is no mere coincidence. He's sure the creepy symbol has something to do with the orphanage where he grew up — and he's determined to find out truth, even if he has to go back into the Beyond to find the answers to his missing past.

A GENTLE NOBLE'S VACATION RECOMMENDATION, VOLUME 1

Misaki, Momochi & Sando

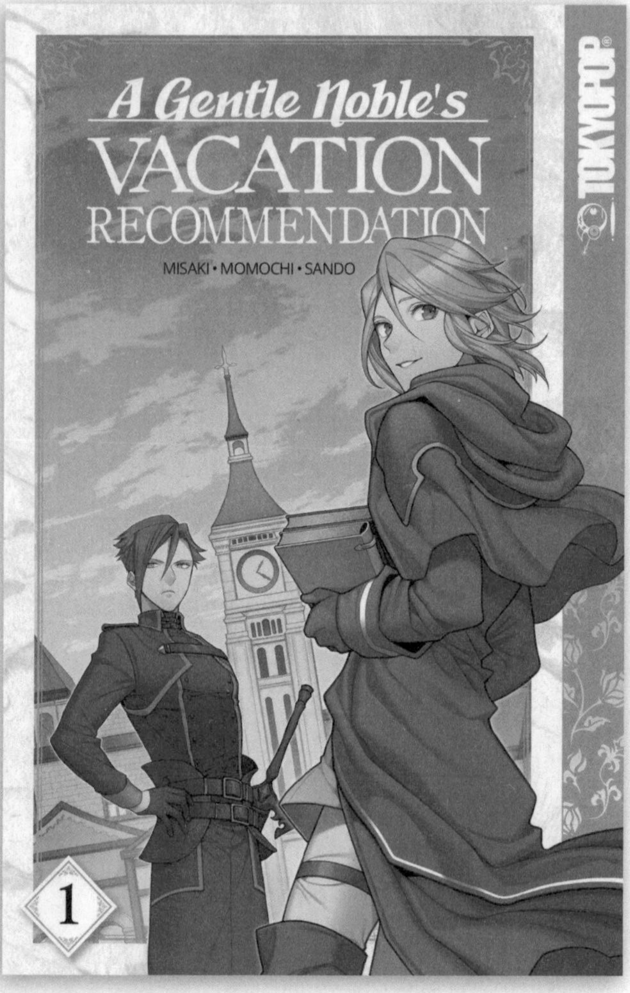
A Gentle Noble's
VACATION
RECOMMENDATION
MISAKI • MOMOCHI • SANDO
TOKYOPOP
1

ISEKAI

When Lizel mysteriously finds himself in a city that bears odd similarities to his own but clearly isn't, he quickly comes to terms with the unlikely truth: this is an entirely different world. Even so, laid-back Lizel isn't the type to panic. He immediately sets out to learn more about this strange place, and to help him do so, hires a seasoned adventurer named Gil as his tour guide and protector. Until he's able to find a way home, Lizel figures this is a perfect opportunity to explore a new way of life adventuring as part of a guild. After all, he's sure he'll go home eventually... might as well enjoy the otherworldly vacation for now!

TOKYOPOP

ISEKAI

After their first successful adventure together, Lizel has officially formed a party with his guard and companion, the famous adventurer Gil. A renowned swordsman known by the moniker Single Stroke for his ability to take down any enemy with just one swipe, Gil has promised to protect Lizel as they become an official part of the adventurer's guild — and the two are already making waves!

Lizel's charming personality has earned him a few friends by now, among them a young appraiser named Judge, the grandson of a rich merchant from the mercantile capital of Marcade. When he asks them to accompany him as guards on a trip to visit his grandfather, Lizel happily accepts the opportunity to sightsee and explore in such a famous country. Gil, on the other hand, is more excited about seeing if there are any super-strong monsters to fight in Marcade's Labyrinth. It's time for the newly-formed party to prove their mettle!

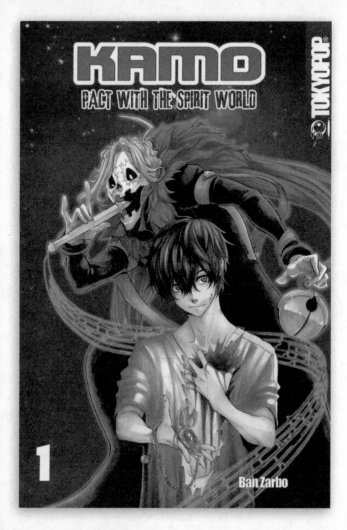

KAMO
PACT WITH THE SPIRIT WORLD
TOKYOPOP
1
Ban Zarbo

KAMO: PACT WITH THE SPIRIT WORLD, VOLUME 1

Ban Zarbo

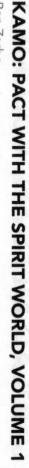

INTERNATIONAL **WOMEN** *of* **MANGA**

Born with a failing heart, Kamo has fought death his whole life, but to no avail. As his body weakens and he readies to draw his final breath, he's visited by a powerful spirit named Crimson who offers him a deal: defeat and capture the souls of twelve spirits in exchange for a new heart. It seems too good to be true... and maybe it is. A pact with the spirit world; what could possibly go wrong?

TOKYOPOP

UNDEAD MESSIAH, VOLUME 1

Gin Zarbo

TOKYOPOP
UNDEAD MESSIAH
1
Gin Zarbo

INTERNATIONAL
women of manga

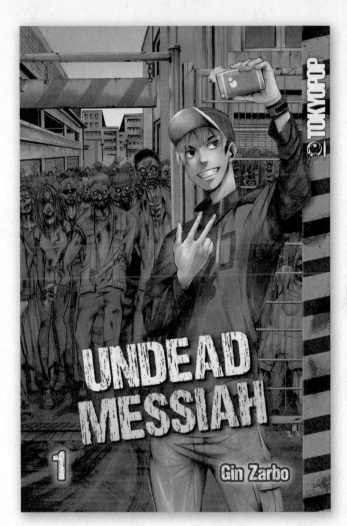

A pregnant woman is pursued by a supernatural creature. On the internet, videos of a bandaged hero surface. 15-year-old Tim Muley makes a terrible discovery in his neighbor's garden. Three seemingly unrelated events, all of which seem to point to an imminent zombie apocalypse! But this time the story's not about the end of mankind; it's about a new beginning...

TOKYOPOP

Nana Yaa

GOLDFISCH, VOLUME 1

ADVENTURE

Say hi to Morrey Gibbs! A fisher-boy in a flooded world overrun with dangerous mutated animals known as "anomals," he's got his own problems to worry about. Namely, how everything he touches turns to gold! Sure it sounds great, but gold underpants aren't exactly stylish -- or comfortable! Together with his otter buddy and new inventor friend Shelly, Morrey's on a quest to rid himself of his blessing-turned-curse and undo the tragedy it caused. That is of course, if they can dodge the treasure-hungry bounty hunters...

SCARLET SOUL, VOLUME 1

Kira Yukishiro

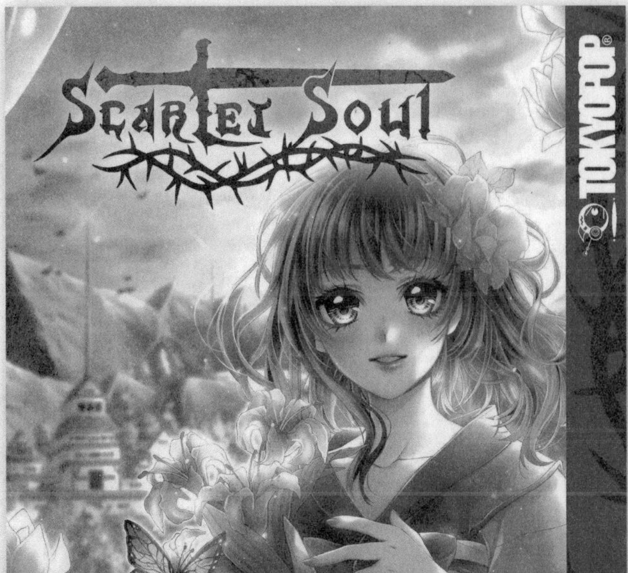
Scarlet Soul
TOKYOPOP
1
KIRA YUKISHIRO

LOVE-x-LOVE

TOKYOPOP

The kingdom of Nohmur has been a peaceful land for humans since the exorcist Eron Shirano repelled the demons and sealed the way to the underworld of Ruhmon. Generations later, sisters Lys and Rin are the heirs of the illustrious Shirano family, the most powerful exorcist clan charged with watching over the barrier and maintaining balance between the two worlds with the aid of Hikaten, the Sword of a Hundred Souls. Until one day, for unknown reasons, demons begin slipping through once more... and suddenly, Lys vanishes without a trace, leaving the sacred sword behind for her little sister to take up. As the underworld threat grows, Rin sets out alongside her companion, the mysterious Aghyr, to find her missing sister and figure out how to fortify the weakening barrier between her world and that of the monstrous creatures that threaten her kingdom once again.

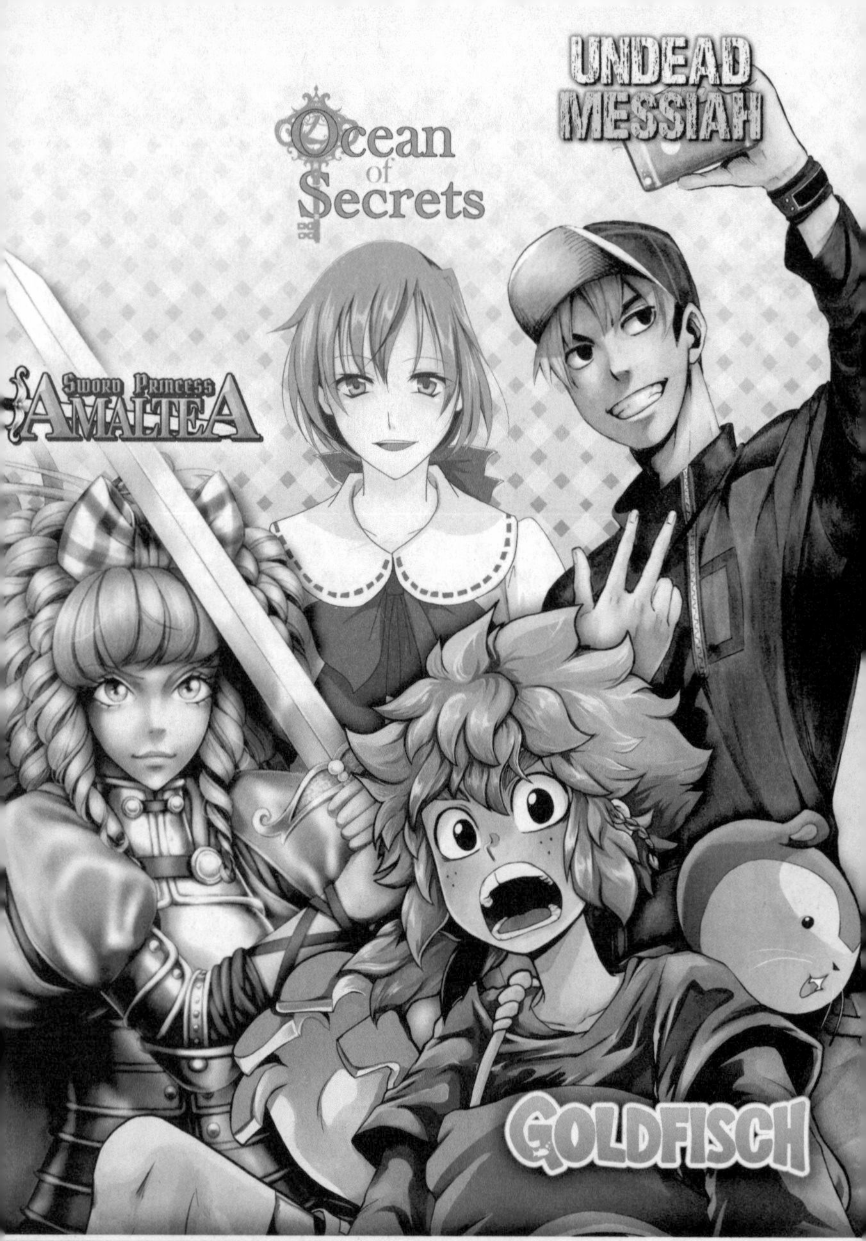
UNDEAD MESSIAH
Ocean of Secrets
SWORD PRINCESS AMALTEA
GOLDFISCH

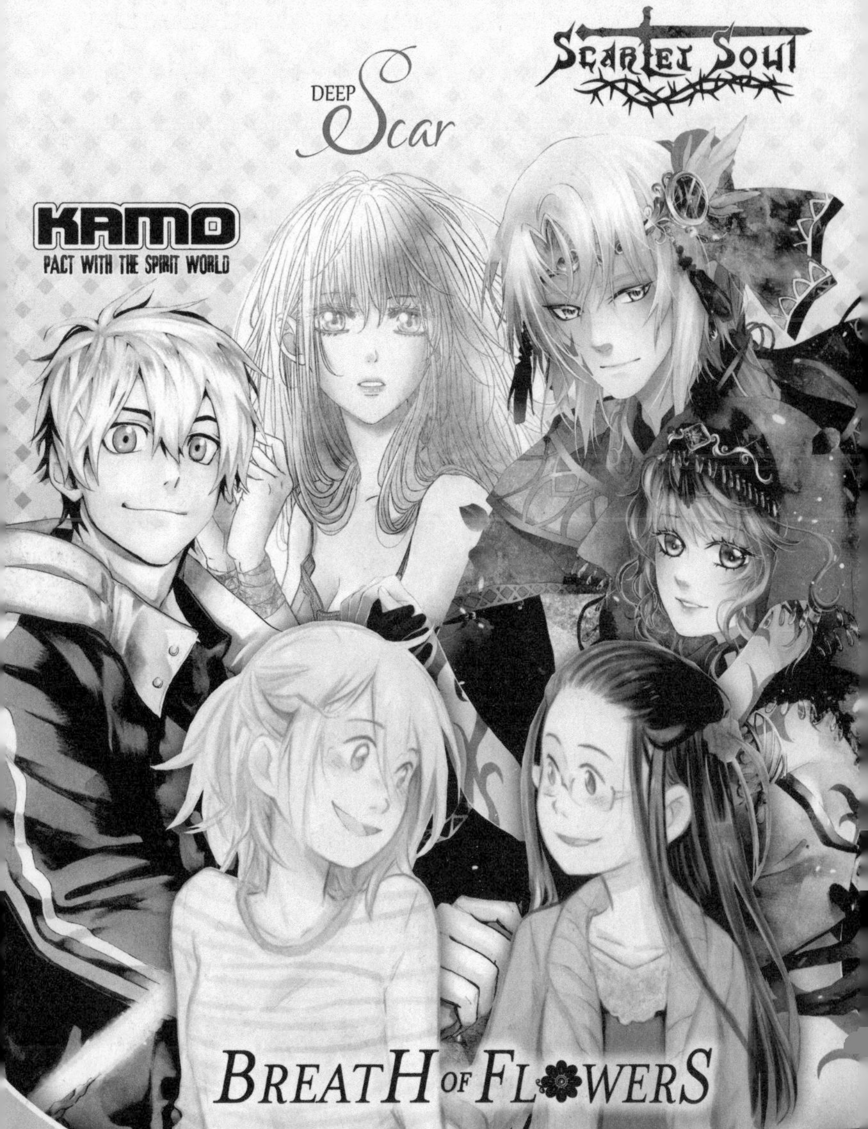
Scarlet Soul
DEEP Scar
KAMO
PACT WITH THE SPIRIT WORLD
BREATH OF FLOWERS

INTERNATIONAL WOMEN of MANGA

Futaribeya Volume 8
Yukiko

Editor	-	Lena Atanassova
Marketing Associate	-	Kae Winters
Translator	-	Katie Kimura
Copy Editor	-	Massiel Gutierrez
QC	-	Daichi Nemoto
Cover Designer	-	Sol DeLeo
Licensing Specialist	-	Arika Yanaka
Retouching and Lettering	-	Vibrraant Publishing Studio
Editor-in-Chief & Publisher	-	Stu Levy

A  Manga

TOKYOPOP and 🎧 are trademarks or registered trademarks of TOKYOPOP Inc.

TOKYOPOP inc.
5200 W Century Blvd
Suite 705
Los Angeles, CA 90045 USA

E-mail: info@TOKYOPOP.com
Come visit us online at www.TOKYOPOP.com

f www.facebook.com/TOKYOPOP
🐦 www.twitter.com/TOKYOPOP
ⓟ www.pinterest.com/TOKYOPOP
📷 www.instagram.com/TOKYOPOP

ISBN: 978-1-4278-6784-1

First TOKYOPOP Printing: June 2021
10 9 8 7 6 5 4 3 2 1
Printed in CANADA

STOP

THIS IS THE BACK OF THE BOOK!

How do you read manga-style? It's simple! Let's practice -- just start in the top right panel and follow the numbers below!

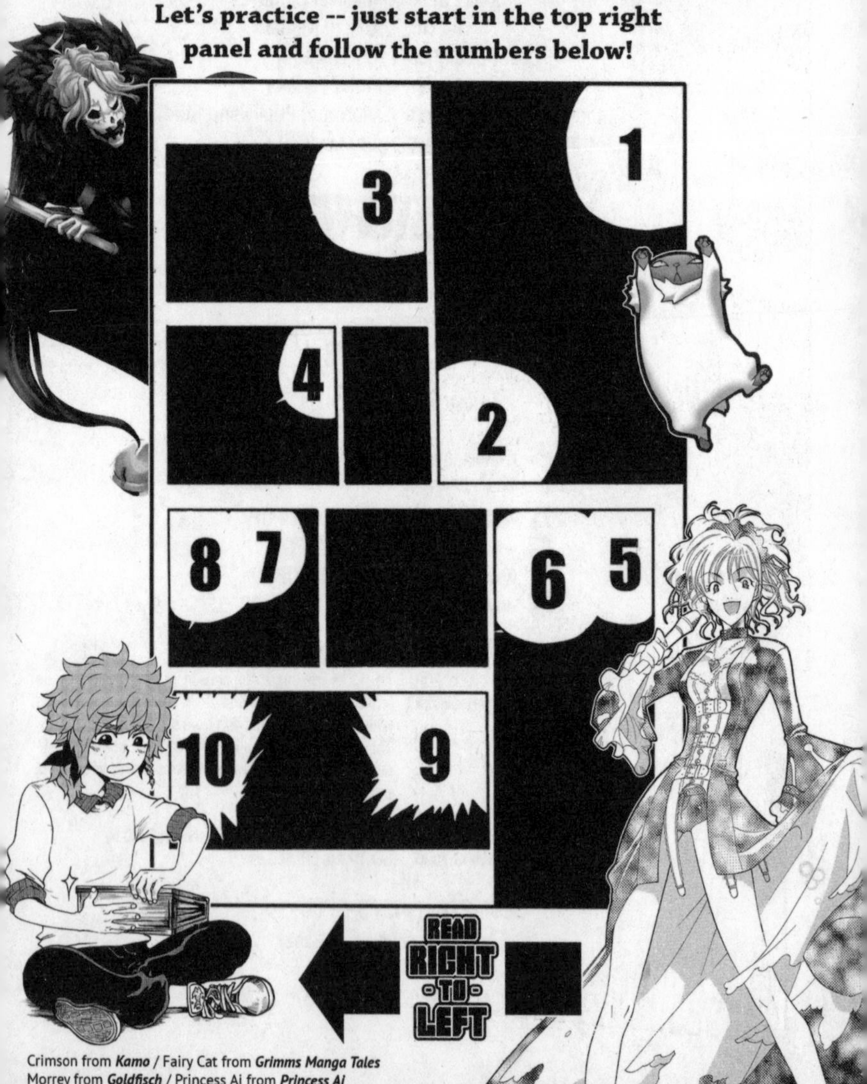
1
2
3
4
5
6
7
8
9
10
READ RIGHT -TO- LEFT

Crimson from ***Kamo*** / Fairy Cat from ***Grimms Manga Tales***
Morrey from ***Goldfisch*** / Princess Ai from ***Princess Ai***